STUCK in the '80s

20 Years of Conversations with Pop Culture Icons Who Defined a Decade

STEVE SPEARS
Creator of the *Stuck in the '80s* podcast

**FOR EVERYONE LISTENING
AROUND THE WORLD
WHO MADE OUR PODCAST
A SHARED MEMORY.**

Stuck in the '80s: 20 Years of Conversations with Pop Culture Icons
Who Defined a Decade
© 2026 by Steve Spears.

All rights reserved. No part of this book may be reproduced or transmitted in any form or by any means whatsoever, including photocopying, recording, or any information storage and retrieval system, without written permission. For permissions or bulk sales, contact the author directly: steve.spears80s@gmail.com.

Editing: Lisa Hochgraf, Top-Notch Text, LinkedIn: @lisahochgraf
Proofreading: Peter Vogt
Cover and interior design by Tamara Dever, TLCBookDesign.com

Stock Image Credits: Cover art created by Tamara Dever using Fotor; Steve's face courtesy of Melissa Braverman Spears | soundwave: YayImages, vikalost

Published by Benjamin House Press

Paperback: 979-8-9945983-0-6 | Ebook: 979-8-9945983-1-3

CONTENTS

Introduction 1
1. Calling Our Heroes (and Trying Not to Throw Up) 3
2. Inventing a Time Machine 15
3. What the Hits Teach You After the Hits Are Over 17
4. The Reunion That Broke Me Open 29
5. Two Dicks, One Backstage Pass 33
6. Thirteen Minutes of Panic 45
7. The Nicest Man in the Loudest Band 49
8. Old Magic, New Projects 55
9. The Face of the '80s 75
10. The Breakup That Became an Episode 83
11. Hits, Humility, and Hand-Built Synths 91
12. The Second Act 115
13. The 80s Cruise 125
14. The MTV Veejays 129
15. Legends, Without the Limo 141
16. The Power of Love 161
17. Off Days and Wrong Questions 169
18. When the Music Was the Movie 183
19. The Rivalry That Wasn't 195

20.	The Man Behind the Mask	203
21.	Conversations Between the Hits	215
22.	Voices from Live Aid	233
23.	Those We've Lost	245
24.	Patiently	257
	Postscript	269
	Acknowledgments	287
	About the Author	291

INTRODUCTION

The '80s really began for me on the evening of October 22, 1981, and it happened as I stepped inside the Lakeland Civic Center in Central Florida. Journey was in town that night to promote their new album *Escape*, and some band named Loverboy was the opening act—a name I barely registered at the time.

The venue was a generic, concrete box that smelled vaguely of stale popcorn with a whiff of cheap tobacco and other then-mysterious smoke products. The civic center—capacity about 8,000—would become the site of the first concert I attended, starring a band that I was enamored with. I wore my favorite navy blue corduroy pants and a knock-off REO Speedwagon concert jersey. In my hand was a partially torn ticket that set me back $9.95. In my pocket I had another $15, which would just barely cover the cost of the Journey concert shirt I was determined to purchase and wear to high school the next day.

Despite having the aesthetic charms of a breadbox, the venue was a cathedral to me and I was about to go through my pop culture communion.

A rightly administered dose of nostalgia can make even the faintest of memories seem wildly intoxicating. I should know. I've been hosting a podcast called *Stuck in the '80s* for 20 years now. Over the course of 750-plus episodes, I've used the show as a time machine to go back and relive those moments—usually with a smile or a laugh, but other times with regret, tears, and, ultimately, acceptance.

The podcast has also opened the door to meeting many of the heroes of the '80s from my younger years—an unlikely phenomenon I still can't wrap my mind around some days.

"Never meet your heroes," the French writer Marcel Proust once said. Like, totally not cool, Marcel!

Alas, he wasn't stuck in the '80s.

This book is a collection of conversations—unforgettable to me—that have made the first two decades of our podcast so special. *Valley Girl* actress Deborah Foreman consoles me over a breakup. AC/DC's Brian Johnson explains how an afternoon on a Bahamian beach led him to write "Hells Bells." Soundtrack king Kenny Loggins sings "Nobody's Fool" to us. John Oates tries to explain the mystique behind his mustache. Carl Weathers shares his favorite moment filming *Rocky IV*. Patty Smyth reveals she could have been Van Halen's next lead singer. Steve Perry talks about his doubts on making new music. It's all in here and more.

Between the conversations, I'll share some of the stories behind the podcast and talk to those who helped create it. The '80s was much more than a decade of hairspray, MTV, Jell-O Pudding Pops, and designer jeans. Let me show you why.

CALLING OUR HEROES (AND TRYING NOT TO THROW UP)

When the *Stuck in the '80s* podcast got its start in 2005, I never imagined we'd stick around long enough—or have the required clout—to do any interviews with our heroes from the decade. My expectation was we'd gather once a week, share some stories, defend some opinions, and call it a day.

When we got to late July 2006, then co-hosts Sean Daly, Cathy Wos, and I were coping with the realization that maybe this podcast was going to hang around a while—and if so, we needed better content. Thankfully I worked at a newspaper, and press releases about '80s-related news were making their way to my desk, including one we didn't expect.

ANDY WICKETT was one of the original Duran Duran singers—before Simon Le Bon, obviously—and he had just remixed a version of "Girls on Film," a song he reportedly had a hand in crafting, the emailed news release said.

I was fascinated by the revelation but incredibly gutless about asking for interviews. Eventually, the three of us decided to do a Duran Duran episode about the entire history of the band. In retrospect, it was a naïve and spectacularly fool-hearted goal. But with the email from Andy's publicist, we now had a connection to a rare piece of the history.

We emailed an invitation for Andy to chat with us, fully expecting never to hear a word back. When an acceptance email arrived a day later, we were all shocked. I spent the night before the interview sweating in bed and the morning after dry-heaving in the sink. I was nowhere near ready to do an interview that actually mattered.

Andy was still living in Birmingham in the U.K., where the band was founded. While Sean numbed him up with questions about why his British home didn't have working air conditioning, I was more curious about the music scene in the region that nurtured one of the most beloved bands of our decade.

"It was just coming out of the Punk Era, and they were getting disco creeping in," Andy said. "You got the new so-called New Romantic scene going on, where people were dressing up and slapping the makeup on and stuff. It was like a coming out of that, really."

Andy didn't start with Duran Duran. He was handling lead vocals in TV Eye, a prominent band at the time and still a favorite with those who remember the scene. Future Duran Duran keyboard player Nick Rhodes was a friend of the band and would hang out with them at a house where they'd record. A song called "Stevie's Radio Station"—a TV Eye original—would later be adapted and become "Rio" for Duran Duran, Andy said.

A late-night job at a chocolate kitchen led Andy to another familiar tune.

"I was working at Cadbury's on the night shift. I used to write songs. It was so boring. And I wrote this old melody, so I carried it in my head till I got home, put it down, and found some words, so we got 'Girls on Film.'"

For that moment in musical history, Andy says he was paid 600 pounds sterling, about $1,100 at the time.

"I try to stop myself from feeling sad, but that's the music business, ain't it? We have to be philosophical, don't we? At least I don't get all the hassle of that beautiful group, all that money to worry about."

While he's followed their career since leaving the band in 1980, he's also kept his distance—at least as of 2006 when we chatted. He had gone, however, to a recent Duran Duran tour stop.

"I took my little three-year-old, Oliver, to see it. And he thought it was great and all the lights [laughter]. But he sort of started falling asleep halfway through [laughter]. But, yeah. No, I thought, 'That's quite good.'"

Did he go backstage?

"No [laughter]. No, I thought best not to. I thought I just, no, because...No. No."

When the interview was over, we congratulated ourselves on the unlikely milestone. An actual musician...from the actual decade we worshipped. This, surely, was the high-water mark for the podcast, right?

ADAM CURRY, the former MTV video jockey, was our second interview. Adam had become known as "The Podfather" for his pioneering work with the medium. Did you know he originally bought and registered the domain mtv.com? We should have asked him about that.

We invited him on the show primarily to talk about MTV's 25th anniversary. The butterflies were still in full force, but at least it felt like we were talking to a kindred spirit with Adam, who seemed to want to help us find our way with podcasting.

"I wasn't there for their first sign-on, which was August 1, 1981," Adam said. "I came in around the time that MTV moved from 9 million households to over 40 million households, which of course was, for a lot of people, the first time they ever saw MTV. I actually came in a good six years after MTV started."

Adam is a pro at storytelling. It didn't take much prompting to get him talking about a 3 a.m. visit to Russia's Red Square with Skid Row's Sebastian Bach, or his assignments—as the only VJ who could ski—to cover snowboarding tournaments and the Pro Mogul Tour.

If you're wondering why any of those non-music events would interest an MTV audience, you've already anticipated my next question.

"Were you happy with the direction of MTV?" I asked Adam. "Could you tell that it had taken a definite turn away from showing music videos into doing something completely different?"

"I wasn't happy with what MTV was doing from day one," Adam replied. "I thought it was like, 'What the hell are you guys doing? It's pretty lame.' All the good shit never gets on the air. Anything that was funny, especially a joke about an artist, would never air."

Still, Adam was realistic.

"Do I think MTV made the right business decisions? Yeah, absolutely," he said. "They clearly saw the writing on the wall. The video outlets were widening and the distribution of music videos would be really widespread, which they already knew around the time that Michael Jackson started giving his world premiere or planetary or intergalactic premiere to the BET. So MTV all of a sudden was competing with BET [Black Entertainment Television] and like, 'Whoa, wait a minute.'"

And then came *Remote Control*.

Remote Control was a game show—on MTV. It ran from 1987 to 1990 with Ken Ober as the host and Colin Quinn as his sidekick. (Later, Adam Sandler and Denis Leary would join the staff.) The show's premise was that Ober was a guy so desperate to host his own game show that he invented one in his home's basement. At its heart a trivia show about music, movies, and TV, it nonetheless had a bit of a dark edge to it.

"*Remote Control* did something really unique in 30 minutes every single weekday," Adam said. "They scored a 1.0 or sometimes a 1.1 rating and that was anywhere from twice to three times what video programming would get. Double the ratings means more money. That's just a fact."

Adam continued to dazzle us with his stories. He appeared in Madonna's *Truth or Dare* movie back in 1991. "I get $2.93 every four years for my appearance," he confessed.

He talked about sitting in the waiting room at Sony Records in New York alongside Simon Le Bon, who goes unrecognized by the receptionist. She tells the Duran Duran frontman to take a seat and wait to be called.

"It was just horrific," Adam said. "It was so sad almost to have witnessed that. It was something so wrong about it."

Now Adam was on a roll.

"I got in a huge fight with Richard Marx once," he then told us. "There was something that I said in the *Top 20 Video Countdown*. I think it actually had to do with his hair. He gets so bent out of shape, and he tries to get me fired. And he's running around the office up on Broadway and telling everyone they got to get me off the channel or he'll never do anything for MTV. I was scheduled two weeks later to do a radio interview with Richard Marx on a show called *Hitline USA*, which was coast-to-coast live on Sunday nights. And he goes off on me. I got to dig up this tape. He says, 'I hope you die of lung cancer.'"

We all guffawed and exploded with laughter and a hefty share of just plain disbelief. This is what makes for a great podcaster. Adam will always be "The Podfather."

"I hope he's doing fine," he said of Marx.

A gracious guest to the very end.

STAN RIDGWAY, the former frontman for Wall of Voodoo, is the face of an epic MTV video. To this day, every '80s teen can sing along to "Mexican Radio" and picture Stan crooning about eating barbecued iguana in Tijuana.

We interviewed Stan about a month after Andy Wickett, and it was an entirely different experience. I felt more at ease this time. Stan wasn't promoting any particular record or tour, so he was ready to take questions pretty much about anything. I think we had him on the phone for a good 45 minutes, after which we could tell he was all talked out. God bless Stan for putting up with us.

Like many people we interviewed, Stan began our chat by questioning why we were "stuck in the '80s."

"I try to live in the present day, but are you guys stuck there most of the time?" Stan asked.

"Yeah, I guess it's a bad thing," I replied.

"Well, somebody's gotta do it," he reasoned.

Stan is one of the most interesting subjects out there and one of the most willing to share. He got started in music at age 12, crafting a homemade banjo from a cigar box, rubber bands, and sticks.

He grew up on a solid diet of gunfighter ballads and trail songs and listening to the great Marty Robbins, maybe the first crossover country/pop singer of his time.

But in 1976, Stan started a movie soundtrack company called Acme Soundtracks in Hollywood.

"I was way past insane at this point," Stan said. "I had a desk in there and a phone and a blackboard and a file cabinet. My idea was that I was going to start a science fiction, kind of low-budget soundtrack company."

When a music rehearsal hall opened across the street—beneath the Pussycat Theater in a space that would later become the punk club The Masque—Stan jumped on it as the perfect spot to create some original music.

"Acme Soundtracks turned into the group Wall of Voodoo, with me doing my best to lead it and drive the train," he said. "We started to play live shows out in the hinterlands and we found that there were at least 25 people that wanted to hear something original. So it was kind of a blast at that point, and started up a whole kind of new creative period that I guess took us into the '80s that we're now stuck in."

Way to bring it back, Stan. I used the opportunity to ask about "Mexican Radio," a song off the band's *Call of the West* album from 1982 that peaked at No. 58 on the U.S. charts. (It performed far better in Canada, New Zealand, and Australia.) The music video on MTV made it a cult classic.

"It still seems to have some resonance," Stan said. "The jam of the song came from Marc Moreland, who recently passed away three or four years ago from a liver disease, unfortunately. We would sit in the car and drive to rehearsal, and we would try and find a Mexican radio station on our AM dial there in my old '67 Mustang. And when we would find one, we would say, 'Hey, great, we're on a Mexican radio.'"

I love tapping into a story like this. I just let go and enjoyed it.

"We used to like to listen to the sound of something we didn't understand. Marc had the lick. It kind of hankered back to the '50s for me, when rock 'n' roll was prohibited in the United States and jockeys like Wolfman Jack were across the border just south of Los Angeles playing kind of outlaw music on AM dials."

"Mexican Radio" would become the first song recorded for *Call of the West*.

"When we finished it, we all kind of knew, like, this is pretty dang catchy, now what do we do?" Stan recalled.

Did he remember creating the video, I wanted to know.

"Yeah, it's hard to forget," he said. "When MTV started off, I said to myself, I said, 'Well, this is an opportunity to get something like a film up there instead of just us on a blue screen or some picture of an egg frying or something.' I think it was $10,000, and that's all we spent to make that video."

The video was shot in Mexico, where the band traveled on a Labor Day weekend.

"We were rolling around taking kind of a cinéma vérité approach, you know," he said. "Now, the end of the video is really an amalgamation of a lot of ideas that were tried out or sketched out for a song called 'Factory' that's on the *Call of the West* record. On 'Factory' it was my desire to masquerade as a meatloaf in the end of the tune, if we were gonna do a video for that."

The band ditched the idea for the "Factory" video but still had a desire to work with food, Stan said.

"We quickly wrangled up this idea that we'd get a big salad bowl and cut a hole in the bottom of it and get a lot of beans, and then I would come up through the beans at the end of the song and sing that 'Mexican Radio' line there and hopefully scare the pants off everybody. But I actually scared my own pants off because it was such a mess. I was breathing with a straw for about five minutes. It was a little bit like scuba diving."

I told Stan about buying *Call of the West* in a Gainesville record store when I was at the University of Florida. The clerk lit up when

I brought it to the register. He opened up the album, put the vinyl on the store sound system, and we listened to it together that afternoon. Every five minutes, a customer would come up to ask about the record, and many would buy a copy themselves.

"Never dreamed I would actually have the opportunity to tell you that story," I told Stan, my voice quivering in the moment. My hands tremble now recalling it.

"I thank you for listening," Stan replied. "It's funny about records and the people who make them, you know? When all is said and done, at the end of the day, if it's taken a while to make a record, the person that's made it is probably the least likely to enjoy it because they hear the flaws in it and some of the things that maybe could have been improved or other things. As you get more distance from anything you do, of course, things always sound better, but finishing something is really the be-all end-all of an art."

As our 45 minutes came to an end, I was struggling to let go of the connection we'd made. The stress of preparing for the interview had given way to the bliss of the moment.

"This has been…" I paused, "fantastic."

"I never know what to expect when someone calls, saying that they're stuck in the '80s," Stan said. "I'm happy to have found out that the view is a little wider than I'd prepared myself for."

I still hung on the line. I wasn't ready to hang up.

"Okay," I stumbled. "All right," he replied. And then he summed it all up just right:

"Over and out."

The Stan Ridgway interview was important for *Stuck in the '80s* in another way: A lot of new listeners came to the podcast because of that conversation. I still get emails every year from people who are just now discovering that episode—or listening to it again for the 10th time. Stan's fans are true blue, loyal to the bone.

PATTY SMYTH was one of the very first artists I interviewed solo. I remember hearing the recording of our phone call afterward and cringing at my heavy breathing, which was loud enough to make someone think I'd just finished a 5K run. Patty is best known to '80s fans for her stint with the band Scandal. Hits such as "Goodbye to You" and "The Warrior" were chart favorites in the early MTV days. Her solo duet with Don Henley—"Sometimes Love Just Ain't Enough"—was another highlight of her career.

Patty had set her music career aside after marrying tennis god John McEnroe—a childhood hero of mine—and devoted her time to raising six children. In 2006, she was reuniting with Scandal to play the We Are the '80s show at Ruth Eckerd Hall in Clearwater, Florida, along with Rick Springfield, Eddie Money, and Loverboy, so I had the chance for a phoner to help promote the evening.

I asked Patty the same question I'd soon ask Rick Springfield on the night they performed: "What was it about the '80s that makes it so endurably popular?"

"That's the question that keeps coming up," she began. "You can compare the early '80s with the late '80s and then the mid-'80s, and that whole 10 years was a real different thing, you know? I think it's all about the songs. And if it's a good song, it holds up. And even with all the cheesy sounds with the synthesizers and all that, I think the kids are amused by that now. Plus, there's a lot of rap artists and hip-hop artists that have sampled a lot of stuff. So it kind of piqued the interest of the younger generation."

"Would you want your music sampled by today's artists?" I asked.

"I would absolutely let them," she said. "I don't believe that that's happened, but I would be honored and completely complimented.

I happen to be a hip-hop rap fan, though. I love Dr. Dre and Snoop, and I like Eminem. I like Jay-Z."

I didn't see that coming. As a hardcore '80s fan, I'm not sure I could even name a Dr. Dre or Eminem tune. But that was hardly the last time Patty would surprise me. "Sometimes Love Just Ain't Enough," which topped out at No. 2 on the U.S. charts in 1992, also had an interesting beginning.

"I only knew who Don Henley was because of 'Dirty Laundry,'" she said. "I wasn't a big Eagles fan. I got a call from my manager asking me to sing background on his record. And I said no, because I wasn't really a background singer. But they kept calling, even though I kept saying no. And finally, the last offer was, 'Okay, we'll put you up at the Beverly Hills Hotel.' And I'm like, 'Okay, I'll do it.' And then it was like we were separated at birth. I wound up singing on five songs on that record. And then when I wrote 'Sometimes Love Just Ain't Enough,' I called him and pleaded for him on the phone because I was so excited because I really felt like it was the best song I had ever written."

Time was beginning to run short on our allotted 30-minute conversation, and after bragging up the '80s show coming in a few weeks, there was one urban legend I wanted Patty to confirm or deny.

Did Van Halen offer her the lead singer spot after David Lee Roth left?

"Yeah," Patty answered. "Valerie [Bertinelli, Eddie Van Halen's wife] was a big fan of ours. And we met. It was right after David Lee Roth had left, [Eddie] said, 'I want you to sing in the band. I want you to be the lead singer in the band. And I really want you to think about it.'"

A year would go by before Patty bumped into Eddie again. This time she was eight months pregnant. Eddie gave an ultimatum. "He said, 'Listen, you have to give me an answer now because I've got to start making this record and you've got to tell me if you want to sing in the band or not.'"

Patty had an answer.

"I said no," she confirmed. "Right off the top of my head, without even thinking about it, I just said no. Because it was just not the right time for me. I was a New Yorker. I did not want to move to L.A. I was about to have a kid. Those guys were drunk and funny all the time, him and his brother, which was just not where I was at in my head. And in retrospect, I probably could have given it a little bit more thought. And I can't say that there haven't been moments when I have regretted not doing it."

Sammy Hagar would inherit the role instead.

"[Eddie] requested that I really not speak about it because it would make Sammy Hagar look like second choice," she said. "And so I never spoke about it. You know, I mean, every once in a while people would ask me here or there and I'd have to answer honestly, but I never did speak about it. So that's why it's sort of been this kind of an urban myth, but it's an urban myth that's true."

By the time I hung up with Patty, I wasn't fighting my nerves as much. I was hooked. This wasn't just a podcast that might hang around. It was turning into a place where the '80s could talk back.

INVENTING A TIME MACHINE

Let's back up a little. What's a podcast? I'll admit I didn't know the answer myself when I started. In the early days, I'd explain it as simply as possible:: A podcast is an on-demand "radio show" that you can download—usually for free—anytime through the internet.

In 2005, I was tasked by my boss at the *St. Petersburg Times* to start up a podcast so our internet department at the newspaper could understand the process and learn the finer details of what makes a show tick. I had two suggestions: a podcast about high school football refereeing—I'd been a high school ref for five years at the time—or a show about why I still love '80s pop culture. The boss wisely steered me toward the second option.

I'm not naturally outspoken, and I've never worked as a full-time writer. My career up to this point had been largely as a copyeditor, the unfortunate soul who worked the night shift grammatically correcting other people's writing. I describe myself as introverted. But I enjoy telling stories. Actually, I like retelling stories. Over and over again. And that is essentially what *Stuck in the '80s* is. It's a device for me to retell stories—either in podcast form or via a blog item or even a conversation during the many trivia sessions we host every year on The 80s Cruise.

The trouble with retelling a story in podcast form is that there's a feeling of "downloading" the memory. I transfer the story from the darkest corner of my brain to the MP3 file. Once downloading is complete, I tend to wipe the story from my memory.

To that end, I decided to write this book as a final record of all the stories that reflect a part of me that's been shaped—and sustained—by nostalgia. But I was careful, too. I employed a professional transcribing company to give me complete and accurate transcripts of my chats with my heroes. When I retell a story, I've tried my best to compare my current memory of the tale with the version that was previously recorded on a podcast episode.

I've reached out to some of the people who were with me behind the scenes, asking about their memories. You'll read their stories here too.

At the end of the day, I just want to emphasize that *Stuck in the '80s* has never been part of any job description I've held. It has been—since the day of its inception—a labor of love and a method for me to reach a cease-fire agreement with my past.

Now let's continue.

WHAT THE HITS TEACH YOU AFTER THE HITS ARE OVER

Lately I've been reading Cameron Crowe's memoir *The Uncool*. It's an incredibly insightful look into the start of so many legendary rock stars through the eyes of an ever-curious interviewer. With *Stuck in the '80s*, I find I'm looking at careers from the other end of the tunnel. Though many of the people I've interviewed are still making new music—Duran Duran comes to mind—most of the artists are still selling out venues but are no longer topping the charts.

From all their years of recording and touring, they're able to offer a level of wisdom that I never tire of probing.

MARTIN FRY doesn't get nearly enough credit for being a statesman of British pop and new wave. Thankfully he tours often these days so music fans can show their appreciation in person. But before 2008, I'd never had a chance to see ABC live. I was gifted two opportunities just three years after we began the podcast.

ABC scored 10 U.K. and five U.S. Top 40 hit singles in their first decade. Their debut album, *The Lexicon of Love*, is an enduring classic and quickly opened the door to fame via MTV videos for "Poison Arrow" and "Look of Love."

Fast-forward to June 2008. ABC—with Martin Fry as the only founding member still performing—was preparing to tour America on the Regeneration Tour alongside The Human League, Naked Eyes, and Belinda Carlisle. I got a chance to talk with Martin before the tour began. I was curious about how friendly the bands are with each other on tours like this. It's a question I've asked scores of musicians, but I like Martin's response best.

"Back in the '80s, everybody hated each other," he confessed. "They'd stand on each side of the TV studio and glare at each other, because everybody was chasing that No. 1 spot, weren't they?"

"I think all these years on now, we've got a lot of respect," he continued. "It kind of works well because the audiences love the show. I mean, it is like standing inside a human jukebox and collectively, there's a lot of hit records there to perform."

For the Regeneration Tour, depending on the night, ABC performed a short setlist of its hits, including "Poison Arrow," "(How to Be a) Millionaire," "Be Near Me," "When Smokey Sings," and "The Look of Love."

Fry has been the only constant member of ABC, which got its start in 1980 in Sheffield, England.

"Sheffield—north of England—was where we sort of formed, out of frustration, really," he said. "We were always trying to make a connection between the records we'd hear in the clubs and the music we'd play at home."

In the '80s, the city would give us The Human League, Def Leppard, Heaven 17, and others.

"As the years roll by, there's a great deal of respect for any musician that's been around for more than 15 minutes," Martin said. "Also, to stand on a stage in 2008, it is a privilege and an honor, and in my case, to perform 'The Look of Love' and 'Poison Arrow' and 'When Smokey Sings' and 'Be Near Me.' So, I think there's a lot of respect about the way people carry themselves in 2008."

Did he find it surprising that the '80s has had this resurgence? "There is an element of looking back to an age when life was less complicated, less debts, less confusion," he said. "Also, when you look at all those kind of crazy homemade '80s sort of pop videos, they're kind of quaint, aren't they? They're kind of amusing and entertaining. Whereas today people seem to take it a lot more seriously, and it's a lot more professional and a lot more corporate in the way people operate."

I objected. "But your videos—the ABC videos—I mean, to almost anybody from the '80s, those really stand out. I mean, you guys did hellaciously great videos back then."

From the animated amusement of "(How to Be a) Millionaire" to the extravagance of the theatric "Poison Arrow" to the affectionate anthem "When Smokey Sings," ABC's videos still feel timeless. Speaking of "Smokey"—which ABC once performed on *Soul Train*—what did the great Smokey Robinson think of the tune?

"I met him originally in Holland. He was doing a TV show there," Martin began. "And then, about four weeks later, I met him in Los Angeles. And by then his record and our record were both in the top five. So, he invited us over to Motown. He was the managing director of Motown at the time in Los Angeles. But, you know, for a kid that's grown up listening to 'Tears of a Clown' and alongside Smokey, Marvin Gaye, and Stevie Wonder, it was a great honor."

Years later, actually just a year before our interview, Martin had parlayed his experience into coaching Hugh Grant in the movie *Music and Lyrics*.

"Hugh Grant was playing a singer who was writing songs who started off in the '80s," he said. "So they figured if he was a singer, he would sound like me. So they got me down there to show him a couple of moves, really, and to kind of encourage him. He wasn't really a natural singer. I mean, he's a much better actor than he is a singer, but he worked really hard."

"So it was a fun gig?"

"They paid me a lot of money. It was great," he laughed. "And I ate well, and the air miles were fantastic."

MARTHA DAVIS of The Motels is one of my favorites because she's been so charitable with her time and stories. She and bandmate Marty Jourard joined us for Big 80s Trivia on the 2020 voyage of The 80s Cruise. Despite being seasick from the rolling seas on the way to San Juan, Martha was a trouper and regaled us with amazing stories from her days decades ago.

Like other bands from the early '80s, The Motels earned a label as New Wave though their moody sound is harder to pinpoint. Their singles "Only the Lonely" and "Suddenly Last Summer" both penetrated the Top 10 in the U.S.

In 2024, The Motels were touring North America on the Abducted by the 80s lineup, and I got a chance for a more formal conversation with her for the podcast.

"That was a wild time, wasn't it?" Martha said, recalling the cruise. "We were rocking, and I mean rocking, on that ship because it was very, very, very rough seas when we were out there. And then we got off the ship straight into the arms of a pandemic."

Martha has been writing songs for so long, I think a lot of people are surprised that the roots of the band go back to the early '70s, when they were originally known as The Warfield Foxes in the San Francisco Bay Area.

"If you listen back to that old stuff, it was like punk funk or something," she said. "The Bay Area had Sly and the Family Stone and all that stuff, so we were heavily influenced by that, even though we were very white children."

In the '80s, when The Motels were running up the charts, the sound and message of the songs seemed more wistful. How did her writing evolve?

"I think most of us that write are very happy to have a psychoanalyst that we don't have to pay because it's kind of what you do," she explained. "You're kind of taking all of your pent-up emotions and laying them out, and it's almost like having that discussion with a therapist. You're putting it out there; now you're looking back at it. I don't necessarily ever know what I'm writing."

"When I'm writing, I'm a very stream-of-consciousness sort of writer. I just 'spew and edit' is what I call it, the process. And nowadays, I don't even edit that much. I'm just so used to spewing, but it really is a purging of a lot of emotions."

Do the meanings of the songs and the writing change over the years?

"Yeah, I think they do change," she said. "I mean, there's some songs that I'm not as comfortable playing just because of their origin story. 'Shame' is one of them. But it's like the 40th anniversary of the *Shock* album, so old 'Shame' got wheeled out lately, and it's okay. It's good for me to reconnect with those things and those emotions, and a lot of times you're still sorting stuff out. You don't just, like, go through it and go, 'Oh, I have that figured out.' It takes a long time to actually ingest and figure out what impacts situations have on you in the long term, short term. Some are traumatic, but a lot of the life-changing thing is a process that takes years."

"Suddenly Last Summer" is another song that reflects Martha's process of going through change.

"I remember very vividly sitting in my backyard in Berkeley, California," she began. "It had to be the early '70s, and it was sunny, and all of a sudden this really cold wind sort of picked up. It was that first autumn-like snap, and I heard the ice cream truck, and I knew the ice cream truck would not be back that year, that it was over for that summer."

"That feeling I had was a melancholy sense of loss. It wasn't about the ice cream truck; it was about a whole other part of me that I had felt that I had lost over a summer. And that probably went back to when I was a very young girl and lost my virginity or something. I mean, who knows. That's what I mean. The process is fascinating, and we're always growing, we're always changing. And if you're lucky enough to be able to somehow have this vehicle like I do, it's important to pay attention to it and sort of notate it. I always think of my songs as like a diary. I don't journal, but I do."

Her words connected with me. "Thank you so much for saying that because, to be honest, I'm trying to write a book myself about the 20 years that I've been doing this podcast, and I find that when I write, I have to be in a bit of a melancholy mood. I have to be a little bit more…"

"Introspective," she said.

"Yep. That's it," I answered. "I can't come in and sit down at the computer when I'm feeling jubilant."

"Yeah, you and me agree on that one," she continued. "I mean, maybe there's people that do, but when it's sunny and you're in love, and you just are eating ice cream, you're not writing a song," she said with a laugh. "You're there in the bliss of it, and it's when the clouds roll over and you have a glass of wine and you're sitting there and just, like, pondering and all of a sudden, that's when that stuff tends to percolate for me, anyway."

Speaking of pondering sadness, I asked her about the movie *Made in Heaven*. The 1987 film starred Timothy Hutton and Kelly McGillis about two souls who cross paths in heaven only to be torn apart when they return to Earth. The song that ties the plot together—"We Never Danced"—was performed by Martha. Even thinking of the movie and the song makes me want to cry, I told her.

"Such a good movie. Oh, my God," she begins. On the cruise, she had told us that she worked with the great Giorgio Moroder on it, and it was a story I wanted her to retell on the podcast.

"We worked at Giorgio's studio. And you'd pull up and there'd be his Testarossa outside, and we had Richie Zito actually producing it," she said. "I think it was Richie's idea to get a choir of kids, and these young African American kids showed up and they were, like, maybe six, eight, maybe 10 tops. They just got a bunch of pizza, and these kids are just, like, having the time of their life and, like, staring at the Testarossa going, 'Oh, my God.' It was so much fun."

"But then they sing and—God, it was so beautiful," she beamed. "It is such a gorgeous sound when you hear children singing, and especially when they're happy and full of pizza. Yeah, that's a beautiful song, absolutely beautiful song and a great movie. I've been lucky that way."

WEIRD AL YANKOVIC had nothing but nice things to say about Michael Jackson, whom he parodied viciously in his tunes "Fat" and "Eat It."

"I actually met Michael a couple times briefly," Al told my co-host Sean Daly and me during a 2010 interview. "A very sweet man, very soft spoken, very kind. We didn't talk very long, but he expressed that he enjoyed the parodies. He said that he actually screened my movie—*UHF*—in his private theater at the Neverland Ranch, and all his friends enjoyed it. I'm grateful to Michael for a huge vote of confidence very early in my career. If he hadn't given me his permission and his blessing for 'Eat It,' I may not be talking to you right now. That gave me a lot of credibility in the industry and that—it was a huge, huge help very early on."

Born Alfred Matthew Yankovic, Weird Al's thumbprint is all over the '80s. He had two notable singles—"My Bologna" and "Another One Rides the Bus"—before his debut album even dropped in 1983. Not many MTV fans can forget his videos for "Like a Surgeon" or "I Lost on Jeopardy." But like many comedy-forward artists we've interviewed over the years, Al played it more straightforward during our conversation.

I suppose it's cliché to think of comedians as funny all the time, but they're often more introspective than their musical peers. Take, for example, Al's revelation about his parody of Nirvana's "Smells Like Teen Spirit."

"When I do the parodies, it's my way of honoring [the artists]," he said. "The Kurt Cobain thing was a little bit trickier because I went on the road pretty quickly after Kurt's death, and 'Smells Like Nirvana' was still my biggest hit at that time. So that was a little bit more uncomfortable. I still did the song because everybody was expecting me to play it, but prior to doing it, I had kind of a somber few seconds where I talked about how this was done in Kurt's honor."

How did it play in Seattle? The Pacific Northwest town was Kurt's home and the epicenter of the Grunge movement.

"I was really wondering whether I should do it at all in Seattle, because obviously Kurt had a lot of friends and family in Seattle, and it almost seemed like that might be going a little bit too far," Al said. "But I asked a lot of people in Seattle and disc jockeys and people in media whether it was appropriate or not, and everybody seemed to think that it was, so we went ahead and did it, and it actually got a huge, very positive reaction."

I asked Al if the '80s—a decade that's so readily identifiable by its fashion, music, and pop culture—was easier to parody than the years and music genres that followed.

"Here's the thing about that," he said. "I don't know about the songs themselves being easier, but it was a lot easier to really define what the hits were back then. MTV, if you can remember this far back, actually played music videos."

"There weren't all these radio stations playing certain genres or subgenres. Music and our pop culture has gotten very segmented and compartmentalized, and it's not really easy to tell what the hits are anymore. There doesn't seem to be as much of a sense of community or shared experience. Obviously there are still hits, and there are still superstars, but I don't know if we'll ever find somebody now that's on the level of Michael Jackson back then."

We reminisced about the heyday of MTV as a music video channel—and the days when Al would take it over for a day and rebrand it "Al TV."

"What is almost incomprehensible now is that this was in the days when MTV really was like this guerilla network. They were not corporate at all. They literally said, 'Okay, well, you want four hours of programming? Great. Have fun. Let us know when it's done and we'll put it on the air,'" he said.

These days, the music video and song parody landscape is entirely different, he explained.

"Never again will I be the first person or the only person to parody any given pop hit," he said. "That's just the times we live in, so it's unfortunate. I liked being unique, but that's never gonna be the case again."

The mood had turned perhaps a little too introspective, so Sean deftly changed the subject to a recent *Rolling Stone* magazine reader poll that named one '80s artist above all others that fans wanted to see in the Rock & Roll Hall of Fame. Yes, they named Weird Al Yankovic.

"I would love for that day to come, but I'm really not holding my breath," Al said. "I kind of don't think that The Hall really has enough of a sense of humor to include me in this. Let me put it this way: If some other accordion-playing parody artist makes the Hall of Fame and I don't, I'll be very upset."

JOHN OATES didn't want to grow back his signature mustache. But in 2009, he talked about it a lot with Sean Daly and me.

"I guess the mustache is this kind of iconic symbol of the '70s and the '80s," John began. "That mustache that I had was seen so many times in the pictures and the photos and the videos. And you know, the mustache is kind of back with a younger generation of people. It's kind of like a hip thing to have a mustache again. There's actually a guy who has a website who does pictures of me with the mustache in these really strange ways. So, I don't know, it's just a thing. But it's gone. It's been gone for 18 years."

Eighteen years? Has the Earth stopped rotating?

"Shaved it off in 1990," he said. "It ain't coming back. It ain't coming back. I don't think I'd look too cool with a white mustache. It might look a little strange."

What's strange these days is thinking of John Oates without his longtime music partner Daryl Hall. The pop and soul duo had more than 30 tunes reach the Top 100 charts in the U.S. Their slew of No. 1 hits began in 1977 with "Rich Girl" and would stretch to "Out of Touch" in 1984. Listing all their epic songs would take more than one volume of this book.

In 2022, the pair performed what we hope wasn't their last concert. In 2024, Hall announced the partnership was over as a result of differences in their business decisions. But back in 2009, before the pair was set to perform a show at Ruth Eckerd Hall in Clearwater, those future shockwaves were out of sight and out of mind.

Sean and I, of course, immediately began our conversation by asking John how the pair's friendship/partnership had endured so long.

"It's a very strange thing; duos in general have a very unusual dynamic," he said. "I have to say that I think it has to do with the fact that we grew up on the same kind of music. We had the exact same backgrounds. We went to the same kind of schools, lived in the same part of Pennsylvania, right outside of Philadelphia. We listened to the same kind of music. We were excited, inspired by the same type of music. And then when we got together, that formed, like, a musical bond."

The adage "opposites attract" still applies on some levels, he said.

"We're so different as people," he continued. "We couldn't be any more different in so many ways on the personal side that I think we balance each other out in a kind of strange, weird way."

I saw Hall & Oates for the first time in 1983 on their H_2O tour. I was too young to know the hits beyond the most recent albums. That night, at the now-demolished Bayfront Center in St. Petersburg, Florida, I was introduced to such classics as "She's Gone" and "Sara Smile." I remember scraping together what little money I had from mowing the lawn to buy their compilation album *Rock 'n' Soul Part 1*. After gushing all this meaningless trivia out to John, I called their concert a master class in rock.

"Yes, that's our job," he replied. "We are the nutty professors of pop music."

At this point, Sean and I started throwing out the names of songs we wanted to hear when the duo played Clearwater.

"I wanna put in a request for 'Bank of Your Love,' my favorite Hall & Oates song from *Out of Touch*," Sean said.

"Nope," John answered.

"Why don't you like that? Don't do that to me," Sean kidded. "It's, like, my most played song on my iPod."

"It's not that we don't like it. We just don't know it," John explained. "You have to remember, we have about 400 songs."

Sean pretended not to be crushed. We all know that feeling when our band doesn't play that one tune. So we went back to John's mustache.

"I respect you and your upper lip," Sean said. "Why are people so obsessed with John Oates's mustache?"

"Cause they're crazy!" he said.

Cameron Crowe met his heroes on the way up. I've met many of mine after the rush had passed. By then, the spotlight had moved on. Competition didn't matter much anymore. Gratitude did. Sometimes the best thing I could do was shut up and listen.

THE REUNION THAT BROKE ME OPEN

S*tuck in the '80s* was more than a work assignment. It was a way for me to deal with the unexpected energy and residual emotions of my 20-year high school reunion. Back in 2005, I was dreading the approach of another get-together with my school classmates. The 10-year reunion of Countryside High School's Class of 1985 in Clearwater had largely been a dud—we were too busy posturing and preening to engage in any meaningful connections—and I had no reason to think another decade would improve the situation. But I couldn't leave well enough alone.

I emailed the organizing committee and offered to build them a reunion website. It was the least I could do, I said, but really it was the most I wanted to do. At the time, building individual websites was still something of a novelty, but I had the training. I bought a domain, built a framework of pages, and uploaded some photos and forms for missing alumni to fill out.

Ta-da. Finished.

Cue the fidgeting and second-guessing that are my defining characteristics. I *could* write a blog talking about memories of those good old days. I'd recently written a short-lived blog for the *Times* that covered the Tampa Bay Buccaneers' journey to their first Super Bowl championship. The concept of writing and publishing without editing or word counts appealed to me. Okay, just a few short blog items, and that's that.

I wrote about how our high school's dance team—The Cougarettes—had been disbanded for a particularly risqué performance of Devo's "Girl U Want" at a pep rally. I wrote about a Monty Python-themed homecoming skit that my friends and I had written and painfully performed that was unenthusiastically received. I penned a piece about Lip Synch, a twice-annual event where students dressed up as their rock star heroes and mimed the songs on a stage with all the makings of an actual concert. My friends and I won the final one of our senior year by portraying Frankie Goes to Hollywood singing "Relax." Our performance was allowed—reluctantly—by the faculty on the assurances we wouldn't overemphasize the word "Come!" (We did anyway.)

I got a lot of stuff out of my head and onto the blog. Now, that's that, I believed. On with the rest of my life.

Except people were reading it. And commenting. And emailing me.

The blog grew to daily entries. More photos. More stories. Every memory I could summon—including some I wasn't sure were fact or fiction. (Did one of the cool kids at school really have a prom date vomit all over a table before the prom, only to comment aloud to the waiter: "My compliments to the chef"? I remember the story but now doubt the facts.)

"Are you coming to the reunion?" people would write to me and ask. "No, no," I replied.

In the end, I couldn't resist. I was comped for the weekend's events because of my work on the website, so really the last excuse was now moot.

Any misgivings or last-second regret would be cured with alcohol. I filled my car with boxes of booze. My longtime friend and roommate for the weekend, John, would arrive separately with a karaoke machine. No matter what happened, we would be prepared.

Except that I wasn't prepared. Classmates whose names I hadn't spoken in 20 years came up to me immediately. "I wouldn't be here if it wasn't for your blog," one told me. "You made it all come alive again."

"I was hoping you'd be here—that blog is amazing," I heard over and over again. I kept blogging, in fact, during the weekend. I posted photos of our parties, our dinners, our toasts at the hotel bar, our group hugs. And when it was all over, I wrote what I thought would be my final thoughts on high school.

I no longer have the blog online, but it went just like this.

"The sun is rising now on Sunday morning, and I can see my old classmates and now new friends loading up their cars and heading back to their lives. There are so many lingering memories that I can't begin to sort them all out—karaoke jams in our room, huge drinking fests at the hotel bar each night, walks on the beach, the reunion photo. Oh, and the security guard letting me lock the door at the hotel bar that final night before we all fell drunkenly asleep—I have the photo to prove it. It's going to take me a long time to process this all. Thank you, everyone, for reading this, for saying hi, for giving me a hug."

It was 10 a.m., checkout time, on July 10—my birthday of all days. Later that day, I'd drive up to my parents' condo for a family dinner. But for the next 30 minutes, the entirety of my drive back home to St. Petersburg, I wept the whole way with The Cure's "Pictures of You" playing on repeat on my Toyota RAV4's stereo.

No worries, Spearsy. A new outlet for my nostalgia addiction was about two weeks down the road. On July 22, 2005, the first episode of *Stuck in the '80s* was published.

"What's it like when you walk into a room and most of the women in that room burst into tears as soon as they see you?"

TWO DICKS, ONE BACKSTAGE PASS

I've crossed paths with Richard Marx and Rick Springfield a few times. Both are thankfully easy to talk to and generous with their time. Though they may seem to occupy contrasting genres of '80s music, they've had a lot of fun in recent years touring together on their so-called Two Dicks tours. (Amazing fun if you ever get a chance to catch them together.)

RICK SPRINGFIELD was the first artist the *Stuck in the '80s* team interviewed in person. In September 2006, he was in Clearwater along with Loverboy, Eddie Money, and Scandal for the We Are the '80s tour. Sean Daly, Cathy Wos, and I were invited to go backstage before and during the show to interview the artists. We got our producer, Dave Morrison, to come along and handle the technical side of things while we sweated out what to ask everyone.

It was the first live concert I'd been to in 10 years, ever since a trip to see Eric Clapton in person had so underwhelmed me that I had sworn off live music for a decade. I was exploding with excitement and jittery energy all day.

Rick was the first person to walk into the room. We'd heard he wasn't feeling well, but he had a glass of red wine in his hand, was wearing glasses, and seemed eager to talk.

"I'm feeling okay. I'm getting over a cold," Rick assured us.

"There are thousands of people here—women here—who would drive home very unhappy if you were too sick to [play]," Sean joked.

"I've never been too sick to play," Rick began. "Well, once I was. I've done stuff where I couldn't get the words out of my mouth so I just had the audience sing. It was great."

I'll confess that our conversation with Rick was largely one-sided. By that, I mean it was us making more observations than asking the questions, and him usually just laughing instead of answering. But the idea of us being in the same room with him was overwhelming at the time. We kept looking at each other with the same thought bubbles over our heads: *How did we get so lucky?!?*

"What's it like when you walk into a room and most of the women in that room burst into tears as soon as they see you?" Sean began. Rick only laughed.

At the time of the interview, Legacy had just remastered Rick's first big record, *Working Class Dog*. (It's actually Rick's fifth studio album, but the one that gave us "Jessie's Girl," "Love Is Alright Tonite," and "I've Done Everything for You.") He'd also win a Grammy that year for best rock vocal performance. The entertainment magazines were again toasting the power pop genius of Rick Springfield. It all seemed like an unlikely place to land for someone many first knew as an actor on TV's *General Hospital*.

"It's what I wanted to be," Rick said of his music career. "I wanted to be a writer first. When I was 12 years old, I wanted to be a writer before I wanted to be a songwriter. Long before that, I was a guitar player in a band and did harmonies. I never thought of myself as a lead singer. The only reason I started singing was because I wanted people to hear my songs."

Pretty often, when I'm interviewing an '80s hero, I like to ask about the so-called '80s Revolution. What was it about this time that makes it so enduring, far beyond the nostalgic appeal of previous decades? When I asked Rick, he gave me the best answer to date. It's one I keep paraphrasing when people ask me the same question.

"I think people have a really small window when they accept music into their life to become part of their life," he began. "I think it's early teens to maybe early 20s. And then your career kicks in or you get hooked up with someone, start a family, or other things take over. There's only a short period of time where music is everything. And it also happens to be the golden time of your life, which is the teenage years. So I think as radio alienates itself more and more from everybody, I think they're going back quicker and quicker to the songs that made them feel good and the times that made them feel good. I think the '80s was certainly a great radio time, and there's a lot of stuff to choose from. It was really before all the crap hit the fan, you know, worldwide, I think it's a last safe time. I don't even think you can call the '90s a last safe time. I think the '80s is the last safe time. The Wall fell. You knew by that time that no one was going to be dropping any nukes."

At the time of our interview, Rick had returned to making some guest appearances on *General Hospital*. We were curious about that, given the grief he got in the '80s for straddling both careers. Rick insisted he had no hesitations.

"Now, if anything, you've got rockers forming bands and being on reality TV shows. You've got people coming out of the woodwork making records and getting on a reality show. It's almost like there's no bad publicity anymore," he said. "So I certainly thought doing a recurring role as a character I used to play 25 years ago has some history at least. It wasn't the worst thing I could do. I mean, we're all looking to get new music heard, you know?"

From there, the interview went in a dozen new directions. What song was he opening with? (A new song, he said, called "Who Killed Rock and Roll?") Was he playing "Love Somebody" from the *Hard to Hold* soundtrack? ("Yeah, sure. It really works live.") Had he met Paul McCartney and Elvis? (Yes, to both.)

Then the dreaded "end of interview" question you'd normally only get from a prospective employer: "What do you see yourself doing 10 years from now?"

"If I'm still writing, which I hope to be, and still in shape to be able to do an energetic show, I'll still be touring and writing, and I hope to be recording," Rick said. "I have my own studio now and maybe working with someone else, you know? Working with some young people who I think are great."

"Do you still have fun doing it?" Sean asked.

"Yeah, very much so," Rick said. "I wouldn't do it if I wasn't having fun."

Nearly 20 years later, Rick is still touring, writing, and recording. And it sure looks like he's having a hell of a lot of fun.

RICHARD MARX is one of the best storytellers I've interviewed. Sure, you know him for his extensive catalog of softer rock hits; he's the only male artist so far to have his first seven singles—tunes such as "Right Here Waiting," "Hold On to the Nights" and "Hazard"—reach the Top 5 of the Billboard charts. But I don't think I'm wrong in saying his humor and never-ending supply of tales from the studio and the road really set him apart. His book—*Stories to Tell: A Memoir* was released in 2021—is now a must-read for '80s fans. But in 2010, Richard was prepping to perform his first-ever acoustic solo show, set for the newly renovated Capitol Theatre in Clearwater. The venue was owned and managed by the pros at Ruth Eckerd Hall, which had practically become my second home during the early years of the podcast, so Sean and I were able to easily score an interview.

These acoustic shows have now become a regular part of Richard's touring schedule, but then the concept was brand new to him and his fans. We asked if he had to rearrange the tunes for the stripped-down performance.

"On paper, it sounds like they would be drastically rearranged," Richard began. "But these songs, for the most part, started out this way, and they evolved because I produced my own record. It all started with me probably 99% of the time just sitting either at the piano and writing a song or grabbing an acoustic guitar and writing a song."

We'd gotten the polite first question out of the way, so I leaned back in my chair knowing that Sean had some history with Richard.

"Before we get too much further here, I gotta say, you and I have met before," Sean started. "In about '93 or '94, I worked at a place called the Columbia Inn in Columbia, Maryland. Okay. And that was right next to Merriweather Post Pavilion."

"Right," Richard said.

"I was a bellboy there in an extremely ill-fitting bellboy costume," Sean continued. "You were staying at the Columbia Inn. I also drove the courtesy van. You were the only celebrity rock star that I drove that sat in the front with me in the courtesy van. Instead of me doing my little bellboy shuffle to open the back door and let you go into the van, you said, 'Hey, I want to sit up front with you.' And it was really cool. I remember we talked about how you helped me get laid in college by playing your songs. And you seemed really appreciative, so I just want to thank you."

"I do appreciate that," Richard said. "I had a guy literally at my house. We're having some construction work done, and I just got back from India. There was a note in my studio from this guy that was working here at the house saying, 'I just had to thank you so much because you helped me get so much action in high school.' So, I'm glad to be on the team."

Being part of the team seemed to be a Richard Marx ethos. We were eager to get the goods on all the artists he'd worked with over his career, including how he'd gotten his start with Lionel Richie.

"He was the impetus for me moving from Chicago to L.A. when I did," Richard said of Lionel. "Because my plan, by the time I was in my junior year of high school, was to kind of stay in the Chicago area, take some more music classes at Northwestern, really, just frankly, to bide my time. I'd written a dozen songs or so and certainly wanted to get a record deal and do that, but wasn't exactly on the path, as they say. And in the middle of my senior year, this demo tape of my first four or five songs that I had recorded wound up in Lionel Richie's hands. And this tells you everything you need to know about Lionel Richie."

We were on the edge of our seats.

"Lionel Richie heard the tape," he continued. "The fact that he listened to the tape is mind blowing because this is 1981, '82, and he was just launching his solo career. I mean, the guy didn't have time to listen to somebody's demo tape, but he did, and he called me himself, and he was very encouraging and supportive, and he really liked my songwriting and really liked my voice and could recognize that it was still pretty embryonic. He was the one that said, 'Look, if you end up going to college, look me up after that. But if you decide you want to really get into this, you've got to move to L.A., because there's nothing happening in Chicago.'"

Career advice from Lionel Richie. Received and taken.

"So, with the full support of my parents, I bailed on college, and I went out to L.A., and he hired me as a background singer on his first solo record. So I was doing some session work for him, but more than that, he allowed me whether I was singing on what they were working on that day or not."

It became an open invitation to observe the entire process. A "master class," as Sean put it.

"Then within a few months of that, Lionel recommended me to Kenny Rogers as a background singer because Kenny was working on a new record. So I got hired for a couple of days of background vocals on his record. And one day I overheard Kenny telling his producer that they were still short a song. I went home to my apartment that night and I wrote a song. And literally my whole body was shaking the next day because I knew I could get fired over this. But I told him, 'I overheard you yesterday, and I'm a songwriter and I wrote this song,' and Kenny was nice enough to let me play it for him. And he cut it, and it was a No. 1 country song."

The song was "Crazy." It became Kenny's eleventh chart-topping single and spent 13 weeks in the Top 40.

How did Richard celebrate, we asked.

"I've never been much of a partier," he said. "You know, I'm a drug virgin to this day."

"Come on!" Sean injected.

"No, seriously, not even weed, dude," he said. "When I was doing session work and stuff in the '80s, blow was everywhere. And I remember being offered blow regularly and thinking to myself, 'The only reason I'm not going to do blow is because I know I'm going to love it. And I could see the damage it was doing to people already. And I just thought, 'I don't need that shit.' And weed was never an issue because I'm so smoke phobic....No, I mean, I love a few kamikazes."

If anything, Richard said he wished he had taken the opportunity to celebrate and let it soak in, but he insisted his life just didn't allow it at the time.

"My life consisted of 6:30 a.m. radio performances and interviews and then going and doing in-stores and then going to soundcheck and then right from soundcheck to some more interviews on TV or whatever, and then doing a gig and then immediately getting off the stage and having phoners in Japan and Australia and going to sleep on the bus for a few hours and waking up and doing it all again," he said.

Even listening to him describe his life was exhausting.

"The truth is that it was such a blur that my only regret is that I didn't soak it in," he continued. "You can't appreciate what's really happening. You don't really have a perspective. You're just working your ass off. You're just treading water. Because my attitude was always 'this can go away tomorrow.' Luckily for me, I didn't really hit that wall for a good eight or nine years. But when it did happen, when we did finally put out the record that went double plywood instead of double platinum, it was not such a big shock for me because I never perceived myself as an artist that was going to be innovative for 30 years and all that."

"I knew that you had to have a certain kind of level of controversy and all that stuff that I just didn't possess," he continued. "But I always knew that I could go back and write songs and produce records for other people, because that's really how I started."

What did Richard think of the get-famous-quick world of reality shows such as *American Idol*?

"It doesn't drive me crazy. It's an extension of a bigger issue for me, which is what's frustrating for me is that I still get completely fired up every day to write songs and make records," he said. "But I'm not inspired by the music that's going on right now. My contemporaries were Sting and Peter Gabriel and U2, and a lot of artists that were the antithesis of what's happening right now. These were guys that really knew their craft, that really paid their dues, and they kept the bar high so that when I would hear the new Def Leppard record or I'd hear the new Peter Gabriel record, I'd go, 'I suck. I'm not worthy. I need to do better.'"

"There's a lot of great music out there, but it's mostly by bands that most people have never heard of," he clarified. "My iPod is full of bands like Sick Puppies and The Afters and CAVO and a lot of bands that don't have a huge following. But that's where I draw my inspiration from—new bands that are paying their dues but they're not having the kind of success that Kris Allen and Adam Lambert are having."

"It's brutal and it's really weird for me because [*American Idol* judge] Randy Jackson and I have been friends forever. He played on a bunch of my records. Randy Jackson is about as talented a musician as there is in the world. Because of *American Idol*, he's become almost a cartoon. And I love that he's become very famous and wealthy from that show, but it really doesn't show people how deep his talent is. I haven't watched the show since season one. I just don't pay attention to it. It just is meaningless to me. It's just karaoke."

At this point in the interview, I confess I was starting to feel bad. We had turned a happy conversation with a musical hero into a bitch session about reality TV. God help me, I can't find the bright side to drivel like *Idol* either, but we had far more positive ground we wanted to cover in the 30 or so minutes we had Richard on the phone. Thankfully, Sean felt it too and changed the subject to "Hazard," a song that peaked at No. 9 on the U.S. Hot 100 and topped the adult contemporary charts.

"It was a huge hit for you. It's not like it's some sort of B-side," Sean began. "But it really seemed like it was a drastic, at least to my ear, songwriting change. Like maybe you were trying something different."

"I wrote that in the back of the tour bus," Richard said. "I've always written a lot of songs on the road because I don't party, and so there's a lot of downtime. I had written this piece of music, and all I knew from the music of 'Hazard' was that it couldn't be a love song and it couldn't be a political song, and it couldn't be anything like I had ever written before. And so I started creating the story with characters. I honestly don't remember what the basis was of how I set it in Nebraska. I think that was just a word that came with the melody or something. And the more I worked on the song, the dumber I thought it was. I thought it was the dumbest song I'd ever tried to write."

It was Richard's wife at the time—actress Cynthia Rhodes—who heard the song and thought it was a hit. He finished the song just to prove she was wrong.

"But everybody flipped out over it, and it became a No. 1 song in, like, 12 countries or something like that," he said. "It's one of my most famous songs. So I've never won an argument since then with my wife."

Do people still want to know who killed Mary, we asked.

"I swear to God, at least every month, someone will ask me about it," he said. "And it's just mind blowing to me because I can't believe that anybody gives a shit. But the truth is that I did intentionally write it as an unsolved mystery. It was the record company that tried to sponsor contests on MTV. Who killed Mary? I was like, 'What are you doing? There is no answer to that question. It's not in the song. And I'm not going to contrive something.' I remember just being annoyed by the whole thing. But I loved that people were paying attention to the lyrics and they wanted to know what happened to these characters."

At this point, we were eating out of Richard's hand, but we were also aware our time was about up. I decided to wrap things up with a ham-handed question.

"I have not decided yet who to bring to your concert," I began. "What song should I wait for by the great Richard Marx before I make my big move on my date?"

"Well, how tall is he?" Richard fired back.

"I love it. Thank you!" Sean gushed.

A few weeks later, I met Richard in person backstage before the show—with my date Jennifer—and we took a photo that, sadly, I no longer can find. Fast-forward a few years, when I found myself in an interview with Tubes lead singer Fee Waybill, one of Richard's best friends. I reached out through Ruth Eckerd Hall to see if Richard would give me a few questions to ask Fee that nobody on the planet would know about. And sure enough, Richard delivered two zingers. When I got through asking Fee the unusual queries, he finally shot back, "Who gave you these questions?"

"Richard Marx," I said back with a smile. I heard a huge sigh on the phone line and then…

"Richard!"

Looking back, it makes sense that Rick Springfield and Richard Marx found each other on the road. They're cut from the same cloth—guys who survived the '80s without being trapped by it. They still care about the work. And they still show up curious, generous, and always laughing.

It's very obvious from reading that transcript that we had no idea what we were doing. I think it's precious. ... But, yeah, it's super awkward and goofy.

THIRTEEN MINUTES OF PANIC

To help me cohost the *Stuck in the '80s* podcast, I approached one of the lifestyle writers at my newspaper. Gina Vivinetto was a former music critic for the *St. Petersburg Times* and grew up going to high school in the same county as me. She was a year or two younger, but we went to many of the same concerts of the day. Our intern, Brendan Watson, was the only person on staff who knew anything about audio editing, so he became the de facto producer.

Gina and I looked like a pair of idiots recording that first show. We sat across from each other at a table with cheap, hand-held microphones. Brendan, who I'm not sure was even born in the '80s, wore headphones and held the digital recorder. He was familiar with sound recording, production, and editing, and had hosted what he called "a very nerdy podcast on media research and the future of news media."

GINA SAYS NOW: I was so impressed with what a good host Steve was right from the start. I looked to him to dictate what we were going to do, and he was such a good leader. He came to perfect his hosting style pretty quickly. He brings so much heart to the podcast. It's clear the fans feel that and appreciate it. The listeners know him. That's a beautiful thing.

The first few minutes...they were not brilliant.

GINA: Welcome to *Stuck in the '80s*, our brand-new podcast on TampaBay.com. I'm Gina Vivinetto, columnist for the *Tampa Bay Times*."

STEVE: "Hi. And I'm Steve Spears, the online news editor for sptimes.com."

GINA: "What are we gonna talk about today, Steve?"

[nervous laughter]

GINA SAYS NOW: Oh, my God, I was just rambling! Now I remember I was always very caffeinated when we recorded. I was drinking, like, multiple iced venti soy chais from the Starbucks on Fourth Street back then because the baristas would give them to me for free. I'd probably have a cardiac arrest now if I tried to consume that much caffeine. It's very obvious from reading that transcript that we had no idea what we were doing. At least we tried to provide some interesting facts. We could have just been sharing our own opinion the whole time or something, you know? It's obvious we wanted to make it interesting. I think it's precious. But, yeah, it's super awkward and goofy.

That was the high-water mark of that afternoon. For the record, we discussed our thoughts about *The Breakfast Club*. For about 13 minutes. That's it. (Thankfully, we'd redo that episode for our 10th anniversary episode and put some real thought and effort into it.)

BRENDAN SAYS NOW: God, you were awkward. Kidding! I remember recording in the little office nook with others working with their backs to us trying to ignore us, which made things that much more awkward. Gina was naturally more outgoing and chatty, but I remember Steve's passion and interest in the '80s really coming through from the beginning. But when we had the podcast studio, and you all started having guests on, I think that is when things really took off in terms of the quality of the content. There were some equipment and space challenges, challenges to coaching newspaper journalists to be more natural 'on tape.' But that was also a period when we still had the resources to experiment. We were figuring out digital journalism, and I remember it being an exciting time.

Brendan would soon hand off the production duties to Dave Morrison, one of the marketing photographers of the newspaper but also a guy who was an ace at audio and video production. We would dub him "The Maestro" for turning our messes into proper podcasts.

DAVE SAYS NOW: I'm not even sure I knew what a podcast was at first. I don't think I had heard the first episode of *Stuck in the '80s* until someone on the staff told me about the show. In spite of growing up in the '60s and '70s, I was a huge fan of '80s music and knew I wanted to be involved. I was almost a decade older than Steve and Gina, but I grew up when music radio was still fun to listen to. I wanted to bring some of that fun to the podcast.

Dave taught me everything I know about audio editing. He also served as the designated driver one Saturday afternoon when we decided to do an on-location podcast on "Drinking in the '80s" at a bar in St. Petersburg. I took over production duties when he and the newspaper parted ways a few years later. He still keeps in touch, and he contributed many of the photos you'll see at the back of the book. He even recreated my column photo from my days at the *Times* for the author photo at the end of the book. Safe to say the podcast would never have found its way without his enthusiasm, dedication, and help.

Gina would leave the podcast and the *Times* after the first two dozen episodes. I immediately missed her endless energy, deep knowledge, incredible sense of humor, and the knack she had for putting me in my place. "Google it, Steve!" became her favorite admonishment when I found myself grasping for a forgotten fact. By that time, the brand-new music critic at the *Times*, Sean Daly, had joined the podcast. Gina named her own replacement: Cathy Wos, a news researcher at the newspaper who was "cooler than Steve and me put together," my outgoing co-host insisted.

GINA SAYS NOW: I wish I could have done a few more episodes with Steve before I left our former employer, but I'm genuinely so proud I was there at all in the beginning. It really has been thrilling to watch the podcast grow and grow. Steve had a really great idea, and it worked out more beautifully than I ever could have imagined. He's an inspiration to me and I'm sure to everyone who dreams of starting a passion project.

THE NICEST MAN IN THE LOUDEST BAND

For many people my age, *Back in Black* was the introduction album for AC/DC. I asked for it for Christmas in 1980 without knowing a single song from it—the word-of-mouth praise around school was enough. I had to have it.

AC/DC and Styx were two of the bands that pulled me away from my pre-teen love for acts like Kiss. It didn't take long for me to become obsessed with the music, and I began collecting the albums from the '70s—especially the live album *If You Want Blood You've Got It*. (The cover art depicts guitarist Angus Young being impaled on stage with a guitar, which was an added bonus.)

Captured during a concert in Glasgow, Scotland, in 1978, it was the only live album featuring lead singer Bon Scott, who would die in 1980—the official reason being "death by misadventure," though alcohol poisoning was the likely culprit.

There was something about AC/DC that just ran through me back in those days. I would put on my headphones, put on a record, and disappear in the music. In January of 1982, the band was touring on their follow-up to *Back in Black*, a disc called *For Those About to Rock*. The tour included two stops in Lakeland, Florida that month. Somehow I conned my parents into letting me go—and getting my dad to drive me and my friends round trip.

We got to the Lakeland Civic Center hours early and ran right up to the front of the stage. We had hours to kill before the show began. Some joints began to make their way through the general admission seating area. I was 14 at the time, but it took about two seconds for me to enthusiastically grab one and try it. It was my first taste of marijuana. I inhaled as deeply as I could before coughing the smoke out.

Midnight Flyer opened the show. I only remember the crowd booing relentlessly and the sound waves crashing between my ears. By the time AC/DC took the stage, I was floating three feet off the floor. Brian Johnson, the singer replacing Scott, was ringing the hell out of a Hell's Bell as the show got started.

The rest of the show is a blur—both then and now. It was undoubtedly the loudest concert of my life—my ears rang for a good four days afterward. I remember getting back into my dad's van at the end of the night.

"How was the show?" he asked us.

"Oh, fucking great. Just fucking amazing! You know what I mean?" I slurred back.

Dad might have been surprised by my language, but he knew what I meant.

In 2007, Brian Johnson was coming through Clearwater along with pal Cliff Williams, Robin Zander, Eddie Money, and others for an all-star gig to support the John Entwistle Foundation, which provides free music instruction and instruments to underprivileged kids. Amazingly enough, *Stuck in the '80s* got an invitation to interview Brian a few weeks before the show.

Sean and I handled this one together. I think we were both a little intimidated at the task in front of us—but we needn't have been. Brian was a total joy to talk with. The topics were random, pivoting between swimming with sharks, life off the road, the

Rock & Roll Hall of Fame, and the inspiration behind some of his first lyrical work for the band.

It was a morning interview, not all that rare for us in those days, though we wondered aloud this time how a hard rocker like Brian could be awake so early.

"Yeah, I'm not telling you the real time I get up. I will blow my whole image," Brian said.

Four p.m. was our best guess.

"I am a 7 o'clock in the morning guy," he finally confessed. "And then I go for a run and then a swim. And then work out."

He swam in a pool, not the nearby Gulf of Mexico (he lived in Sarasota, Florida, at the time). Why? Sharks.

"I have this terrible fear of sharks and other little things that bite the end of your freaking toes up," he said.

Sean and I were delirious with laughter at this point. Apparently, Brian had once loved swimming in the Gulf, until a friend of his took him up in a helicopter and showed him all the sharks down below.

The talk shifted to the band's enduring appeal. Apparently that day it meant action figures.

"My daughter phoned us from England the other day and she said, 'Geez, Dad. I've just bought an action figure of you,'" Brian said. "'There's you and Angus and you can sit Angus on your shoulders [laughter].'"

"It's fabulous to know that you've left something well worth something," he continued. "This year was one of the greatest years of my life when I found out that we had just overtaken the Beatles in catalog sales. I mean, that takes some doing and I'm real proud of that."

Speaking of legacy, we couldn't resist asking him what the Rock & Roll Hall of Fame experience was like. AC/DC was inducted in 2003. During the ceremony, Brian had read some of Bon Scott's lyrics.

"I did it because Bon wasn't there and his two nephews were there," he said. "All I said was, 'In the beginning, back in 1955, man didn't know 'bout a rock 'n' roll show and all that jive. The white man had the schmaltz. The black man had the blues. No one knew what they was gonna do but Tchaikovsky had the news.'"

"And I just said, 'Bon Scott wrote that, thanks very much. We accept it on his behalf and his family and ourselves.' And that was it. Basically simple as that."

Brian's so humble and grateful that Sean and I continued to feel caught off guard. It turns out this is a quality I've found in many British musicians. (Though AC/DC is Australian, Brian is English. His Geordie accent is hard to miss.)

When Brian joined AC/DC, he told us, he was thrown into the business of writing lyrics to music the band had already composed.

"I was just so desperately trying to write the words down as fast as I could, because the next day, the next track would be ready," he said.

One day, as the band was recording in the Bahamas, he was told to write lyrics to "Hell's Bells." As for ideas, the band had nothing for him.

"I was sitting in my room, well, it was more like a cell, a little concrete cell," Brian recalled. "It's on the beach, and this big thunderstorm came in and I was going, 'Oh, hang on a minute. I'm rolling thunder.' Then it pissed down with rain…'I'm pouring rain…'"

Sean and I looked at each other in the podcast studio. Our jaws dropped comically like a *Tom and Jerry* cartoon. He was really telling us the backstory of one of our favorite anthems, and the chills were overwhelming.

"And then the wind picked up and I just, 'I'm coming on like a hurricane.' And that was the end of it, really. It was dead easy after that."

When we finally wrapped up, we screamed—thankfully our studio was soundproof—and then we fell to the floor and rolled around like a pair of five-year-olds. Though it had lasted only 26 minutes, it was the first interview where I felt like I was talking to a living god.

A few weeks later, we were invited backstage at Clearwater's Ruth Eckerd Hall to meet Brian and Cliff Williams. We weren't the only ones. Eddie Money was there—he performed at the benefit too—and he slyly stole a beer from a six-pack I was carrying around. Robin Zander was there too. And so was…Wade Boggs?!?

The famous Boston Red Sox third baseman was wrapping up his career with the hometown Tampa Bay Rays. Sean, normally unflappable, couldn't bring himself to say hi—he had grown up a huge Sox fan, and the team was sacred to him. I chatted Wade up for a few minutes and just soaked up the rare air of the evening.

The night ended and I found myself searching the parking lot for my car. My ears were ringing again—almost as badly as they had decades before. The next day at work, coworkers asked how the event went.

"Oh, fucking great. Just fucking amazing! You know what I mean?" I said back.

They knew what I meant.

"I played it very real and sincere, but I know that everybody hated me. It's terrible, terrible."

OLD MAGIC, NEW PROJECTS

The first time I learned you can't interview actors the way you interview musicians, it wasn't from a publicist. It was from the pause. You ask the innocent question—*"So what was it like making that movie we all wore out on VHS?"*—and on the other end of the line you can almost hear the smile tighten. Musicians have to live with their past in public. Kevin Cronin can't take a night off from "Keep On Lovin' You" without starting a small riot. But nobody expects Molly Ringwald to sit down and do a table read of *The Breakfast Club*. (Although, holy hell, we would pay for that.)

So when *Stuck in the '80s* landed an actor from our beloved decade, it was usually for one reason: They had something new to sell—and we had a narrow window to sneak in a question or two about the old magic before we heard that familiar sigh.

MARTIN SHORT had a great run in the '80s, appearing on TV with *The Love Boat* and *SCTV* before tackling bigger projects such as *The Three Amigos* and *Innerspace*. In March 2012, he was visiting Clearwater to do a one-man comedy show at Ruth Eckerd Hall. When Martin says "one man," he means many. During the show, many of his beloved personas—Jiminy Glick, Nathan Thurm, Ed Grimley—would manifest and take turns stealing the show.

My co-host Sean Daly and I got the interview—a phone chat far too early in the morning for reasonable people to be awake, so I wasn't sure what to expect. Even Canadians have to sleep, right? Though we paused the conversation for a few minutes so he could answer the hotel door for room service to deliver coffee, Martin was right on the ball.

I had always been curious about his Jiminy Glick character, a boorish movie critic with a hefty dose of cluelessness and ignorance.

I began: "Martin, I stayed up last night, and I watched you on *Letterman*, and the hardest I laughed was when Jiminy Glick asked Mel Brooks, 'So what's your real beef with the Nazis?' It made me wonder—have you ever gotten a question so absurd or clueless you wanted to end the interview right there?"

Martin's answer surprised me: "Very infrequently. Everyone thought that Jiminy Glick was my way of getting back at them. But I never actually had a rough time with the press. Glick was more like, just to me, it made me laugh that in show business there are morons with power who have assistants who are running out, getting sandwiches, and they're afraid that they screwed it up. And the guy is an idiot. And the same in politics, too."

The conversation evolved into his movies, and Martin is a storytelling machine. Because he and the late John Candy had worked together in *SCTV*, we asked if he had any memories to share.

"Oh, I adore John," Martin said. We could hear his smile through the phone. "John was exactly how you would love him to be. He was funny, and he was sweet, and he was a partier. And he would insist on paying every bill even though he made the exact same money when we were starting on it. He was a deeply, deeply fabulous guy. He's someone that I can just absolutely see walking in right now. He'd always sing when he saw me, 'Marty Short. How are you?'"

When we moved on to Hollywood's insistence on remaking '80s movies, we asked which of his own flicks deserved a redo. "I would say *Three Amigos*. Yeah. Why not?" he answered.

The secret to the enduring—and maybe unanticipated—respect for *Three Amigos* is that it was "an absurdist film for just pure comedy," Martin said. The 1986 movie, directed by John Landis, had been bouncing around the studios for years. The casting changes alone are harder to follow than three-card monte. Dan Aykroyd and John Belushi were originally slated to star. Bill Murray and Robin Williams were also in the mix. Even Rick Moranis and John Candy were once on board. Eventually, through fate and scheduling, the stars would be Steve Martin, Chevy Chase, and Short.

The result was a product that confused audiences and confounded critics. The three stars were sent out to explain in a series of TV appearances.

"I remember Chevy and Steve and I were promoting it. We were doing *The Today Show*," Martin said. "And Bryant Gumbel said, 'So what will you say if someone says that this is a silly movie?' And he just kinda spit the word 'silly' out. And Steve Martin said, 'Well, it depends how you say silly. If you say, this silly movie, that's a compliment.' And he goes, 'This is a silly movie, then it isn't a compliment.' And I actually think that the absurdist…Steve is an absurdist even when he tweets now, they're always, 'A dog is holding a gun on me. What do I do?' It's always that strange 'I'm going to the Oscars to meet Cher, hopefully to get on a first-name basis with her.' And so that script, and that's the invisible horsemen and all these strange things, were just his sense of humor."

In 2021, Martin Short and Steve Martin teamed up again for *Only Murders in the Building*, a reminder that silly, absurdist comedy doesn't age out—it just finds a new stage. And talking to Martin that morning, it was obvious: He wasn't revisiting the '80s out of obligation. He was still having fun.

MICHAEL MCKEAN is a mensch. He not only seems to still embrace his roles from the '80s, he's willing to quote his own character's lines before you can. In April 2009, Michael was touring with *Spinal Tap* pals Christopher Guest and Harry Shearer. The trio were playing the songs from three of their movies together—*This Is Spinal Tap, A Mighty Wind,* and *Waiting for Guffman.*

The tour was called Unwigged and Unplugged and was making a stop in downtown St. Petersburg at the Mahaffey Theatre. Sean Daly and I had a chance to talk Michael up prior to the actor hitting the road.

"No more wigs?" we asked.

"No more wigs," Michael confirmed. "I gotta say that the unplugged part is kind of a lie. You gotta plug these days a little bit but it's just not gonna be in the 11 area. It's gonna be more like eight and a half."

We exploded with delight at the *Spinal Tap* reference.

"I'll try and disarm all these jokes before you get to them, and then we don't have to bother," he kidded.

This Is Spinal Tap is the 1984 mockumentary—or "rockumentary" as it's described in the film—directed by Rob Reiner, his first project behind the camera. The three actors star as aging British heavy metal musicians looking to reintroduce themselves to American audiences with a tour to promote a new album, *Smell the Glove.* Michael confirmed what we always believed: 99 percent of the movie is improvised, with just two lines of actual dialogue being written ahead of time.

Critics nearly universally praised *Spinal Tap* at its release, while the audience would grow to love it as a cult classic once it made its way onto VHS. We asked Michael if that meant he was hounded on the street by doughy white guys quoting the movie to him.

"Yeah. But that's okay. It doesn't bother us," he said. "Everyone is very nice about it. I don't encounter any fans that are of the stalker variety, mainly because they know that Spinal Tap doesn't really exist. The Folksmen [his band in *A Mighty Wind*] are a figment of a very old imagination, and they know that Corky didn't write all those songs in *Waiting for Guffman*. I think our gang, our fans, are very smart, and so we don't really have too much of a downside, I gotta say."

If you ever wondered how Michael McKean—the actor—became Michael McKean—the musician—he offered this background lesson.

"I grew up around music," he said. "My father worked for record companies. He was an A&R man at RCA and Columbia. We always had a lot of different kinds of music around. He himself was kind of a jazz aficionado and classical music fan, but he also loved the blues and kind of the more genuine folk stuff. And he was also smart enough to recognize that the better rock-'n'-roll stuff wasn't just by the numbers. I started playing guitar during the whole folk era of the early '60s, so that's kind of my education. I had my own preferences, of course, and I was always a big fan of music of all kinds."

What did he make of the movie's lack of initial success?

"People didn't quite know what to make of it," he said. "When we would preview the film, they were just, 'Well, who are these guys? I've never heard of them. Why is the camera jiggling around like that? Why is Meathead directing the film?' And that's kind of what we had to contend with. It had spots of success. It ran in one theater in Boston for over a year, which is weird because Boston is not a big college town."

We immediately applauded another *Tap* reference.

For Michael, success in the cineplex didn't come easy or quickly. After becoming a household name as half of Lenny and Squiggy in TV's long-running *Laverne & Shirley* series, he'd find some leading roles such as Dr. Simon August in 1982's sadly forgotten *Young Doctors in Love* and the more widely appreciated *Clue* movie in 1985 playing Mr. Green.

I asked him why actors in his generation didn't have the same success jumping from TV to film like an Adam Sandler or a Kevin James.

"I don't know. It's a good question," he answered. "It's just kind of the accident of the product. How good is your movie? That's all. And I think that if you launch directly from a sitcom into a feature, it's not automatic, no matter how popular your show is. And that continues to this day. I don't think that Kevin James's film career would've taken off if he weren't good. And then he's funny. He's funny in the *Mall Cop* movie."

We had one last ask of Michael. Sean wanted to know about Michael's brief but memorable scene as a state trooper in *Planes, Trains and Automobiles*.

"I think it's John Hughes's best movie myself," he began. It turns out his role was supposed to be beefier, though. "There was a little more to the story, too. I take them [Steve Martin and John Candy] in and to jail and everything."

The scenes were eventually cut as unpredictable weather snowed in some sets, but it wasn't a lost cause, Michael said.

"The first time I heard the Beatles on CD was on that shoot. They had never been released on CD before," he told us. "John

Hughes got a copy from a friend in London, so I sat in my trailer, watching the snow, and listened to the Beatles."
Michael McKean—always the musician first.

DIANE FRANKLIN had always been a bucket-list interview for me. As a teenager, I fell hopelessly in love with her as the girl next door, Karen, in 1982's *The Last American Virgin*. Well, until the final five minutes of the movie, when Karen dumps our hero Gary (played with total devastation by Lawrence Monoson) for hunky but villainous Rick (Steve Antin). Don't mock the soap opera plot here—or maybe applaud it—because this movie, more than any other '80s flick, defined the ups and downs of early love for me and many of my friends of the time.

In 2017, Diane was one of the actors in the lineup of the initial 80s in the Sand week in Punta Cana, Dominican Republic. I stopped her in the buffet line one morning, asked for an interview, and got her personal email address. For reasons baffling to me, I would end up waiting until 2022 to email and book that conversation.

The Last American Virgin was Diane's first big-screen role. She'd also be the love interest in the cult classic *Better Off Dead* in 1985. When she appears at cons these days, she's often dressed as the French exchange student Monique from that film, where she co-starred opposite John Cusack. Other movies included *Bill & Ted's Excellent Adventure* and the underappreciated *How I Got Into College*. Horror movie fans adore her for her work in the *Amityville* series.

My goal in our conversation, however, was finding some sort of peace with what Karen does to Gary in *Virgin*. No, she didn't write the part, but she became the person. And oddly enough, I'm haunted by Gary's heartbreak to this day.

"They hate me," Diane said when I mentioned how fans react about the Karen role. It took very little prodding from me for her to continue.

"*Last American Virgin* was a film that I didn't even know if it was gonna get made," she said. "At that time in the early '80s, you didn't know if a film was gonna even get on the screen. But when I did the part, I remember saying to myself, 'Well, I can bring some sweetness and realness.' I didn't want her to be the girl you saw and went, 'Oh yeah, I don't even want her with him anyway.'"

If you haven't seen it, I'll ruin the movie and ending for you. Rick dumps Karen after she gets pregnant. Gary, our hero, saves the day by helping her get an abortion and recover. In the aftermath, he finally confesses he's always loved her, and we get the kiss we've been waiting for. Is the movie over? Oh, hell no. Gary buys Karen a pendant for her birthday, and when he shows up at her party, he finds her in the arms of Rick again. The look on Gary's face is devastating—the English language needs to evolve to find the right term for the level of moroseness we see. As the credits roll, Gary drives away, tears rolling down his cheeks as James Ingram belts out soulfully, "I did my best, but I guess my best wasn't good enough" from his hit "Just Once."

"You want Karen to be with him, and that's why it hit so hard," Diane said. "I remember, we, all of us, Lawrence Monoson, Steve Antin, and Kimmy Robertson, we all thought that [writer/director] Boaz [Davidson] was going to change the ending. We really thought that was unfair. It just wasn't an American ending; it wasn't a happy ending."

It turns out the director had his reasons.

"Boaz was adamant, 'No, this is my life. I lived this way and this happened to me, so I cannot change it.' I've talked to people about it. I've said I wouldn't have gone with Rick and I certainly wouldn't have gone with Rick after he got me pregnant. My reaction at the end of the film, a lot of people read a lot of things into it. And I like that. I think that's good. I think that if it's ambiguous, it makes it more interesting."

My teenage angst and ongoing trauma is "more interesting?" I wonder today.

"I just think that sometimes relationships, even if you love someone, even if you deeply love someone, they cannot be. That's just life," Diane said. "You can love someone with all your heart, and there's something that's keeping you guys from being together. So from my perspective, I played it very real and sincere, but I know that everybody hated me. It's terrible, terrible."

I told Diane that in retrospect—at the age of 15 when the movie came out—I wasn't ready for something so sad but ultimately realistic.

"For so many reasons, it's a human story. It never goes away, whether it's today or a hundred years from now. Humans will be acting the same, they will have the same problems and same dilemmas, and it will connect," she said. "Obviously, the ending will never go. It'll never go away because it's not cookie cutter. It's a time capsule for the '80s, which is great, so if you don't know anything about the '80s, all of a sudden you're smack in the world of a teenager during that time, in the darker world. In a world, let's say, more realistic than *Fast Times at Ridgemont High* in a way."

Diane's next big role was Monique in *Better Off Dead*, where she plays the heroic and self-confident exchange student—quite the opposite of her turn as Karen. It almost didn't play out that way.

"[Director] Savage Steve Holland wanted me to play Beth—the villain," Diane said. The whole story is recounted in great and loving detail in her book *Diane Franklin: The Excellent Adventures of The Last American, French-Exchange Babe of the 80s*.

Better Off Dead has always held a special spot in my '80s nostalgic heart. I worked the summer of 1986 between semesters from college at a video chain in Tampa Bay called Pik-a-Flik. My tiny store had two copies of *Back to the Future* and two copies of *Better Off Dead*. During our chat, I told Diane this story and revealed that when customers would ask for the never-in-stock copies of the Michael J. Fox classic, I'd steer them to *Better Off Dead* instead. I'd always say: "If you don't like it, you don't have to pay for it." Nobody ever asked for their money back. If they really loved *Better Off Dead*, I'd recommend *Last American Virgin* next.

"Well, now they hate me, right?" she laughed. "I would always tell people to watch *Last American Virgin* first then watch *Better Off Dead*, because you'll end up, it'll be fine. You'll forgive me. Hopefully."

MOLLY RINGWALD is one of the names that defines the '80s. She and director John Hughes had a partnership that created some of the most enduring movies of the decade—*Sixteen Candles*, *The Breakfast Club*, and even *Pretty in Pink*, which though directed by Howard Deutch was still written by Hughes.

In the decades that followed the '80s, Molly and many of her contemporaries seemed ready to move on to different types of projects and careers and leave their teen images behind. In December 2006—for only the 69th episode of the podcast—we got a chance to talk to Molly, easily the biggest "get" so far. Too bad I would bungle my way through this rare opportunity.

Here was the catch: Molly was promoting her starring role in the touring version of *Sweet Charity*, a stage musical that was making a stop in Tampa Bay. Her willingness to answer questions about the '80s was untested, but I just had a feeling that she wasn't going to entertain many queries. To help me, I asked *St. Petersburg Times* performing arts critic John Fleming to join me for the interview. John retired in 2013, but in 2006 he was thankfully willing to talk with Molly. He's easily one of the most knowledgeable critics I ever worked with, and his familiarity with stage work was unmatched. I wanted him to begin the chat.

John asked whether this was her first big-length tour. Her first tour ever, she replied. Molly was performing in eight shows a week—playing Charity Hope Valentine—and had to sing, dance, and act. The production moved towns each week, she explained, giving her the added electricity of having an "opening night" every seven days.

Finally, more than halfway through the interview, sensing our time was running short, I jumped in. I recalled that she had acted on stage before her run of '80s movies.

"I was a singer originally with my father's jazz band, and somebody had suggested at the time that I audition for *Annie*," she said. "I got a part in it, and so that's sort of how that started."

After *Annie*, Molly got an agent. She'd land two episodes on TV's *Diff'rent Strokes* before moving over to the spinoff *The Facts of Life*, where she appears in 14 episodes in that sitcom's first season. Finally, we'd reached the timeline I was waiting for.

"You and John Hughes worked together a lot in the '80s," I noted. "Would you be open to working with him again?"

"I'd love to work with John Hughes again, but yeah, as far as I know he's not really pursuing that right now," she replied. Granted, my question could have been more probing. But maybe I was treading on uncomfortable turf.

"Do you ever get tired of people asking questions?" I began again. Ugh, that sounded bad and maybe too aggressive. I stammered on. "I mean, there's always some buzz about the need to do a sequel to *The Breakfast Club* or *Pretty in Pink*. Does that chatter bother you?" (I sigh reading the transcript today. I should have been better prepped.)

"I was sort of developing a sequel to *Sixteen Candles*, and I still think that that might possibly happen," she said. What? This was news to me, but I was too stunned to follow up. "I don't think I'd want it to happen without John's involvement in some way."

"I often thought that *Sixteen Candles* would make a terrific stage musical," John interjected. A colleague to the rescue! We were in the same room doing the interview, and he could obviously feel I was stumbling.

The Breakfast Club as a stage musical would make more sense, Molly answered, as it's basically all going down in one set.

That's about where the highlights of this conversation end. As I reread the transcript today, I agonize at the missed opportunities. Years later, I would meet Molly in person after a screening of *The Breakfast Club* in Clearwater. After the movie, she sat for a Q&A and later met with some fans at a cocktail reception. I have a photo of it somewhere—me talking to Molly, trying to see if she remembers our *Sweet Charity* interview and her just smiling and saying, "No." Why would she? Another stupid question of mine. Sometimes I can't get out of my own way.

These days, Molly is staying busy with acting. She co-starred in four seasons of *The Secret Life of the American Teenager* from 2008 to 2011. More recently, she appeared in *Riverdale* and *Feud*. When actor Andrew McCarthy produced his 2024 documentary *Brat*, Molly was one of just two actors to turn down the opportunity to rehash the '80s with him. Don't sweat it, Andrew, Molly will always be a tough conversation. But the chance encounter taught me something I still carry with me: preparation matters, especially when time is short.

A MARTINEZ has enjoyed a fascinating career, and it's one that I'm still discovering day by day as he continues to create incredible work on TV and movie screens. He's also played an important and unexpected role in my personal life. Let me explain.

My wife has been a devoted fan of the '80s soap opera *Santa Barbara* since she was a teenager growing up in New York City. To her, the onscreen couple of the show's Cruz Castillo (Martinez) and Eden Capwell (played by Marcy Walker) was the very definition of a smoldering, eternal love affair. Early in her life, she even got the chance to interview A and grew to be good friends with him.

Fast-forward to 2021, and here comes Melissa walking down the aisle to marry me—with A Martinez by her side, standing in for her father, who had passed a decade before. It was this moment that flashed before me when I got a chance to interview A for the podcast in the fall of 2023.

"I have been seeing you all over the place lately, last year in theaters for Michael Bay's *Ambulance* and on Netflix, where I'm obsessed with *Longmire*," I began. "And, of course, we saw each other two years ago, almost to the day, when you walked my bride down the aisle at the wedding."

"That was a great day, man," A replied. "I got to be her surrogate father for that, and I loved it. That was one of those days you go through that just leaps out, not just because of what it meant for you guys, but just what it meant for me....You meet people because of the work you do and have them turn into lifelong friends. That's not something that happens all that often. And I love it when it does."

During our hour-long chat, we covered our mutual love for Jackson Browne, A's own music career, and even how he got his start in the 1972 John Wayne movie *The Cowboys*. But I didn't want to miss the chance to talk about *Santa Barbara* in the '80s, even if it was a show I'd only recently discovered.

"I didn't have a history of watching soaps," A confessed. "But I had this memory one day of walking by the TV. It might've been that Leslie [his wife] was watching a show. But I remember walking by the TV and seeing a soap and seeing an actress doing a scene. And at the end of the scene, the scene was over and the camera lingered on her and lingered and lingered and lingered. And I realize now that what she was doing was just filling time! And the organ music swells, and you watch this actress, who had done a perfectly good job in the scene, now just try to find something dignified to do at the end of it. And I just thought, 'Oh, that's a fate I don't want to ever have any part of.'"

Credit Leslie, A said, with changing his mind. She suggested her husband just rewrite scenes that didn't play well. The opportunity presented itself at his audition, he recalled. "I remember when I got the audition, I couldn't imagine finding a way to get through the scene. It was just a language I didn't understand. I didn't know how to play that way."

So he grabbed a yellow legal pad, went to a park down the street, rewrote his lines, and memorized them.

"It's like anything else: If you can find a way, if you can devise a strategy and hold onto it, chances are something good will happen," he said.

Lots of good would happen. A would later win a Daytime Emmy for his *Santa Barbara* work. From there, he'd continue on to *L.A. Law*, the smart, glossy legal drama that consistently ranked among TV's top 10 shows in the late '80s and won 15 Emmy Awards.

"It was a big change in rhythm and very challenging from the point of view that by the end of *Santa Barbara*, having been there eight and a half years and having gained a lot of trust in the process, I parlayed the fact that I rewrote my audition into a lot of leeway,"

A said. "The writing was phenomenal on *Santa Barbara*, but it's still a big committee of people that's processing this beast that has to be fed constantly. And then you go to *L.A. Law*, a show where they were absolutely sticklers. They wanted you to say the script as written, down to the punctuation. They wanted the rhythms of the commas in it. And of course, the writing is very good. But also the writing was coming at you late sometimes. It was not uncommon to get the script at your door pretty late the night before and you gotta come up early in the morning and be ready to do it word-perfect. And of course, they're lawyers, so they talk in a certain way and stuff. It was a big challenge."

Lest you think of A as a creature of the soaps—both daytime and prime time in the '80s—I beg you to seek out a copy of the 1989 indie flick *Powwow Highway*. A co-stars with Gary Farmer as a pair of Native Americans who make an *Easy Rider*-style journey from Montana to New Mexico.

"I think Gary Farmer is one of the best actors I've ever worked with," A said. "When you're on the stage with someone and you're working really closely with them, you gain a glimpse into a world that's so rarefied, it's hard to put a value on it. And Gary's like that. He does things in the course of going through the work that are so deep, so true, so fluid. He has this quicksilver capacity to get an impulse and go with it."

A would work again with Farmer on an episode of *Longmire*, another series that made the effort to shine a spotlight on the Native American community. A's resume now includes other, similar roles in standout projects such as *Dark Wind* and *Blue Ridge*. But it's a different role that he cherishes when I asked him the podcast's "time machine" question to conclude our chat.

"Here at *Stuck in the '80s*, we like to think of the podcast as a time machine," I began. "And as such, I can grant you a seat on the so-called podcast time machine to go back and relive a moment from your past or catch an event you missed, or even give a younger version of yourself some good advice. If I gave you that seat on the time machine, where would you go back to and what would you do?"

Thankfully, my wife hadn't tipped him off that this question was coming, but A was quick with an answer.

"I think if I could go back in time, I would be a little more serious about my role as a father," he said. "I think by and large, I've been a good father. But as I've gotten older, I've realized that I could have been a better father. I'm a very, very optimistic person, and I tend to want to get to the word 'yes' as often as I can."

"I remember working with Michael Caine 40 years ago and asking him about his career, and he said, 'I try to say yes. I just say yes, even if it looks like it could be a train wreck. If they want me to come and play, I say yes.' And I think 16 years later, he got the *Cider House Rules* and won his Oscar. I think of the great John Patrick Shanley, the playwright, the guy who wrote *Doubt* and *Moonstruck* and these incredible plays that some of which became movies. He wrote a preface to *Doubt* where he says, 'We can't know. We have to learn to embrace uncertainty. Conviction is a resting place.'"

"Being an actor is good for that because it's nothing but uncertainty. You can just constantly have no idea what you're going to do next. Sometimes my kids have come to me and said, 'What do you think I should do? I have this thing in front of me.' And I will just, without thinking twice, just go to, 'I think you should try to find a way to say yes.' And then years later, sometimes saying yes was really maybe not the better option. And you won't know for a long time sometimes."

I wasn't yet sure I knew what A was working through, but I wasn't going to interrupt it. Sometimes the best thing to do in an interview is nothing.

"I worry that I've just sort of defaulted to my knee-jerk, childlike actor staying in touch with his inner child. I've been real good at that," he continued. "If I had to do anything over again, I think I would find a way to develop that part of myself a little better so that when I was asked for advice from my kids, I could give them a more fulsome picture of what the options and the possibilities were rather than just default to the optimistic choice, just say yes. I can't believe I'm actually saying this to you, Steve. But this week I've been feeling it."

I was awestruck. "Of all the times I've asked that question," I told him, "that is the most thoughtful response."

Looking back at me through our Zoom windows, A smiled. "I appreciate you asking the question. It's a good question," he said. "I think as we get older, we start to have to, whether you want to or not, you just fall into the realm of seeing what's gone before with more acute eyes."

GLENN GORDON CARON is the genius behind *Moonlighting*, which turned the TV business on its ear in 1985 and made a star of a young actor born Walter Bruce Willis. Getting Glenn on the podcast was a total surprise. In December 2023, I got an email out of the blue from a publicist I'd never spoken with that began like this:

"Reaching out to you to see about having Glenn Gordon Caron on your podcast."

The email went on for four or five more paragraphs, explaining Glenn's career in TV and movies, though I didn't need a primer. I was all-in after the first sentence. I'd grown up a fan of *Moonlighting* but also appreciated Glenn's big-screen work on *Love Affair*, *Clean and Sober*, and *Picture Perfect*. I still can't believe I was offered time with him.

At the time of the interview, *Moonlighting* had finally made it to streaming TV, and I had plunged myself into rewatching as many episodes as possible. Naturally, the conversation began with the challenges of getting a 40-year-old series onto the subscription services.

"It's been quite a journey," Glenn began. "I started sort of campaigning to make it happen about five years ago. *Moonlighting* fell into a sort of weird abyss because it wasn't made by a legacy studio. It's owned by Disney now. But at the time, it was made by ABC, and that was a moment when the government said, 'Hey, you can't broadcast shows and make shows. You can't do both those things.' So ABC was compelled to hold onto it."

Another factor, he explained, was the use of popular music in the show.

"The outrageous amount of music that I chose to use back in the '80s sort of reared its ugly head and made it very, very difficult for them to wrap their head around the idea of streaming it," he said. "We only did 66 episodes, and we used 300 songs."

There was a darker side, though, to the success of getting *Moonlighting* in front of a new audience.

"When I started this conversation, Bruce and I would talk about it a lot," Glenn explained. "Bruce has had his medical challenges of late, and now it just makes me sad because he was really excited about people seeing [it]. Most people think of Bruce as a guy with a gun who comes into a dangerous situation, and certainly that's part of his kit, that's part of what he can do. But the idea that he was a romantic lead, the idea that he had this extraordinary verbal dexterity, and was also capable of being a stylist in the sense that what we did was in many ways an exercise in style."

"I know somewhere in there it brings him great pleasure to know that it's out there, that his kids are seeing it, that other people are seeing it, and that it's reentered the conversation, if you will," Glenn said. "But I wish we had gotten there a little sooner."

I asked how closely in touch they were.

"I tell people I try and see him once a month. The truth is, I'm not that good. Sometimes the month turns into two months," he said. "Seeing him is tricky because—and I don't like to speak about this—but I'm not sure past the first minute or two that he even knows that I'm there. He's not communicative in the way that...I mean, when you think of Bruce Willis, you think of this guy with this enormous sense of joie de vivre, a man who loves life. The Bruce that I go to see, he's very different than that at the moment. He's not terribly verbal and, like I say, I'm not sure he completely comprehends who I am. But he's certainly happy, and he's certainly surrounded by family. He has a wonderful family."

Glenn and I both wanted to lighten the mood a little, so the conversation turned to the conception of *Moonlighting*. I'd read that Glenn was tasked by Hollywood with creating a boy-girl detective show, an assignment he didn't covet because it sounded like well-traveled territory. If he was going to do it, he needed the freedom and time to seek out the right headlining actors. The female lead would be played by Cybill Shepherd, an actress who turned heads in 1971's *The Last Picture Show*. A series of less successful roles followed in the decade.

"Cybill came on board fairly early," Glenn said. "People always are amazed when I spout off this statistic, but we actually auditioned about 3,000 men for the part [of David Addison]. People don't realize what an extraordinarily verbal part it was, that you had to be really, really on your game as an actor."

When Bruce Willis first walked into the audition room, Glenn recalled, he was sporting a buzz haircut, earrings, and army camouflage clothing.

"The second he opened his mouth, I went, 'Oh, my God, that's him.' And he finished and he left the room. I actually ran out of the room and ran down Pico Boulevard and caught him and said, 'Can you come back again tomorrow? Could you dress a little more conventionally?'"

"He was like a guy from the neighborhood," Glenn continued. "And the idea of a guy from the neighborhood being partnered with Cybill Shepherd, who was one of the most beautiful people on the planet, that was really intoxicating to me. But ABC did not get it. And you also have to remember that ABC at this time was almost exclusively men. Again, it was the '80s. Anyway, long story short, I brought him back 11 times."

Eleven times, I gasped.

Casting *Moonlighting* was the first challenge but hardly the last. The show had timing issues, Glenn said. It took a lot longer to shoot, edit, and finalize than the network had time for. In fact, ABC sometimes had to run promos explaining why they didn't have a new episode for viewers. True to his "control freak" nature, he said, Glenn produced those promos himself.

"I remember doing one, I can't remember the actor's name. He was a wonderful actor. This guy's dressed up in a work outfit. He's standing on a loading dock. He's got an ABC logo on his chest. And the little chyron thing says, '02:45 AM.' And the guy's standing there and you hear a voice from—It's my voice, actually, from offstage going, 'Hey, what are you doing?' And he says, 'Oh, waiting.' 'Waiting? For what?' He says, 'Oh, new *Moonlighting*, maybe.' And that was the whole promo because we needed to communicate to the audience, 'We're trying. We're trying. And we want to amuse you, but if it isn't completely cooked, we can't serve it to you.'"

THE FACE OF THE '80s

Truth be told, the start of any podcast episode is tough. In the early days, I just winged it. "Hey, this is *Stuck in the '80s* and I'm Steve Spears." As time went on, it evolved to "Hey, hey welcome to *Stuck in the '80s*, it's your host Steve Spears…"

Still, I'd fumble it so often that now I write down exactly what I'm going to say. It's on the top of every Google Docs file that I keep for each show. And usually I write the text in such a way as to transition in the random movie quote I've found to use as a punchline. Like this one from Episode 668:

> STEVE: Hey, hey welcome to *Stuck in the '80s*, it's your old pal Spearsy, and today we honor the final songs from 1989 that reached No. 2 on the charts but no further. It's our "Close But No Cigar" series swan song.
>
> BRAD: The '80s are over?
>
> Movie clip [from the end of *Ferris Bueller*]: "It's over. Go home."

Introducing a celebrity at the start of an interview was often a struggle in the early days of the podast. But none so bad as in 2007, when MTV veejay Martha Quinn came on the podcast for the first time. As excruciatingly painful as my introduction was, I kept it unchanged for the final show.

"She is the original…" I started. "Oh, I can't even…This is horrible. Ready? Here we go again. Hey, she's one of the original…"

"This is why I prerecord my show too," Martha said with empathy before breaking up in laughter.

"I know. You should see how painful it is," I replied. "We've done about 100 shows now, and every show still feels like episode two or three sometimes."

Martha took pity on me. "Okay. Can I tell you something about that?"

"Sure," I immediately agreed. "Go for it."

"I read a quote by David Lee Roth that made me feel so much better about this very issue that I wrestle with every week too," she said. "And that is, the way you get a stage personality is through thousands and thousands and thousands of hours on stage. He didn't just walk out on stage the first time he played, or the first 100 times he played, and be that snappy kickass, fast-talking dude. That took years and years and years. So every time I do a show, just like you, I'm getting closer."

Martha was an intern at WNBC in New York in 1981, making ends meet as an actress in TV commercials, when her boss at the radio station recommended she audition for MTV. Though it was the final day of auditions, Martha dazzled the assembled crew and had an offer two days later.

Any teenage boy in the '80s would readily admit about the female veejays this universal truth: Nina Blackwood might have been the girl we dreamed about having on our arm for a splashy party, but Martha Quinn was the one we all wanted to marry. I never asked what she made of her girl-next-door image, but I felt she was comfortable with it.

Martha's been on the podcast three times over the years, and every visit has been a treat. For this first interview, she was promoting the new board game *The '80s Game with Martha Quinn*. She quizzed us on the names of each member of New Kids on the Block. Though technically an '80s band—formed in 1984 believe it or not—I've usually dismissed them as a '90s phenomenon. Boy bands, girl bands, Spin Doctors...all '90s in my head.

Martha is one of the kindest celebrities I've interviewed over the past 20 years. She's probably been thrown every question in the book over the decades, but she still delivers. I did this interview with Sean as a co-host, so the questions were more personal than usual. We asked if guys often came up to her and revealed that she was their first big crush.

"No. This is what happens, and it's always a double-edged sword to me because I know people are trying to be nice," she said. "Somebody says, 'Oh, Martha, I used to have the biggest crush on you.'"

Sean and I both groaned.

"I was like, 'Well, who do you have a crush on now?'" she continued.

We assured her she was just as cute that day as she was in 1981, which wasn't a lie. Find a photo of Martha today, and you'll be swooning again.

I decided to take a swing at another question. "When MTV started 25 years ago, do you think anybody at the network, or even among that first group of VJs, could foresee that you would become the face of the network and, really, the decade?"

Let's face it—Martha is indeed the face of the '80s. You can throw Cyndi Lauper, Madonna, and Molly Ringwald all into the top 10. But Martha's the undisputed champ.

"God, you know what? I've gotta congratulate you because you are the first person to ever ask that question," she replied. "Where

I thought that you were gonna go was, 'Did you foresee that MTV would last this long?' Which I've heard a million times."

To this point, it was the most satisfying moment of my career.

"I'm going to pass out now," was my reply.

"It's funny. I will say that every once in a while I'll read an article and if they're talking about the '80s, I've actually seen them referred to as the Martha Quinn years," she said. "And I'm like, 'Oh my God, that's incredible. It's amazing.' No. I'm quite sure that nobody had any idea because I was just some goofy kid off the street, basically, and it just worked out that way. I can't explain it. What can I say? It worked out great."

I followed up. "Is it almost a weird burden in a way?"

Now, I was feeling the connection growing. Whenever this happens in an interview, and it's not that often, it's like a flower is tickling your brain. There's a rush that just takes over.

"Well, I try not to drink and drive," she said.

A joke is always a great way to give yourself time to think of a deeper answer.

Martha continued. "So that I don't let the '80s down, I try to be a good role model. You know how I feel about it? It's so great I have *The '80s Game with Martha Quinn*. It's totally reconnecting me with this group of people who I really feel like we came of age together. And I'm not one of those celebrities, this will probably shock you to hear this, who's mysterious and alluring…I don't have that Angelina Jolie kind of slithery rap about me. I'm very, very approachable. It's wonderful. It's great."

I knew exactly what she meant. There's something transcendent about '80s nostalgia. I can be great friends with someone I have nothing else in common with, but we have the '80s.

"People are passionate about the '80s," she said. "Even though there was Reaganomics and the Reagan years and there was a lot going on in the world, there was also a lot of real hardcore optimism."

Martha called it a safe time.

"My brother was in the military during the '80s and he was never in any kind of combat situation—it was always considered a peace time," she said. "Somebody listening to this is going to go, 'She's such an idiot, doesn't she remember?' But as far as I remember, it wasn't like we had the war on terror at that time...People always love the period of time that they grew up in. Before they took on adult responsibilities, before they were driving. Their formative years. When you're a tree growing up as a sapling, you kind of grow around what you're up against. And you always love those years. I do think that the people who grew up in the '80s are more passionate about the '80s than any other decade. When the '50s came back, it was kind of a kitschy, cute revival, but more like, 'Oh, aren't these clothes wacky?' People love the '80s."

I told Martha that Rick Springfield said something largely along the same lines when we interviewed him.

"People identify with the music from the period when they're in their formative years," I told her. "He also talked a lot about the Cold War being the last safe war we ever had."

She replied, "Ah, interesting. I'm going to steal that if you don't mind."

When we eventually wrapped up, it felt like we'd just had cocktails with an old friend. Sean and I couldn't stop smiling. If Martha had been in the room, I'm betting it would have ended in a group hug. It's a great feeling when your heroes are just as genuine as you dreamed they'd be.

In 2009, as the podcast was figuring out a way to mark the end of another decade, Martha returned to the show. We wanted to know how she marked the end of the '80s.

Martha had spent December 31, 1989, at a Fuzztones show in L.A. Her future husband, Jordan Tarlow, was the band's guitarist.

"That's what I was doing—going out of the '80s the same way I went in, which was rocking," she said.

For many of the New Year's Eves of the '80s, Martha spent her time co-hosting MTV's *New Year's Eve Rock N' Roll Ball*. She likened the events to a "roving band of gypsies"—she was usually paired with such celebrities as Weird Al Yankovic and Pee-Wee Herman—that eventually got slicker and slicker over time.

"It just was a crazy fun period. I know for a fact that I handmade my outfit," she said. "We didn't have deals with Patricia Fields or anybody fancy. It was just us...You'd walk by J.J. [Jackson's] room, and he'd be in there putting on his makeup."

Any dreams I'd had of backstage shenanigans in those days were immediately dispelled by Martha during this chat.

"In the very beginning we were super, super-duper toeing the line," she said. "We were very kind of goody goodies in a way, in that we were just, at least, especially me, Nina [Blackwood], and Alan [Hunter]. We were called the Junior VJs. And we were always studying and doing our thing and showing up on time to work."

In 2011, Martha helped me out with a story I was writing about the 30th birthday of MTV. Let's face it: The network bears little resemblance to the place where Martha once worked. Music videos have been replaced by reality shows. And veejays? There is no point in having those anymore. I needed some perspective from the person whose face once symbolized the entire phenomenon.

"Here's the thing about MTV today vs. MTV then," she wrote me. "Let's say MTV [still] played videos 24/7, all music...it still wouldn't be our MTV. It'd be Pitbull and Rihanna and the *Glee* cast. It's not like they'd be playing The Fixx."

Music videos are no longer the way today's generation of youth communicates, she said.

"The spirit lives on in MTV as an ode to its scrappy start. Each and every one of us on the original MTV crew—VJs, cameramen, secretaries, executives—were rebels with a cause. Today, the rebel bit is an act. Nobody's job is on the line, and the dream has long since been realized. The 'we're crazy kids' routine has become shtick. It's totally expected for MTV to be unexpected."

As usual, Martha nailed it. It didn't make the truth hurt any less. But it helped knowing she was at peace with it.

In 2017, I had my most recent chat with Martha. She was just celebrating a year at her new job at iHeartRadio. Bob Pittman, who had hired her for the MTV veejay gig decades before, was now running the online media giant and wanted Martha to host the first branded iHeartMedia station, to be named iHeart80s. She couldn't turn it down, but it meant saying goodbye—professionally at least—to Mark Goodman, Alan, and Nina, who stayed behind at Sirius/XM, where they hosted 80s on 8.

"It was a super hard decision because I love my VJs," Martha told me and my co-host Brad, who, like me, grew up a diehard Martha fan. "There is never any doubt if I ever reference my VJs on Twitter or Facebook. It's always Team VJ forever. Forever and ever, we are a linked family. And that was a little hard, but the truth is, we're in different parts of the country anyway, so it's not like the old days when we were going into the VJ office and sitting down and watching Eurythmics videos while we were eating Chinese takeout from the restaurant on the corner."

Ouch, another tough dose of reality. She was right. Things have fundamentally evolved. Nina lives on a farm in Maine and records her contributions from there. Alan is based in St. Louis. Only Mark still lives and records in New York.

"I can still call them and email them," Martha said. "I wish that that element could somehow still be in place because I do love being a part of that gang, but I'm always a part of that gang no matter what our jobs are. No matter where life takes us, we will always be together."

I miss talking to Martha. I never left a conversation with her without feeling like she had given me a great big hug. She has a warmth that shines in every broadcast and social media post. If the 1980s do indeed have a person who embodies the best of it, I'm so happy it's Martha Quinn.

THE BREAKUP THAT BECAME AN EPISODE

When people ask me who my favorite interview was, I usually blurt out Steve Perry. But then I noodle on it some more, and I think the real answer is Deborah Foreman, the actress who first caught the attention of '80s fans in *Valley Girl*. She really saved my life—emotionally, anyway.

Back in 2009, I was in the process of getting my second divorce. In an effort to spend more time away from home—I still co-owned a house with my soon-to-be ex—I decided to head to Las Vegas for The Regeneration Tour, a traveling show that featured The Human League, ABC, Naked Eyes, Belinda Carlisle, and a few other acts. I was meeting up with a small band of podcast fans for the show. One of them would later be known as VGF—the Vegas Girlfriend.

VGF was from Detroit, and we hit it off immediately. Despite the long-distance nature of our relationship, we were together for nine months. She'd come down to Florida one weekend a month—I was never invited up north because she was still living with an ex-boyfriend. First red flag.

We had mulled the idea of a permanent relationship, but she was finishing up pharmacy school and was financially obligated to work for Kroger for a number of years after graduation as the grocery chain was footing her school bill. Alas, there were no Krogers in Florida. Maybe not a red flag, but certainly a bad omen.

The likelihood of me moving to Detroit wasn't high. Newspapers were then—as they are today—a dying brand of communication. Detroit wasn't exactly in a region that was growing. It didn't take long for us to see our situation was bleak. Still, I wanted to believe things would work out.

One weekend, instead of getting my regular morning phone call from her followed by a longer nightly call, the phone didn't ring at all. I texted. No answer. I called, but just got voicemail. This continued on for three days before she finally called back. She didn't say much, but it was clear through the silence that our relationship was over. She left me to connect the dots during the short call. I remember driving a half hour that night to my mom's condo to borrow two Xanax.

At work the next day, I talked to Sean and Cathy—they were both co-hosting the podcast with me then—about how to handle this. Because the relationship had been discussed ad nauseam on the podcast, the breakup should be public too, we agreed. But it couldn't be a pity party—it needed substance—so we agreed on a topic: breaking up in the '80s, featuring our picks for the best breakup songs and breakup movie scenes of the decade.

We needed one more thing: some expert help.

Deborah Foreman had largely retired from acting at this point, but she was running a Pilates studio in California. I found the website and emailed her, telling her about my breakup and the podcast idea. No chance I'd hear back, I thought.

When the phone rang a few hours later, I heard a sweet, friendly voice. "Hi, Steve, this is Debbie Foreman. I got your email."

"Hi…Debbie…Foreman," I stammered in disbelief. Sean looked up from his cubicle with his mouth open.

"Yes," I mouthed back.

Debbie and I talked for 20 minutes about my email and the idea of coming on the show. She wanted to know what kind of questions I would ask. I sent her a half dozen via email. She wrote back and told me to wait for her call. I ran up to the podcast studio and sat at the control board, my heart thumping out of control. The phone finally rang.

"I got to admit when I first started this podcast four years ago, I had two questions in the back of my mind," I told her. "One was, 'How soon can I do a show about *Valley Girl*?' Which I did in the first month. And my second question, which I never thought I would answer, was, 'I wonder if I'll ever get a chance to talk to Debbie Foreman on the phone.' And today it comes true."

She fired back gleefully, "Because you wrote me!" She had a wide smile I could feel over the phone line. "And also because I shared the email with my mom."

What? Really? I asked what her mom said.

"Yeah. I said, 'Okay, you have to hear this email,'" she continued. "And so while I was reading the email to my mom, she was giggling through the whole thing. And I thought, 'Oh, okay, there's something to this.' Because my mom, she's very psychic, she's very intuitive about stuff."

It was pity, I'm sure.

"I think that the beautiful thing is that you reached out," Debbie continued. "You stuck your neck out doing something you probably would have never done otherwise. And I think that's probably going to continue to happen in the next six months, so don't be surprised if you start doing things that you wouldn't naturally do, because I think that's the blessing of what's going to come out of this. I know it's hard to see that right now because it's really fresh. But you know the saying, 'Time heals all wounds,' blah, blah, blah. You're going to have to go through all the emotions until you get to that place of finally going, 'Okay, I actually do have fond memories and fond feelings for this person, and I wish them well.' I doubt that's what you're feeling right now, though."

Actually, I'd been walking on clouds since Debbie called. *Valley Girl* was a special movie to me. My mom taped it off HBO on a night when I was on a date with a high school friend. The date was memorable because when it was over, I stood outside her door for two hours unwilling to say goodnight and unable to summon the courage to attempt a kiss. It remains the third most agonizing memory of my youth. Later on, my college roommate would meet that same girl by chance at a club in Tampa and would frequently have sex with her in the room next to mine in our apartment. One time, they even coated his waterbed mattress with baby oil for the night. The fragrance of that oil still makes me a little nauseous. His relationship with her and the baby oil incident remain the top two most agonizing memories.

Valley Girl, as it turns out, is partly the device I'd use to forget about the trauma. The oft-imitated Romeo and Juliet storyline felt new again with Debbie and Nicolas Cage as the leads, and the music made repeat viewings of the film on VHS a weekly ritual back in 1984. But now I could add the memory of talking with Debbie Foreman.

"It was just another audition, just like all auditions," Debbie told me. "I had gone to a go-see with a very reputable casting lady. We just had a short meeting, just a go-see, just so that they can in the future—maybe she could think of me for projects. And she goes, 'Look, I know these people over here, they're doing this film called *Valley Girl*. I think you'd be perfect for it. I want to send you over there.' I think everything happened in one day."

I was curious what Debbie made of her co-star and future Oscar winner Nicolas Cage when they first met.

"I loved his eyes," she said. "I thought he had great energy. I thought he was scary to me. He was triggering stuff in me that I had never experienced in my life. I didn't even have a boyfriend prior to that movie, so that's my memory of him. Even when I had the audition with him, and even when I worked with him, there was this kind of, like, this thing inside you that you can't control, those sort of butterfly feelings, and you keep just squashing them down thinking, 'We're professionals, we're working. It's a movie, it's not real.'"

Debbie punctuated the retelling of her memories with laughter and giggles. She had an amazing laugh that was intoxicating. She and I would go on to talk frequently on the phone in the coming years. During all our chats together, I loved the laughing the most. When we each were single, our phone conversations would become like therapy sessions.

Right now, though, I just wanted to explore the chemistry of this movie. I still wanted to believe that another failed relationship on my part didn't mean it was the universe punching back at me.

"There's a chemistry that's between you guys in this movie, and I think I saw it for the first time when I was 15 or 16 years old, and so it made a big impression on me," I told her. "And I don't think at that point in time, I'd ever seen a movie that I could relate to the characters and the chemistry and the story. I think for people who were my age at that time, there's something about *Valley Girl* that will always hold a spot in our hearts. Maybe it's the chemistry, because you two really have it."

When you go too personal during an interview, some writers would say you're being unprofessional. Subjects can just shut you down and end the interview abruptly. At this point, I had put my notes away.

"I still haven't been able to figure any of that out," she said. "I know that when we were working, there was an undeniable energy between the two of us that was sort of…"

She was choosing her words more carefully here. I didn't blame her. We' were in uncharted territory for two people who had never met face to face.

"We just fed off each other, and I allowed it to happen, too," Debbie said. "I think that in real life, we're very cautious. We put our guards up. We're very cautious of what we say and what we do around the people that we really like. And that environment allowed me to not have any of those walls and any of those boundaries because now, I had text to deal with, the script that just lent itself to it, and I just allowed myself to be taken on that journey."

To this day, when I rewatch *Valley Girl*, I still marvel at Debbie and Nic and their journey, their connection. Watch them closely and you'll see it unfold.

"Those environments just lent themselves to the beauty of falling in love for the first time, or even your 10th time in life," she said. "It just allowed that to happen. So, maybe that was it. I can speak only in that respect in terms of Nic, that he allowed it to happen as well."

So was there a relationship, I asked. The conversation was coming faster than I could control it.

"I'll only speak for myself," Debbie said. "I had strong feelings for Nic, and when the film ended we had a conversation. I actually went up to San Francisco with him for a weekend, and then when we came back an ultimatum was made, let's just put it that way. And I decided not to go with the ultimatum. And we inevitably never were together after that. So I think it only lasted during the shoot of the film, which was only between 17 and 21 days and a weekend afterward."

I remember feeling buzzed at the intimacy of what she was sharing. I get shivers today rereading her words. People may give the '80s grief as the decade of excess or an era of artificiality. Those of us who grew up and spent our formative years during that time know otherwise.

There was a particular moment in *Valley Girl* that still haunts me. When Debbie's character, Julie, breaks it off with Nic's Randy, the pain is palpable. I wanted to know how Debbie felt when delivering the bad news.

"You give him the most painful words known to the English language—'I don't love you anymore.' And that strikes a chord with me," I said. "I heard those same words three days ago."

Debbie replied, "I think as a young person, you say things that you don't really mean, and you don't really understand the impact of the words. And then when we become adults, we do have an understanding of those words. I think it's important to take responsibility for what we say, right? So there's a big difference between the two—between what happened with you and what may or may not happen in a movie."

At this point, I could barely keep things together. I have a reputation for wearing my emotions on my sleeve. My voice by now was shaky. You can hear in the audio that I was fighting back tears. Debbie was trying to triage a fresh wound.

"From my heart, I'm deeply sorry that this happened to you," she said. "But on the other hand, congratulations because you are going to do some things that you've never done in your life, period. It's going to make you become courageous in meetings and on the phone and in email and in person with people in your future because this happened. I know you can't wrap your brain around it because there's time that was involved with this person. And you have to sort of go through those emotions to cleanse it all out of you. But in the end, something huge is going to happen with you."

"It really means a lot. I appreciate that," I stammered out with whatever strength I had left. Listen to the podcast audio and you'll hear me falling apart. Her words were the only thing keeping me upright. "Really, listening to you tell me that, it just helps a lot. It does."

I told her I wanted to give her—and her mom—the biggest hugs in the world.

"Good," she said. "And continue to pass it, to pass it forward."

"I will," I said. "Seriously, you've healed a lot of wounds today."

"You never know what the future holds, so stay open," Debbie said.

"I will," I said. "I promise."

Debbie would appear a few more times on the *Stuck in the '80s* podcast in the following years. We continued to trade stories about our relationships and look for brighter skies with the other's advice and guidance. She would appear in the 2020 musical remake of *Valley Girl*, offering a new Julie some advice in a short cameo.

My advice for all the Julies and Randys out there: Listen to Debbie Foreman. You indeed never know what the future holds, so stay open.

HITS, HUMILITY, AND HAND-BUILT SYNTHS

As the months and weekly episodes came and went, I had more chances to handle podcast interviews on my own. I didn't have the natural chemistry that my cohost Sean had with those he interviewed, but I found my way by bingeing on YouTube videos with the artists and reading every article I could find ahead of time. To this day, the 24 hours before any solo interview is just excruciating for me. But when I'm able to relax, I've scored some memorable conversations. Here are a few that come to mind.

THOMAS DOLBY was one of the first artists I interviewed solo. The artist best known for "She Blinded Me with Science" and "Hyperactive," Thomas had an eclectic career. After his run through the '80s, he switched things up and founded Beatnik, a company that would create ringtones for the exploding cell phone market. Now, after years away from music, he was touring the U.S. again as a one-man band, and his upcoming stop in St. Petersburg gave me the chance to speak with him. Sean bowed out, but I was all in.

I'd done a lot of research—reading previous interviews and such—and what caught my eye first was that Thomas had hand-built much of his musical gear. Why? It didn't yet exist.

"In the early '70s, it was very expensive to get into electronic music," Thomas told me. "You could do it if you're at an art school or a university music department. But for the average musician, synthesizers were really prohibitive. And so the first one that I ever had was actually built from a kit out of a magazine, and it was called a Transcendent 2000. And then you could actually link different boxes together. And this came in very handy because I didn't have a drummer. I used to use my finger to play the drums, and I'm not that in time and it was laborious. So one day, I was actually out at a nightclub and I was watching this empty dance floor with these flashing red and green lights, and I thought, 'Wow, that's just gotta be positive and negative voltages being sequenced in time for the music.' I had used that to play my drums. So I bought myself one of these units and hooked it up to my kit synthesizer. And the next time you listen to the drums on the end of 'She Blinded Me with Science,' you're actually listening to a disco lighting console."

That song was his highest-charting song in the U.S., peaking at No. 6 in 1982. Yet, he admits he has mixed feelings on it.

"It's one of my fluffiest songs," Thomas said. "I've always been a little bit schizophrenic in the moods of my songs. A lot of my songs are very personal, intimate, atmospheric, things like 'Screen Kiss' or 'Budapest by Blimp' or 'I Love You Goodbye.' But then I also have this wild exhibitionist side as in 'Science' or 'Hyperactive.' And I think it's okay for a musician to have different styles. Novelists are allowed with each book they write to pick a different era of history in a different geographic location as a setting. And yet musicians are somehow expected to stay true to kind, and I think that's a shame."

"She Blinded Me with Science" did make Magnus Pyke a household face—at least to fans of MTV.

"Magnus Pyke was kind of a TV scientist in England when I was growing up," Thomas explained. "He'd always go on the BBC and when there was some scientific topic, a kid would call in and go, 'Why does the moon affect the tides?' And he'd go, 'Well, the moon revolves around the earth...' and he sort of did this whole spiel while wildly waving his arms around. And he was sort of an inspiration for the song "She Blinded Me with Science." Conversely, when he came to the States after my video had been on MTV, people would walk up behind him on the street and yell out 'Science!' [chuckle] and get him out of his shoes. And he didn't like this because he took himself actually very seriously as a scientist, and he always objected to the fact that over here people assumed he was some two-bit actor that had gotten the part in the video."

These days, Thomas continues to perform the song along with his other favorites for his My Personal Recollections Tour. He also, impressively enough, teaches at Johns Hopkins University, where he's led the Music for New Media program at the school's Peabody Institute. In essence, Thomas remains exactly what he's always been—a curious mind and restless innovator, still bending sound and ideas into something new. Science, indeed.

CARL PALMER was one of the more unforeseen interviews over the past 20 years. When the supergroup Asia reunited for a 2007 U.S. tour, one of the stops landed close to home—Ruth Eckerd Hall in Clearwater. That put me, unexpectedly, on the phone with Carl, the band's drummer, who turned heads in the early '70s as part of Emerson, Lake & Palmer.

Asia had been one of my favorite bands in the early '80s. Their self-titled debut album was a Christmas gift from my parents in 1982, and I played that cassette so relentlessly it eventually wore out. It's one of the few albums I've owned in every format imaginable—tape, vinyl, CD, and digital.

In 1983, MTV announced it would broadcast Asia live from Tokyo. I stayed up into the wee hours to watch, only to feel crushed when the concert began and I realized John Wetton had been replaced at the last minute by Greg Lake. Even then, Asia was teaching me a lesson about expectations.

Critics loved to sneer at the band's glossy, radio-friendly sound. The teenager in me didn't care. I loved the songs about heartache and betrayal—subjects that were only just beginning to creep into my own life. Three decades later, I was finally about to see the band the way they were meant to be seen. But first, I had 30 minutes alone with Carl Palmer.

I began by asking how drumming in an early prog-rock trio differed from his time with Asia.

"Well, it was a change of pace to have an album No. 1 for nine weeks," Carl said. "Emerson, Lake & Palmer never had that in the whole of their career. We never ever reached that kind of instant success and acclaim that Asia had on the first album. But [Emerson, Lake & Palmer] were a box office draw, and people always wanted to see the band, whether we had a new album or not. So that was a nice thing to have. To go from the larger audiences down to where Asia was was really, for me, a sign of the times."

It also was a sign of how FM radio still controlled concert audiences in the U.S., where prog-rock bands such as Rush, Yes, and Genesis hadn't yet released any pop-friendly albums. Give Asia some credit for easing that transition.

"Progressive rock wasn't being played on the radio. Progressive rock wasn't part of MTV," Carl agreed. "I have a real strong idea that the reason why that first Asia album was big was because it was a mixture of, like, six-minute kind of proggy type tunes like 'Time Again' and 'Wildest Dreams' with the pop songs like 'Only Time Will Tell' and 'Heat of the Moment.' It was a wonderful crossover happening on that one particular product."

I asked Carl what the future had in store for Asia. Would the reunion endure? Were new albums on the way? Today, we know the band would release four more albums before the death of John Wetton in 2017. In 2006, Carl didn't see any of that happening.

"We've decided that we might record some retro material—nothing has been decided on yet, exactly. And we'll look at the new material," he said. "We are in no rush to do it. I mean, the world is not waiting for an Asia album. We all know that."

After the interview, I got an invitation to visit Carl backstage before the show. This was a first for me. I was a mess beforehand—I had no idea what the etiquette would be or how long I was expected to stay. My friends at the hall led me back to the door behind the stage, where Carl was waiting. We shook hands and I repeated my thanks for the interview. I wasn't sure what else to talk about so I just asked what they were planning on opening with that night. Even Carl wasn't sure but he handed me the setlist on paper. It was "Time Again." I remember buying a concert tee that barely fit me and settling in for the show.

When the band finally walked onstage and launched into their show, it felt less like a concert opener and more like a quiet closing of a loop that had started decades earlier in my bedroom, a worn-out cassette spinning one last time.

NANCY WILSON is one of a dozen members of the Rock & Roll Hall of Fame who have been on the show over the years. Heart was doing a tour of theaters, and Clearwater's Ruth Eckerd Hall had made the cut again. I wouldn't be totally alone for this interview; Cathy Wos was a big Heart fan and decided to join me.

CATHY SAYS NOW: I went into the Nancy Wilson interview with pure dread. Nancy is one of my heroes, so I was very nervous and certain I was going to make a fool of myself. Thankfully, going against the cliché of never wanting to meet your heroes, she was incredibly gracious, and there was so much more I learned about her in our conversation. This was easily one of my favorite episodes that we did.

It was another restless night before the interview. I was sick with anxiety—this was a band that had a long, distinguished career, but I only knew their '80s catalog. Please don't sniff me out as a rookie fan, I pleaded.

Nancy couldn't have been more gracious on the phone. After a few minutes of catching up on the band's most recent projects and appearances, I got a chance to ask about the musical redirection during the '80s, when Heart took a left turn from a hard rock sound to a power pop feel.

"Yeah, it was very much the style of the time," Nancy said. "The fashions, they do shift around, and every five years, every ten years it's something else coming down the pike. And in our case, we thought it would be fun to kind of put on the lace gloves and the corsets and the hair spray."

Cathy asked if it was true that one tour had been informally dubbed "The Leave It to Cleavage" tour.

"Yeah, we did!" Nancy confessed. "We had a backstage laminate that just was a frame of just our two cleavages next to each other in corsets, and we called it the 'Leave It to Cleavage' tour. We never got too serious about it all. But it was really the fashion of the day."

As for the musical direction, that too was the fashion of the day, she said.

"There was a lot of new digital equipment that was coming out in the studios then, and everybody had to use it," she said. "It was kind of an interesting shift in music because it really took on its own identity that is clearly the '80s sound."

"Also, the big 'corporate-ness' of everything really latched on. Everyone was kind of under the thumb of the man at the record company and the management companies and the image makers and all that stuff, kind of like it is right now.

"It was so much about image, with MTV having just sort of happened as well. And so there was a whole image idea that took away, ultimately, I think, from the actual music, but not entirely. There's some really beautiful and great songs from those times. We were lucky enough to have a few of those, I think."

Another interesting facet of Nancy's life back in the early 2000s was her marriage to filmmaker Cameron Crowe. The two had been set up by friends and married in 1986. For years, I had been telling people that Nancy and Cameron met on the set of *Fast Times at Ridgemont High*. (He wrote the script while Nancy made a cameo.) Wrong. I had also told anyone who listened that Cameron and Nancy were the couple singing to each other in a hotel room in a quick scene in *Almost Famous*. Wrong again, Nancy said. Those were Seattle musicians Pete Droge and Elaine Summers.

A few years after this interview, Nancy and Cameron would divorce, citing the standard irreconcilable differences. Similarly, right after this interview, I stopped telling stories that I couldn't factually verify.

In any case, I had been obsessed with Crowe since *Say Anything, Singles,* and *Jerry Maguire*. But his projects *Almost Famous* and *Elizabethtown* made me truly fanatic. It turns out that Nancy handled the musical duties for some of Cameron's biggest films. I was too nervous to even bring up Cameron's name during the interview so Cathy handled it instead.

"You've pretty much made a career out of working with your sister but scoring movies for your husband," Cathy said.

"First of all, me and Ann are really close. We've always been really close, I think because we started really young doing music together. And so we were kind of fearless about what we were aimed at, and even without a gender identity root necessarily," Nancy said. "And then with Cameron, too, I guess I really enjoy collaborating musically with people that I really love and understand and [who] get me too. And so you know, in that way I've been really lucky because the people in my immediate family are cool."

How do making music for a band and making music for a movie differ, I asked.

"Working on the soundtracks and the scores for movies is completely different," Nancy said. "I mean, especially the score music, which is not the songs, it's the rest of the music that happens in the movie. And doing that kind of writing is really cool. It's not easy, but it's really cool for me especially since I got to do it for Cameron's stuff."

"You have the scene itself and the dialogue that's happening in the scene and the mood of the scene to support. And it's interesting because you sort of have to be invisible and support what's happening at the same time. So I find that the hardest thing is to almost be simple enough sometimes and stay out of the way and still be in there musically."

By the time we hung up, my nerves were gone—replaced by the quiet realization that Heart's '80s reinvention wasn't a compromise at all, but another chapter of fearless creativity. Trends fade, formats change, but artists who trust their instincts always find a way to sound like themselves.

ANDY TAYLOR brings back a lot of mixed memories for me. On one hand, there was no more important band in 1984 than Duran Duran. On the other hand, it brings me back to being a bag boy at Publix Super Markets. Give me some room to explain.

When I was 16 years old and finally got a driver's license, I went out in search of a part-time job that would pay my gas bills and feed me on dates. I was hired to be a bag boy at Publix Super Markets after filling out maybe three pieces of information on an index card and being offered the job on the spot. The store was in Dunedin, Florida, the town next to the one I lived in, and was full of teens who went to the rival high school. On my very first day, I met the object of many odd decisions I would make.

Her name was Alisa, and she was a grade ahead of me. She wore heavy eyeliner and a scent that I would still recognize today. She spotted me watching training tapes in the break room and just gave me that smile. I think my heart stopped completely.

Within a month, we had our first date—to see *Footloose* in the theater. (She later bought me the soundtrack on tape to commemorate the event.) A few weeks later, I gave her my class ring in the first of many teary moments—on my end—that our relationship would cause. A few weeks after that, at an overnight birthday party at a mutual friend's house, she took my virginity while Thompson Twins' "Hold Me Now" played on repeat in the background.

Before you start to think this is an after-dark Hallmark movie romance—or at least a very disappointing HBO miniseries—you should know this twist: My mom hated Alisa. And probably for good reason. Alisa smoked. She worked at a job—a grocery store cashier—that she seemed perfectly willing to keep long after high school graduation. And, my mom suspected, she would lead me down the pathway of bad decisions.

Mom wasn't wrong. I was already skipping my SAT prep course twice a week to see Alisa. We'd sneak off to the movies or make out in the back of my car for a few hours before I'd return home with lipstick hastily removed from my cheeks and my clothes reeking of cigarette smoke. Suddenly, the idea of me staying home and working my way up to be a grocery store produce manager at Publix seemed like a good idea.

So when Alisa found us two tickets to see Duran Duran playing a few towns away on their Seven and the Ragged Tiger tour, Mom put her foot down. "Absolutely not," she insisted. Mom was the judge and jury when it came to all concert decisions, but this denial seemed more like an execution. Duran Duran was as hot as they'd ever be. I didn't know it at the time, but it would be the last time the original lineup toured for decades. My failure to justly earn my freedom that night—or to thwart Mom's sentencing and go anyway—lost me a lot of respect in Alisa's eyes. We'd break up a few weeks later. (Oh, sure, it was mainly because she already had a boyfriend back home in Ohio, where she had recently moved from, but I still associate it all with the band.)

Decades later, when my love for the '80s was reignited, Duran Duran became the band I could still enjoy with no guilt involved. I remember buying their reunion concert DVD—*Live from London*—and playing it endlessly at home while enjoying a cocktail or two and just letting the memories flood back without any care in the world. I would air-guitar to "Careless Memories" like I was on some sad reality TV competition, imagining myself as Andy Taylor while legions of women gasped in delight in front of me as I pouted on stage.

So imagine my surprise in 2008 when Andy actually wrote a book—*Wild Boy: My Life in Duran Duran*—about those days and was open to doing interviews. Literally every moment with Alisa flashed through my head as I prepped questions. Because this was still pretty early on in *Stuck in the '80s* history, Sean took the lead with questions. I can't even tell when I listen to the interview today if he even bothered introducing me. We were still pretty awkward at this point.

For reasons I can no longer fathom, I had staked out the areas of the band's political experiences and messaging. Formed in Birmingham in the late '70s, Duran Duran had come of age during a particularly heavy era of violence and terrorism between the British government and monarchy and its struggle with the Irish Republican Army. It was a good place for Andy to jump in.

"In the '70s and '80s, we had the British government and the Irish Catholic community who were represented by the IRA, and that was the military terrorist wing that wanted to basically set Ireland free from the British and the English Parliament," Andy began. "There was masses and masses of bombings in the U.K. and Ireland, thousands of people, a similar figure. About 3,000 people were killed in The Troubles. It was a terrible thing to grow up with because it happened so regularly. And the biggest target, to the IRA, was the British royal family because they represented everything that the Irish Republicans were against. So, in 1983, we had the honor of being asked to play for his Royal Highness and Princess Diana."

Yes, the infamous gig at the Dominion Theatre in 1983, where there was a foiled attempt on the lives of Prince Charles and Princess Diana. Andy was there with the rest of the band to perform.

"The whole story came out in the media eventually. The guy who was the bomber was a double agent, total James Bond stuff. He was a double agent for the British government. He has since wrote a book about the whole thing," Andy said. "And it was foiled, and I just thought…well, in the world we live in today, there's always been very, very evil people on your doorstep. It's not just a new thing."

I asked about the seemingly missing messages in Duran's music. Unlike some bands, they seemed to ignore politics.

"I was 19 when—I think Nick was 17—when we signed our first contract. And I think we had probably grown up more in the fantasy world of Bowie and the Beatles. We were all basically working, middle-class kids, but none of us had suffered and made us have a strong opinion about social issues," he said. "The lyrics of Bowie and more of the poetry of it and the Pop art culture and the glam rock thing and punk—that's when Simon [Le Bon] came along, and he had lyrics that sort of meant something. I still don't know what some of these lyrics are about. Sometimes he just won't tell you."

Andy, Sean, and I covered a lot more topics in our 45 minutes on the phone. Early influences, the struggle of being a guitar player in a band known for synths, and the possibility of a reunion. Our conversation—recorded back in September 2008—was before Andy would be diagnosed with stage 4 metastatic prostate cancer in 2018.

Andy had called his breakup with the band "a divorce," but we had to ask.

"If John and Simon and Nick call you up tomorrow and say, 'Look, you were right. We were wrong, we want the old Duran Duran back,' what would you say," I asked.

"Only if we could go and do that on Oprah," Andy joked in return.

I pressed: "What if they say, 'You pick the manager, you bring your music, we want we want…' Will you be open to it?"

"The trouble is you just never get an a là carte opportunity to put things right like that," Andy said. "Because you've went past trying to make those points with people, and they didn't want to hear."

I blurted out that I regretted never seeing the original lineup. The memories—the nightmare—of Alisa was paying a visit.

"Well, then, just for you if they'd call," Andy laughed. "But I said you never say never, but as it is now, making an album, doing the things the way that they've been done, it's the creative relationship hit a difficult patch, and the result of the things having to be done in a way that was still not, still didn't work, and that the core of it was our creative relationship. We didn't meet as friends. We met as fellow ambitious young wannabes, and that's what got us together when we—the personality test, if we had done a personality test, we probably wouldn't have been able to get together. We did it on a creative basis, and within a very short space of time of getting together, had written the basis of what the first album is, and that's the bit that's difficult to get to now."

"Playing live is great. I love playing live. I haven't got a problem with it at all," he said. "It's where you make your money, but if you can't make a record, then you have to explore why, and you can't outsource creativity to somebody else. It remains a creative relationship that I think is perhaps irreparably damaged or has done everything it can, and that's really what led to the tensions—not concerts."

As I think back now on this interview, it strikes me how neatly Andy's story of fractured creative relationships echoed the way some people—and some moments—slip out of your hands, leaving only songs behind to remind you they were ever there at all.

I have no clue what happened to Alisa after her graduation. I tried looking her up a few times over the years, but she left no footprint behind. I wonder if she has a lingering association with me and Duran Duran or if it was just a careless memory.

PHIL OAKEY and The Human League visited the U.S. for the first time in about 20 years for the Regeneration Tour in 2008. Phil, along with bandmates Joanne Catherall and Susan Ann Sulley, shared the stage with other '80s icons including Belinda Carlisle, ABC, A Flock of Seagulls, and Naked Eyes. I was able to score an interview with Phil before one of the opening dates in Las Vegas. I was full of nerves and nausea before, during, and afterward, but thankfully I don't notice it in the transcript more than 15 years later.

"We tour Britain at the end of every year," Phil began. "We've got all those traditional Christmas things that we go and do every year, and we've extended that into Europe, and we go to Australia. Yeah, but we haven't done a sustained tour of America for a little while."

That was a surprise to me. THL had six Top 40 hits in the U.S., beginning with the chart-topping "Don't You Want Me" in 1981. "Human" also hit No. 1, in 1986.

"I think because no one's ever quite sure what the market is, and to be straightforward, it's very financial," he explained. "As the money markets go up and down, sometimes we just can't make money coming over there [to the U.S.]. It's mad little things, like the cost of hiring buses, and then you can't go. It's really strange."

I was baffled. "I never thought of it that way," I stammered.

"I never wanted to think of it that way, but this is what my manager tells me," Phil said. "He could be just lying, of course. In fact, everyone hates us. No."

Nobody hates The Human League here, I assured him, though I doubt he needed my reassurance. Phil's humility was throwing me off, though. It seemed contrary to his on-stage persona.

"We mainly stick to hits," he said of the band's shows these days. "I think maybe because we never quite expected to be in a band. We're pretty grateful for people liking what we did. And we tailor the shows to what people want to hear, and blatantly so. We don't include new songs, for instance, that are less popular. We just try to make the audience enjoy themselves, really, or at least nod off with a pleasant sound in their ears."

"You're so humble," I blurted out. "It's taken me by surprise."

"Well, we're pretty ordinary, really, so we just get on with it," he replied.

The conversation shifted to Sheffield, the industrial town a few hours north of London where The Human League got started. The town can also lay claim to ABC, Def Leppard, Heaven 17, and Thompson Twins. What makes that region so conducive to forming bands, I asked.

"It's not particularly flattering to Sheffield: I think it was because there wasn't much else going on," he answered. "It's funny because it's quite a big town. It's the fourth biggest in the U.K. And we did have two art colleges, which maybe got people a bit inspired. But really, it's never been as exciting as some of even our neighboring towns, like Manchester. In Sheffield, everyone just drifts. So it's easy to go into a studio and try to make records."

Now that we were onto the topic of records, I wanted to get his thoughts on the album *Dare*, which went triple platinum in the U.K. and gold in the U.S.

"Everyone you talk to, especially the critics, consider it to be just a defining album in pop and electronica," I began. "I'm just curious: when you were making that, was there a point during the process where you thought, 'This is something special'?"

"I didn't really understand that until last year, I don't think," Phil said. "I've always thought that maybe the album wasn't quite what people thought it was. And I tended to think of the run of singles that we did as more important. It was only through doing the tour last year that I suddenly got that somehow the 40 minutes of the album meant more than the individual songs."

"Don't You Want Me"—the big hit off *Dare*—seemed a little out of step with the rest of the album, I said. I had heard Phil wasn't a fan of the song and that he didn't want it released as a single.

"It seemed a little bit populist," he said. "We were such a left-field band, and as we've sort of had pop success over the years, people have forgotten that. But we were like Devo or someone for a couple of albums, and it was surprising to me to find how mainstream we'd become. I've always liked pop; it just wasn't where I thought we were."

Because we were now firmly on the group of the band's poppier hits, I had the opening to talk about one of my favorite tunes from the decade: "Together in Electric Dreams" from the *Electric Dreams* soundtrack. At the time I was doing the interview, it was the ringtone on my phone. I'd heard a rumor it was recorded in a single take.

"There might have been two takes; I had to insist," Phil said. "Giorgio Moroder, who did all Donna Summer's hits and so on, he didn't like to work on things too much. He believed it should be instinctive. I went in and sang it and came out and expected him to say, 'Okay, now we'll do it properly. I understand how loud your voice is and things.' And he said, 'Oh, okay, that's done. That's done. You can go.' He let me do it once more, but I think he used the first one. He thought if you can't sing it in one take, it's not the right song for you."

Though it's technically a solo song for Phil, the band performs it live regularly, often at the end of their set.

"We run out of songs otherwise, so we have to do that [song]," he said. "Actually, to be straight, in Europe, I would say that's probably more popular than 'Don't You Want Me.'"

Since the band's formation in 1977, Phil has remained its only constant member. I wondered if he was ever tempted to call it a day and leave music and the road behind.

"There are things about being in the music business that can be harsh, and sometimes it sort of takes away from you," he began. "But I've got to say, the best thing about it has always been the people in the group. I love being in the group. Over the years, I've come to realize that I couldn't possibly have got better partners than Joanne and Susan, who, I think—everyone thinks they're the backing singers, sort of. But, for instance, Joanne handles a lot of the financial side of the stuff. Susan's really good at publicity and things, and we just look out for each other. Then the guys in the band are excellent, and we just have too good a time to give it up, you know? So we can't afford to pay to play anymore, but so long as we make enough money to just get by, we'll keep doing it."

Years later, it strikes me how little rock-star mythology had entered the conversation at all. Phil Oakey didn't talk like someone guarding a legacy—he was tending to it, quietly and carefully, with the same people he'd always trusted. And somehow, that made the music feel even more human.

ROBBIE GREY has a memorable face. We remember him best as the frontman behind one of our decade's most recognizable anthems—"I Melt With You." The song—about an amorous couple's last moments as an atom bomb is dropped—and its video were mainstays on MTV in the earliest years of the cable music network. Would you believe Robbie once considered the song a mixed blessing?

Though today considered a signature tune of the decade, "I Melt With You" was only a modest hit on the U.S. Billboard charts, and it didn't perform as well in the band's hometown U.K. markets.

In 2011, Robbie and Modern English's original bandmates reunited for an American tour, which afforded me a chance to talk with him before an appearance in Tampa Bay.

"There's always been, like, a love affair between the United States and Modern English," I began. "You see just a handful of English bands that seem to really connect here almost better than they do at home. How do you explain that?"

"I think MTV helped us, you know, back in the day of videos," Robbie began. "We recorded a video for, like, a thousand bucks, and it was one of the most played videos on MTV when it was still a music channel rather than a style channel. And also, 'I Melt With You' had been used in the film *Valley Girl*, which was Nicolas Cage's sort of breakthrough movie. And that did really well with the youth of America. So I don't really know why that certain bands from England do really well in America. I can understand why U2 would do well because of their sort of anthem, sort of stadium-type music. I think the song 'I Melt With You' just hooked into so many people, not just in America but worldwide, really."

Valley Girl was indeed a nice break for Nicolas Cage, as well as actress Deborah Foreman, whom I'd already befriended at this point. How did the song end up in the 1983 movie?

"The band were on the road. We were doing a tour of 80 concerts in a hundred days," Robbie recalled. "They were working us like dogs, basically. We were living on a massive bus with beds on it. And we got sent this film, and we just sat down one night after a concert and watched it. And they used 'I Melt With You' in it, I think three times. And in one scene it was used all the way through, like the whole song, which is really unusual. It would have been to do with our management, I'd imagine."

The band would go on to re-record the tune for its 1990 album *Pillow Lips*. It's been covered as well by a handful of artists, including Jason Mraz and Bowling for Soup (who changed the words "making love to you was never second best" to "being friends with you was never second best" for the kid-friendly flick *Sky High*).

The success of the song caught the band off guard, Robbie said.

"It's been kind of a fantastic thing. I mean, I'm not going to complain about 'I Melt With You.' It pays my bills every year," he began. "But it has been a bane in a way as well, because sometimes you'll play a club or a venue or a concert somewhere, and it's the only song that some people know. And a lot of our other stuff, it's a lot edgier."

"There's a lot more to Modern English than 'I Melt With You.' But we were taken completely off guard. We were recording some fresh songs, and we heard that in America they were playing 'I Melt With You' on import. It wasn't even released there; the radio stations just picked up on it. And then there was a kind of bidding war between all these record companies to sign us to get it out on a release in America. We can't complain about it because every time we play it, it's just fantastic audience reaction, you know."

These days, if you're not hearing the song on SiriusXM's 80s on 8 or First Wave channels, you're likely hearing it on a TV commercial.

"God, yeah, I can't tell you how many commercials it's been in," Robbie said. "It's been in so many commercials. T-Mobile. And then we had the Hershey bars thing that's still going on now for the third year."

Did the band get a say-so in its commercial usage?

"They do ask us," he said. "I don't have a problem with any of it. There was a problem when we did the Burger King one because at the time our keyboard player was a vegetarian. So he did a little complaining, and when I told him how much the money was, he seemed to quiet down, though."

With the band now touring regularly—and making multiple appearances on The 80s Cruise—everyone seems to have a Modern English story now. But I'd heard there was an infamous show back in the '80s in Daytona Beach. I wanted the scoop.

"Yeah, that was a big one," Robbie recalled. "We were just breaking at that moment. This is how naïve we were as Englishmen. We got off the plane in Daytona Beach wearing coats. You know, we were wearing winter clothes. We were literally walking down the gangplank taking all our clothes off. You know, it was like bloody hot. And that night, I remember we went to the venue in Daytona and the guy said, 'You can play outside in the open air.' We'd never done anything like that before. We were a club sort of venue band in England, 200 people. So we got a bit scared by that and we said, 'No, we want to play indoors.' And God almighty, did we. They couldn't get all the people in there. It was about 5,000 people outside. There's 5,000 people inside the wall. All the moisture coming off all the walls was incredible. And, I mean, the crowd just went absolutely nuts. That's probably why people remember that. I remember coming off stage and just—I'd never seen a crowd reaction like it before for us. It was incredible."

Please don't bring your coats again to Florida, I implored him.

"I'll try not to this time," he assured me.

PETE BYRNE of Naked Eyes is one of my favorite people in the *Stuck in the '80s* timeline, and he's one of the few I've met several times in person. Naked Eyes was part of the Regeneration Tour in 2008.

I'd only vaguely known of Pete as the glowering hero in the band's video for "Always Something There to Remind Me." I had zero idea what to expect when I saw him perform live.

The lights dimmed, the audience at the Planet Hollywood theater in Las Vegas began to hoot and holler, and then a smiling, bounding Pete Byrne took to the stage and opened with... "Always Something There to Remind Me."

The unusual upfront appearance of the song was one of the first things I asked him about when we talked on the phone a few days later.

"I think what really surprised me when I saw you live was, I mean, of course I knew the videos and I knew the hits, and in the video, you're sullen, gloomy," I began. "And when you came on stage, you brightened the place up. You had this great smile. You came out, you played that one chord, and the audience, I think, was just blown away."

Pete was as exuberant on the phone as he was on the stage. "It occurred to me that doing such a short set and going on first, it might be a nice way to open the whole evening with possibly one of the most well-known songs," he said. "I just thought it would go down well. And I've been proved right. I guess it's unusual for people to open with their most well-known song. But I'm having fun with it."

I remarked how Naked Eyes never seemed to hit the road in the U.S. back in the '80s at the height of their popularity on the radio and MTV.

"Back in the early days, EMI Capital considered us to be a sort of video band," he began. "I think from their point of view, it was a better option for us to do videos and promos. I mean, I did all the big TV shows in America. I did *Solid Gold* and *American Bandstand* and all those things. But we never did tour. I think it hurt us a great deal. I've been back on the road for about three years, and everybody knows my songs, but there's still a lot of people that don't know the name Naked Eyes because of that fact. So the marketing of Naked Eyes wasn't the best thing ever."

Of course, everybody in America—probably everybody around the world who grew up in the '80s—knows "Always Something There to Remind Me." Not as many know it's a cover of a Burt Bacharach song. I was curious how Pete heard the original version.

"Oh my God, when I was a little kid," he said. "I just knew that ['60s British pop star] Sandie Shaw was, like, this killer 19-year-old chick doing it. And she used to walk around in bare feet. That was her gimmick. And she was very sexy and everything."

The song's construction caught the eye of Pete and his bandmate, the late Rob Fisher. Plus, it was a chance to cover a song popularly sung by a female voice.

"Rob started playing it on the synth, and it just happened very quickly," he said.

Extremely quickly, as it turns out. I'd heard that the tune was recorded at one in the morning and in a single take.

"Oh, God, yeah," Pete realized. "In fact, it may have even been later there, maybe three in the morning. We were quite wasted at that point. There was a big party at Abbey Road where we were recording the album. And Paul McCartney was there and Linda [McCartney], and a lot of big English pop stars like Billy Fury. We were working in the studio, but the party was downstairs and they said, 'Why don't you come down and have a couple of drinks?' And of course, one thing led to another. And so by about the middle of the night, it seemed like a great time to do the vocal."

It didn't always come that easy, Pete assured me. Recording the vocals for the follow-up hit "Promises, Promises" took three days.

"It's difficult stuff, but 'Always Something There to Remind Me' was one of those just, like, magical moments," he said. "There's so much luck involved in it. I mean, the things like the intro, the tubular bells that we use, we were just sitting around in Abbey Road and we discovered these bells and they were in the studio and we thought, 'Well, why don't we try them out?' And we did."

The music video—the one that mistakenly convinced me Pete was an ogre—wasn't quite so magical.

"It wasn't that I was acting in that film," he recalled. "I had actually been up all night and we started at like six in the morning and it was raining and I was absolutely miserable shooting it."

In 2007, a year before the Regeneration Tour hit the road, Naked Eyes released an album, *Fumbling with the Covers*. A cover of Elton John's "Rocket Man" caught my attention. Pete's version was ethereal, each note hanging in space, mirroring the song's sense of isolation and wonder.

"What do I have to do to talk you into playing it in Clearwater?" I asked. The Regeneration Tour was wrapping things up in my hometown a few weeks after our conversation.

"You know, I'd love to do that," Pete said. "It's really difficult on this tour. I mean, I love doing it, but it is frustrating in that I can't relax and do a couple of acoustic numbers and that sort of thing."

"Well, I'm actually going to be backstage in Clearwater because I think I'm handling the stage introductions," I told him. "So if I come up to you, and I beg you to play, like just a couple…"

"I'll do it!" he said, stopping me in my tracks.

"'Rocket Man'? You'll do it?" I said in disbelief.

"I'll do it," he promised.

A few weeks later, Pete and I were standing at the side of the curtain at Ruth Eckerd Hall, and he watched as I shuffled nervously to the center of the stage to introduce him. I have zero recollection of what I said. I might have finished by proclaiming triumphantly to the audience, "Please welcome my good friend Pete Byrne and Naked Eyes!"

I skipped back to the side of the stage as the rest of Pete's bandmates shuffled out to their spots.

"Steve…." Pete said. I turned to him, surprised and wondering why he was still standing there. He lifted his guitar and began to play, whispering the opening words to "Rocket Man" to me as my jaw dropped. After he finished the first chorus, he smiled, patted me on the shoulder, and strode out to start the show—again with "Always Something There to Remind Me."

Out on stage, Pete gave the crowd what they wanted. But behind the curtain, for just a minute, he gave me something else entirely. Twenty years on, it's still the most personal performance I've heard—and the one that's stayed with me the longest.

THE SECOND ACT

I never thought I'd leave the *St. Petersburg Times*. Florida's largest daily newspaper, it was also one of the country's best publications. Those who worked there were among the best writers in the business. *Stuck in the '80s* was born there. But after 17 years, I felt like I'd hit a wall. The podcast was popular outside the building, but it still seemed like a misunderstood and underappreciated project inside it. Digital was the future of journalism, but the *Times* was a writer-focused institution devoted to print. And while I'd won a slew of awards for my digital accomplishments from various state and national organizations, a lot of my office time was relegated to menial duties best suited to an intern.

In 2012, a former supervisor recruited me to leave Tampa Bay for Orlando, an area of the state I never wanted to live in. Disney, traffic, and tourists? No thanks. But he offered me what the *Times* never did: the chance to take what I'd learned from building up *Stuck in the '80s* and apply it to another media organization. And so that October, I packed my boxes and left for a magazine publishing company based in Winter Park, a tony suburb of Orlando.

I found living in Orlando more of a struggle than an opportunity. It probably took me a good nine months to a year to find my footing, both with my new job as a digital content director and as a resident.

The podcast went through its own growing pains too. Sean Daly, who stayed at the *Times* a few more years, would have to depart as a co-host. I had to give up the podcast studio the *Times* had built and the high-tech gear that came with it. But I did have Brad Williams, a longtime podcast fan and friend who is a genius at tech challenges. I invited Brad to join as the new co-host. We bought some decent USB microphones and decided to record the show via Skype.

What a nightmare. Skype might have been great a decade ago as a free video chat service, but it had no built-in recording mechanism, so we had to use third-party software programs—usually with names we couldn't even pronounce. They were sketchy and unreliable at best. The quality of our audio went downhill, and there was a time lag between our East Coast and West Coast conversations, making for never-ending talkover gaffes. And, from time to time, the software wouldn't record at all—and not tell us until the call was over. I lost interviews with a handful of artists as a result. (A memorable chat with The Tubes' Fee Waybill would be in this book had Skype been working properly one evening in 2016.)

Brad and I had to work on our chemistry as well. For the first time, I was recording with a host who wasn't in the same room with me. We also had to record later at night when Brad was home from the office in SoCal. It was a slog. It would take us about six months to find our new voice.

To develop our rapport and create the friendship that is needed for a project like this, we started with phone calls—lots of them. With Brad working three hours behind me, he'd call me in my evening on his drive home from the office each night—a one-hour drive that we filled with stories from our teenage years, my adventures to date with podcasting, and the usual guy talk. I'd usually have a drink in hand, and the stories would grow bawdier as each night's drive went on.

We were becoming two people who could trust each other—we were becoming good friends.

The podcast was pretty much the only positive thing I had going on in my life. My personal life had dried up. I tried online dating. While the results in Tampa Bay had been largely poor, they at least provided some really great stories. Here in Orlando, even the stories were boring. One night, I had a coffee date with a woman, and in our half hour together I learned she hated the '80s, loved jazz, and never read a newspaper. So much for a match. We spent the rest of the date sharing restaurant recommendations.

I had inherited a cat from my previous relationship—"Cat Benatar"—who took to me more warmly than the ex-girlfriend. She was pretty much the only female to spend considerable time in my apartment. She would sit on my desk while I conducted interviews with Adam Ant, Mike Reno of Loverboy, and others.

MIKE RENO and Loverboy were the first voices I heard from a stage. It was October 22, 1981. I only remember the date because it was my first concert—Loverboy opening for Journey on Journey's Escape Tour. In 2014, when Loverboy released a new album of music, I had a chance to talk to frontman Mike Reno. Mike was an amazing storyteller. Do you remember the MTV contest where the lucky winner got to make a music video with Loverboy? Mike does. He related the whole story, beginning with how Loverboy ended up on MTV.

"You're gonna laugh, Steve," Mike began. "We were told by the record company in New York: 'We want you guys to pull into Albany, New York, and we want you to play a whole pile of songs off your record, and we're going to add some funny clips and stuff from different things and hand them to this new company out of

New York that's doing a 24-hour music television show.' And we went, 'Okay.'"

"So we pulled in and recorded a whole bunch of stuff. We just played live, they filmed it, and they sent all these clips...I think they sent three finished five-minute clips...and this is how funny this is, Steve...they didn't even know what they were called back then. They were just 'music clips.' It turns out they were called videos because that's how it was created one day. The day before, there was none and the day after, they were called videos. They sent them to a company called MTV, which had a two-hour license to play music on the television. Only about 13 bands jumped on that and so they played us and the 13 bands 24 hours a day. We became television stars. Our faces were famous. Before that, things were kind of faceless unless you got a show on *In Concert* or the rock 'n' roll concerts they played on the weekends. Nobody knew what you looked like unless they looked at your album covers."

I told Mike I certainly remembered Loverboy in 1983, when MTV promoted a new contest: The winner got to appear in the video for "Queen of the Broken Hearts."

"Ohhh, I remember that. Do you know the backstory to that?" Mike asked. "She [the woman in the video] is actually the mother of the girl who won. The girl who won was SO freaked out, she never even showed up to get flown in to the Mojave Desert video shoot. So the mother went, and they limoed her out to the desert, and on the way out there, she got so drunk from all the liquor that was in the limo that she wouldn't get out of the limo. So finally, they almost crowbarred her out of that limo and put her in a scene somewhere because she had to be in a scene. That was part of the contest. She just didn't even want to do it. So, they sat her down and filmed her as she was trying to get up and back into the limo because she didn't even want to be part of it. So, that's the back story. That's funny, huh?"

Likewise, the story behind the power ballad "Almost Paradise" will surprise fans. It nearly destroyed the band, Mike explained.

"I got a call from Bruce Allen, my manager, who said, 'Listen, I got the opportunity to put a song in this new movie *Footloose* they're making and they want it to be a duet. What are you thinking?' And I said, 'I'm going to pick Ann Wilson from Heart,' because Heart kind of grew up in Vancouver, same as us. They were a group from Seattle but they came up here for about 10 years and lived here in the '70s, played here all the time in Vancouver. So, we kind of considered them one of our own, and I learned to love Ann's voice."

"So, I get to the studio and we start. The song's all ready to go. We both kind of learned it. She was three hours late for the session and they were just about ready to shut the session down, and she walked in and she was sorry for being late. But she'd slipped on the ice or something. She'd hurt her wrist, and she was kind of holding an ice bag on her wrist, and I felt really bad for her. And I said, 'Do you want to just forget about this, or do you just want to sit down and relax for a little while and then cut this track?' So, I got her to relax a little bit and we sat there and got to know each other a little bit. This was out in the studio with the curtains closed, just her and I sitting there. I think we had a glass of wine or something to calm us down. Then, after about an hour or something, I said, 'Did you want to give this song a try?' She said, 'Yeah, it's a beautiful song.' So, I asked the guys in the studio to open up the curtains and they ran the track. We sang it once, facing each other on the same microphone. Boom! That was it. Magic, baby!"

"One take!?" I marveled. But I was curious what effect it had on his bandmates.

"Oh, Paul (Dean) thought we were finished," Mike said of his bandmate and lead guitarist. "Paul thought we were going to turn into a ballad band. He got all pissed off. Turned out, he was a little bit premature on being angry because that album went and sold

27 million copies. It was like, No. 2, or something. So, whatever makes noise makes the band famous, right?"

With the success of "Almost Paradise" and the *Footloose* soundtrack, Hollywood came with another movie project.

"Next thing you know, they're knocking on our door to do *Top Gun*. So, Paul's tune changed immediately. We got together and wrote "Heaven in Your Eyes" and that also went on to sell something like 27 million albums. So, he now has a whole new appreciation for the love ballad."

I asked what the bond was that kept the band together for so long when other bands found it difficult to make more than one or two albums tops.

"Well, there's one thing that Paul and I did when we first started," Mike said. "We took our time finding the guys who we wanted in this band, and it took us over a year to find the exact blend, and we went through a few blends before we would put out a record or did any videos or anything," he said.

The original lineup is still together today, minus bassist Scott Smith, who was presumed dead after a boating accident in 2000. ("He was a pivotal member of the band and was my best friend," Mike told me. "It took a while to get over that.") One key to the longevity is the rare equal share of the royalties among bandmates.

"Paul and I decided to just make everyone equal partners all the way down the line so everybody is just as responsible as the next guy," Mike said. "Paul and I took time finding the people we wanted to be with because we were hoping this band would be around for a while. We didn't know it would go 35 years, but we thought, 'You know, let's work with people we enjoy being around,' right?"

The interview with Mike Reno was a great boost to my confidence. It was one of the first "gets" after leaving the *Times*, and it showed me the podcast had a life beyond the walls of the newspaper.

ADAM ANT was another. The British New Wave standard-bearer was touring the U.S. in 2013 for what seemed like the first time in forever. He had a stop in Orlando at Hard Rock Live, a medium-sized venue just outside Universal Orlando in an entertainment district called CityWalk. I had snagged second-row tickets. The show was incredible—of all the '80s icons, Adam is a vastly underrated frontman. He oozed charisma that night on the stage, and I wrote up a review on the *Stuck in the '80s* blog that caught his publicist's attention:

> *If you think punk rock is dead. If you believe the fire of '80s magic has been extinguished. If you just stumbled on this blog because you were searching for a weekend weather report instead of fulfilling your commitment to the life-affirming ideals of the soul-warming nostalgia, then allow me to introduce you to Stuart Leslie Goddard, better known as Adam Ant. He's now going to claw your heart out, have it incinerated and scatter the ashes over Orlando's Hard Rock Live, with the last flake landing on the ground some 36 hours after he finished the final note of* Antmusic *during Saturday's classic concert.*

Adam's publicist reached out to me shortly after I published the review. She offered me the first U.S. interview for his upcoming tour. I was stunned. Aside from Steve Perry, I can't think of anyone who was as reclusive as Stuart Goddard. It was a challenging interview to prepare for because Adam hadn't done as much press as his peers. Still, one weekday afternoon, I faked being sick at work so I could be home to get his call.

We spent the first part of the interview talking about how everyone has an "Adam Ant story," even MTV's Martha Quinn.

She told me before the interview with Adam that she and fellow VJ Nina Blackwood had shared a bowl of rice pudding with Adam at a Sheraton in New York back in 1981.

"Oh, right, yeah," Adam said. "I like rice pudding. It's one of my childhood delicacies."

It turns out the most unlikely of Adam Ant stories was the time he lived fairly anonymously in Tennessee. It was there that he had written much of the album he was touring to support—*Adam Ant Is the Blueblack Hussar in Marrying the Gunner's Daughter*. He found the house—nestled at the top of the Tennessee Valley—in a property magazine while driving through America.

"It was the most spectacular view you could ever—probably one of the best views in the world. It was so beautiful. And I just thought, 'If I don't do this now, I'm never going to do it.' We settled there for two years and it was a lovely experience. We had a very good neighbor who eventually became my daughter's godmother. And people kind of left me alone. They had no idea who I was. It was only my next-door neighbor who kind of knew that I was a singer, and that was the nice thing about it. So it was a real sabbatical as it were. It was a lovely period of time in my life."

We went on to talk about Malcolm McLaren, the promoter/artist who helped form Adam and the Ants. McLaren had only recently passed away when Adam and I spoke. I asked if there were still hard feelings about the way McLaren had ditched the Ants to move on to other projects. Not so, said Adam, who actually wrote a song about his old friend—"Who's a Goofy Bunny?"

"Certainly there was bruised egos, but in hindsight, I think Malcolm was a great mentor to me as someone who sat down with me and talked about the structure of songwriting and the history of music. He had a great knowledge of rock 'n' roll. He got me to sit down and discipline myself as far as the songwriting was concerned, and also to simplify things and help me to decide if

I wanted to continue making records like *Dirk Wears White Sox*. No one else had really sat me down before and talked to me about music. So it was, I think in the history of rock 'n' roll, in my opinion, he's one of the greatest rock 'n' roll managers with Colonel Tom Parker, Brian Epstein, and Peter Grant. He was very much a unique character."

I think a lot about that afternoon with Adam when I look back on the years of podcasting. It was an unlikely conversation, but listening back, it sounds more like two friends catching up than an interview. That had become my new goal, and whenever I reached it, I knew I'd done something right.

My life in Orlando was starting to feel comfortable—at least in terms of continuing the podcast. In terms of my job and my relationships, it was still a shipwreck. I wasn't enjoying my day job, and my social life was nonexistent. That put a lot of pressure on *Stuck in the '80s* to fill in the holes.

Eventually Brad and I found things were buzzing again when we did the 10th anniversary of the podcast—a tribute to *The Breakfast Club*, the subject of our first-ever episode. But something was still missing. We needed a force to really give us a kick in the butt.

That came with the arrival of The 80s Cruise.

I wrote up a string of questions so difficult that we were threatened... in the hallways between trivia sessions.

THE 80s CRUISE

Back in 2015, the novelty and energy of the podcast was beginning to wane. It'd been three years since I'd left the *St. Petersburg Times* for a job in Orlando. In the process, the podcast became a hobby that I had to schedule for evenings and weekends. We needed a spark. We got that with the creation of The 80s Cruise.

That year, I saw a social post about this new '80s-focused cruise. Three of the MTV veejays—Alan, Mark, and Nina—would be the hosts. (Martha doesn't do water, she has said before.) The music lineup was incredible—Huey Lewis & The News, Richard Marx, Kool & the Gang, Starship, Naked Eyes, Wang Chung, A Flock of Seagulls, and Biz Markie as the DJ.

I immediately posted about it on the blog. The next day I got a call from Michael Lazaroff, the owner of ECP, the company putting the cruise together. It turns out he was going to contact me about participating on the cruise too. I bounced from the floor to the ceiling with energy. Brad and I signed on immediately.

It was more than a year between signing on and sailing.

BRAD SAYS NOW: I saw the cruise as an opportunity to spend a week with people that would be built-in fans—an easy way to connect with 3,000 possible podcast listeners every spring. I thought our listener numbers would explode from the immersion with the '80s Nation faithful. While we've definitely made connections with some amazing people, we've never really seen a big listener bump, even though we circulated a "how to listen to the podcast" flyer to every cabin one year!

It wasn't an entirely free ride. We had to market the cruise to our listeners and host a few trivia sessions onboard. No sweat, we thought. The trouble was we assumed the guests on the ship would *really* be into the '80s and would thus be able to answer questions beyond the most elementary ones. We assumed wrong. I wrote up a string of questions so difficult that we were threatened—presumably in jest—in the hallways between trivia sessions.

I will admit that people had a valid argument. Among my more ridiculously hard questions:

- What was the original name of Huey Lewis & the News? (Huey Lewis & The American Express)

- What was the name of the Australian boat that defeated the Americans in the 1983 America's Cup? (*Australia II*)

- What was the name of the school the girls attended in *The Facts of Life*? (Eastland Academy)

Holy hell, I must have been deranged. In the years that followed, we progressively made the questions easier and easier. (You are on a ship—true or false?)

The highlight of any cruise is when we get artists to be "VIP guests" for our Big 80s Trivia sessions. For that first year, it was Modern English. Thankfully I had interviewed their lead singer, Robbie Grey, years before, so I knew he was a friendly guy who spun some great stories. In future years, we'd have actress Claudia Wells, singer Katrina Leskanich from Katrina and the Waves, Howard Jones, Midge Ure, Paul Young, and others. The guests usually help us draw larger, more focused crowds.

On one of the more recent voyages, former Skid Row frontman Sebastian Bach was a last-minute addition to our trivia lineup. I'd been gently warned by my friends who were fans of his music that Brad and I should resist any temptation to joke around with him, so we planned to play it very straight with our interaction.

BRAD SAYS NOW: There's no other way to say this—the moment we handed Sebastian a microphone, we ceded control of the session. He would chat with Steve and me (mostly Steve) for a bit after every question, and then he would turn to me and say, "Okay, ask the next question." He was not bossy or controlling, he was just setting tempo. At the end of the session, he treated the crowd to an impromptu rendition of the theme song from *WKRP in Cincinnati*, video of which was on YouTube within about 15 minutes.

Another memorable trivia moment came in 2025, when we asked the following question: "Pass the Dutchie" by Musical Youth is roughly based on several songs, including "Pass the Kouchie" by The Mighty Diamonds. What is "Dutchie" slang for?

BRAD SAYS NOW: As we were in a generous mood, this was presented as a multiple-choice question, with the following options: A) Chocolate dessert; B) A Dutch oven; C) A cannabis pipe; and D) A Netherlands resident. When the answer was revealed to be "B) A Dutch oven," the room surged with angry energy, and with the crowd loudly insisting that the answer was clearly "C) A cannabis pipe." Ah, but here we had an ace in the hole, because who was onstage with us that day but Dennis Seaton and Michael Grant from the band Musical Youth! Of course we turned to them and asked, "Hey guys, what is this song about?" The answer was unequivocal: the song is about food, full stop. Dennis said, "We were 12 years old! We weren't writing songs about drugs!"

Everyone I count as a good friend now is someone I either know through the podcast—like Brad—or someone I met on an 80s Cruise. Each year, we end the trip with a group toast at the final dinner. Brad always does the honors—I'm possibly the worst dinner host you could imagine.

One thing that always amazes me is how many people recognize me on a cruise. I get a lot of "Hi, Spearsy" greetings everywhere I walk. I never get used to it. I'm horrible at remembering names, though the faces are always familiar. Even my wife likes to tell the story about how she almost said hi to me on the first year of the cruise when she saw me walking across the pool deck, but she decided against it. "You looked like you really wanted to be left alone," she later told me. Melissa and I formally met on the 2019 cruise and got engaged on the 2020 cruise. We married in 2021.

The best thing about The 80s Cruise has always been the history we didn't realize we were building in real time. Somewhere during that first trip, the people we met stopped being a group of strangers and became a family. ECP threw *Stuck in the '80s* a much-needed lifeline all those years ago. But even more than that, I'm grateful for the people who showed up and stayed.

THE MTV VEEJAYS

Everyone has an MTV story.

Millions probably claim to have been awake just after midnight on August 1, 1981, to witness the event, but they're most likely stretching the truth. When MTV began on that fateful day, basic cable was a luxury for much of America. It's believed only a few thousand people in northern New Jersey were actually able to see MTV on day one.

The first spoken words—"Ladies and gentlemen, rock 'n' roll"—weren't even delivered by one of MTV's original five video jockeys. Rather, they were uttered by John Lack, a 33-three-year-old news radio executive in New York, who would catch lightning in a bottle as one of MTV's cofounders.

Of all the heroes from the 1980s, I don't think there are any I place above Martha, Mark, Alan, Nina, and J.J. The original MTV veejays deserve "one name only" status far more than Madonna. When MTV arrived for the slimmest of national audiences, I was living in suburban Tampa Bay, far from the nearest cable market. To allow me to watch MTV, my mom got a friend at work who miraculously lived in a cable neighborhood to record it for me. So about once a week, I'd get a six-hour VHS tape, recorded at some random timeslot of my beloved music television. It was this way that I saw my first ever MTV video ("Be Good Johnny" by Men at Work) and the first MTV video I was never allowed to watch again at home because it was deemed too violent by Mom ("The Twilight Zone" by Golden Earring).

If you'd asked me in 1981—hell, in 1991 or in 2001—if I'd ever conceive of a time when I'd have one-on-ones with these people I grew up with, I'd have laughed until I passed out.

NINA BLACKWOOD has the biggest heart you can imagine. In 2013, when the surviving veejays collaborated to write the book *VJ: The Unplugged Adventures of MTV's First Wave*, Brad and I got the chance for our conversation with Nina. When she learned Brad was calling in at 6 a.m. California time, Nina's first words were out of concern for the wildfires that were destroying large swaths around the southern parts of the state.

"Oh, God!" she began. "Have you been affected by the fires?"

The fires were indeed near his home, but he assured her there were "about a thousand concrete shingled houses between that and me."

BRAD SAYS NOW: When we interviewed Nina for the podcast, I'd been cohosting for about six months and was just starting to feel comfortable in the seat. This was one of the early instances of what I'll call "Talking Heads moments" in which I found myself musing, "Well, how did I get here?" I'm just some guy that grew up in a smallish town in western Oklahoma. Please explain to me why I'm interviewing MTV veejays. We were having some wildfires in L.A. at the time, and I was so touched that she asked how I was doing, how my family was.

The two continued to chat up his precarious situation for another minute before we remembered we were on the phone to talk about a book.

"We've read the book cover to cover and enjoyed every second of it," I said, interrupting the conversation.

"Actually, it goes back eight or nine years ago when J.J. was still alive, and we thought it would be a good idea to write a book because we have a unique vantage point that nobody other than the five of us had," Nina began. "The last time, sadly, I saw J.J. was when we were in a lawyer's office signing paperwork to start shopping the story, and then J.J. passed away."

J.J. Jackson—sometimes known as "Triple J"—was a prominent radio DJ before setting foot in the MTV studios. After five years at the cable network, he returned to radio and continued to work until he passed on March 17, 2004.

"When J.J. was alive, I think all of us deferred to J.J., and he had that beautiful, booming voice and his presence that when he would speak, everybody would shut up," Nina said. "He was kind of the leader in that regard."

The other VJs had their roles to play too, Nina said. "Alan was the funny one. He was the jokester. We had Mark, who was the older FM brother. You had me, who tended to be the quietest, because I didn't wanna try and over talk everybody because everybody else was talking. Martha, of course, was the little sister."

The dynamics have changed over the years, especially with the absence of J.J., she said. It really became noticeable when the foursome was promoting the *Unplugged Adventures* book.

"I can say, for Martha, Mark, and myself, I felt an extra, deeper bond with us. Alan, I kept telling him to shut up, you know [laughter]. So I guess my bond was a little bit different with him. It's like, 'Would you let somebody else talk?' You know, but like brothers and sisters, I mean, the love is still there. It's just I'm an only child, so this is my experience of having a family of brothers and a sister. And you could get really annoyed, but you still love the person."

When Brad and I interviewed Mark, Alan, and Nina for our 500th podcast episode in 2019, the irritability between "the quiet one" and "the jokester" was still palpable. If we'd only gone back and listened to this interview with Nina, we would have expected it.

"Alan, I know, he's more of a comedian mentality, and comedians tend to try and fill all the spaces, like dead air is, like, bad. And I think that's what he's doing," Nina said. "And I think that's why he seems to be more vocal than he used to be. Because I never remember ever going, 'Would you shut up?'"

Nina herself has always been a little more guarded and private with her stories. But there was one she was eager to share: the female subject of John Waite's song "Missing You." It's Nina, she said, and she detailed the story behind it in the MTV book.

"I couldn't not talk about John because he was very much a part of my time at MTV," Nina said. "When I think of my life in New York in the MTV days, John is the person I think about.... He contacted me after the book came out, and it was weird because we had been in contact but all of a sudden, it's a Monday and I'm getting these messages from my manager and from other people saying, 'John Waite's looking for you in a very public way.' I had been in communication, forewarned him about the book, and explained where I was coming from."

"Missing You" would become a No. 1 hit for John Waite in 1984. The inspiration and spark for the song came from his impending divorce and several loves, he had told interviewers at the time. Nina said she finally wrote him asking, "Are you looking for me?"

"He wrote back and he clarified. He said, 'It is your song,'" Nina told us. Brad and I were unable to follow up with any questions—we were a bit hypnotized—so Nina kept going. "He said, 'I never would've said that if it wasn't.' So there you go [laughter]. I was very happy about that. I believed him, but then there were all these other people saying stuff, and I'm going, 'Well, maybe it's not the truth, you know?' So there you go."

It was about this time during our interview that Brad and Nina discovered they're both crazy for British cars. I'd try to give you a taste of the back and forth they had during the call, but frankly it's beyond my comprehension. Still, I remember smiling, sitting back, and enjoying the connection they'd made. I hated to break up the chat, but I knew time was running short.

"I know, Nina, that you're probably asked this all the time, but today's MTV doesn't bear much resemblance to the MTV that we grew up on," I began. "Do you recall a time when you worked there, when you began to think that something was changing? And also, I'm kind of curious to know, what is your verdict on where it is today?"

"It was something that was kind of intangible, but it was starting," she said. "I left before any of that reality TV hit—*The Real World, Remote Control*. Obviously it's a bottom-line financial thing. Obviously they're making a lot of money. Martha and Alan will be very diplomatic about it. I think it sucks. Make money, but at least keep some core of what music television was about."

"That's why it was unique. You can't have what it was back in the '80s. Of course not, progress," she continued. "I'm disappointed, that's the word. Disappointed that it went into the direction that it did. But hey, it did [laughter]. And I don't think it's cutting edge anymore. I really don't. It's kind of like part and parcel of the disposable pop culture society, really."

We ended the call shortly after that bummer note. But we'd meet Nina in person a few years later. She was a regular on the first few years of The 80s Cruise. And the conversation had only just begun.

▶ ▬▬▬||||||▬▬||||▬|||▬|||▬|||▬▬▬||||||▬▬||▬||▬||▬||

MARK GOODMAN, ALAN HUNTER, and NINA BLACKWOOD joined us in person on the 2019 voyage of The 80s Cruise to mark our 500th episode of the podcast. I can't overstate the combination of shock, panic, delirium, and delight that overtook us when we found out we'd landed this group interview.

BRAD SAYS NOW: I was more than a little freaked out at the prospect, but these folks have been interviewed about their role in MTV to within an inch of their lives. What could possibly go wrong? When the day came, I was as close to completely freaking out as I would allow myself to be. Steve and I were waiting in the backstage area of the venue 15 to 20 minutes before showtime when the VJs started trickling in. I chatted a bit with Nina about old British cars, and we were joined by Mark and Alan. The corner of my brain still housing 15-year-old Brad was flipping out. I leaned over to Steve as we walked out and whispered, "How did we get here? Is this actually happening?"

The interview played out in front of a live audience of '80s Cruisers, who were so close to the stage they could probably count the sweat drops falling off my face as I gurgled out the worst introduction.

"How we doing?" I began.

Ugh, I cringe still at reading this.

"I guess this is our 500th podcast, and so thank you for being here. We started this 14 years ago as a way to remember some good times and maybe someone would listen to us."

"And here we are," Brad said, finishing my thought.

"As Brad is fond of saying, when you're 14 years old, nothing in your life is more important than music. And in 1981, MTV became the conduit to the connection that we had with music," I continued. "The people that are going to come on the stage right now are the faces and the voices that became our older brothers, our older sisters, and they became our sages to the medium that we loved. And like it is here on The 80s Cruise, we consider ourselves a big family. We gather every year, we renew friendships, we share hugs, we make the reconnection. So here it is. We're nearly 40 years since the launch of MTV. Our older brothers and sisters are back, the '80s family is back. Please welcome to the stage Mark Goodman, Nina Blackwood, and Alan Hunter, the MTV family."

Alan, Nina, and Mark made their way to the stage while I tried to get my heart to stop beating 200 times a minute. My throat went dry, my legs were no longer working. Eventually we all found our chairs and sat, nervously thumbing the blue note cards with neatly printed questions that we had been organizing and rewriting for months.

"First question right off the bat: set your minds back 40 years," I began. "What seems more unlikely, that you would become the faces of music in the '80s or that 40 years later there would actually be the fourth year of the '80s cruise?"

"The cruise," Nina quickly answered.

"I didn't understand—none of us did—what MTV was going to become when we got the job," Alan said. "I was just glad to have a job that got me some new clothes. And I wanted to be a Broadway actor, and it paid me more just by a couple of dollars than that. I think it's an unusual decade, one of the more unique decades."

Brad jumped in next: "I have to think that you guys get endless invitations to many concerts from the bands that we love from the decade. Are there '80s artists that are impressing you with what they're doing now?"

"Well," Nina began, "somebody that I think has impressed me enormously, not quintessentially an '80s artist, per se, but Rob…"

At this point, a little chaos ensued. Mark interrupted to clarify the question. Nina tried to restate her answer (Robert Plant, by the way), and Alan egged the disruption on.

"If I can get a full phrase out with these two, we'll be lucky. As I was saying…" she continued.

Alan fired back: "It truly is nap time for Nina." Brad and I implored Mark and Alan to let her talk, to no avail.

"Brothers," Nina said emphatically. "It's why I'm happy I'm an only child. No, they're my brothers and I love them even though they drive me nuts. Anyway, but what was I saying…"

More interruptions came from Mark and Alan. Brad and I shot each other a look. We'd lost control, and this thing had only just begun. Finally, Nina was able to finish her answer.

"Everybody, let's hear it for Nina so she feels good about the rest of the day here," Alan said. "Glad she got it out."

"Horrible. Horrible," she replied.

I don't think I'd ever felt so low before. I wanted to throw up. We'd managed to enable this fight between our MTV heroes. This is not how I saw our 500th episode going. But there was no pulling the plug, so I took a deep breath and waited for the sniping to end. Was it good-natured ribbing or signs of deeper issues? To this day, I don't know.

"I'm so sorry you have to see this," Mark said after a few more moments into the back-and-forth conversation. I didn't know if he was joking or serious.

"Are you kidding me?" Brad said. "This is solid gold."

"We haven't interfaced on the trip yet," Alan explained. "This is the first day we've ever done anything together, so you're catching it fresh. We've got to work some shit out, I'm telling you. Some familial stuff coming out now."

It didn't stop, though. We talked about Duran Duran, Pet Shop Boys, U2, and Peter Gabriel, but only in fragmented sentences. I tried some low-hanging fruit and asked about the second song to ever appear on MTV on its first day ("You Better Run" by Pat Benatar) as well as the last song that day ("Lonely Boy" by Andrew Gold).

"See, I wouldn't have known that," Nina said.

"Wow, I didn't know that," Alan answered next.

"Andrew Gold? Nice," Mark finished.

Maybe we were back on track. Good timing because I had been ready to just dump my note cards on the floor when I tried this one: How quickly, I asked, did MTV change the way that people listen to music and how bands charted on *Billboard*.

"Oh, man. That's the sort of thing that everyone around the country could see," Mark began. "It probably took a couple of years, I think. But in the first six months, as we would go out—they would send us out to do appearances and things—and I went to Cheyenne, Wyoming, in the first year, and 1,000 people turned up at a record shop to see me. I couldn't believe this, and neither could the driver. But I think the real change was when it started to affect, by '83, '84, when it started to affect fashion. People were dressing like Cyndi Lauper, or Madonna, or Pat Benatar."

"As MTV grew, and as we started to do more and more things, I think that they wanted different things from us," he continued. "And my thing was, I love music. I'm going to be passionate about music, I'm going to want to talk about music. Not that Alan didn't, but Alan, you may have noticed, is a bit of a joker. He's a bit of a, 'I want to fuck around and act crazy.' So Alan was the guy because he could go to spring break and he could be nuts and act crazy with all the kids who were down there."

Alan picked up the thread: "The evolution of MTV was after '84, '85, '86 in the prime years. After things started to evolve, and we all started moving on elsewhere, MTV changed from a video jukebox because it started to lose its luster. Then MTV became more about people's lifestyles and what you liked beyond just music. That's why spring break was tons of fun, that's why *Remote Control*, the game show, came on. So you loved watching videos, but you didn't want to do that all the time now, you wanted to watch specialty shows. People ask nowadays, 'Isn't it terrible what happened to MTV?' And I go, 'Well, one, I don't really care, because I got a life, and two, evolution.' That was normal and natural for it to move on."

"Imagine interviewing us," Mark said. "What a fucking nightmare."

"I know," Nina confessed.

There was so much more to cover and time was running short. It was time to talk about Live Aid. Did my generation overromanticize it?

"I don't think it's overromanticized at all," Nina said. "It was a very serious problem, and I thought it was a wonderful thing, that Bob Geldof got all these people together and there were no egos. Everybody was hanging out; you'd see Bill Graham hanging out. Queen, of course, that was the epitome of their performance career. But getting together to actually help the world. And there are smaller things that still go on, like the rainforest benefits, and Bon Jovi was down doing something for the Everglades. But something on that big of a global stage, I wish there were more of them."

"Sure, it was the Woodstock of the times," Alan said. "But it was a lot bigger because of the outlets, the distribution of it. It was worldwide. That was planned from the beginning."

"It was a really amazing moment," Mark added. "I think part of the reason that we romanticize it is because of U2's performance that day, Freddie Mercury's performance that day. Although it was shocking, [Bob] Dylan that day really started Farm Aid by saying, 'I wish that some of this money would go to American farmers.' There were so many things that happened that day, and I know, for us who were in Philly, we really did feel like we were part of something. We really did. And I think that the people there did as well. And I think it was like a social-cultural high point for the music business."

We covered a lot more that day, and I encourage you—if you're really masochistic—to go listen to the full podcast sometime. The banter between the VJs is indescribable. Familial is definitely a good and kind verdict. But we had time for a final question—along with the myriad jokes and deflections that followed every one of our queries—so I felt it was time to trot out the "Podcast Time Machine" question. It's a final question we use often on the show to wrap up interviews.

In this show, it went like this: "If our podcast is a time machine, and we could offer you a seat to go back in time to either relive a particular moment or change a decision you made or just witness an event you missed, how would you use it? When and where would you go?"

"Let's hear the ticking clock now, while the VJs try to come up with something witty to say," Alan said.

"I try and live no regrets, so there's nothing that I would go back to try and change," Mark said. "There are great moments that have happened to me. Sitting down and talking to Paul McCartney, that's a moment that I would love to do over and over again."

"There's a personal situation, but I don't want to share it," Nina said. That was it.

"I think mine's probably more philosophical, to be honest," Alan said. "If I could go back, probably to the day Mark and I looked at each other after Martha and Nina and J.J. had all departed from MTV around '86, something like that—Mark and I were the last ones left, and we were standing in the hallway and we were thinking, 'Man, the writing is on the wall here.'"

"Are you saying that you would've gone back to the day that we both quit together and not quit?" Mark asked.

"Yeah, I would've just left your ass in the dust," Alan said. "I had two more years to go on a contract, and I should have just kept that. No, I think I frittered away the last year of my time there, thinking it was all going to be rosy, and I should have really plotted the plan, either to logically say to you, 'Man, we just need to hang on another year and get the next gig going. Don't just quit and think it's all going to happen.' So, don't take things for granted. That would be my really not cliché piece of advice."

With that, we called it a day. Alan offered a toast to The 80s Cruise, which had brought us all together. Mark had one last thing to add.

"Round of applause for these guys!" he said with his arms around our shoulders. My legs grew weak, and my heart began pounding again.

Ladies and gentlemen, rock 'n' roll.

LEGENDS, WITHOUT THE LIMO

Some chapters of this book start with a voice on the phone; others begin with a knock at the door. These four artists made me feel like the '80s weren't some far-off decade—we could still reach out and touch those years, one conversation at a time.

ROBIN ZANDER came to visit us in our podcast studio in 2011, and the image has stayed with me ever since. I can still picture him walking alone down a quiet downtown St. Petersburg sidewalk, climbing the steps to the front door of the *Times*, where Sean and I were waiting—equal parts excited and slightly awestruck—to welcome him inside.

Robin lived in nearby Safety Harbor with his family, and his wife had driven him there and dropped him off. No chauffeur. No hired car. No bodyguard. Just his wife, who was going to park and wait for him.

The frontman of Cheap Trick wanted to promote a New Year's Eve show at which the band would play its *Dream Police* album in its entirety.

"Thanks for everything you guys have done for Cheap Trick down here," Robin began. I remember feeling faint from surprise.

A future Rock & Roll Hall of Famer—Cheap Trick was inducted in 2016—was sitting next to us, wearing a knit cap and sunglasses. And he was thanking us.

"Do you consider *Dream Police* the ultimate Cheap Trick album?" Sean asked.

"No, not necessarily," Robin answered. "But it was sort of a turning-point album or a door-opening album for us because it was diverse, you know, with a song like 'Voices' and a song like 'Gonna Raise Hell' back to back. Really, we started stretching out a lot, and it sort of opened up new horizons for our music."

After a few more minutes of conversation, I finally worked up the courage to join the party.

"Is the fact you're stretching out with *Dream Police* a product of the times?" I asked. "I mean, 1979 to me is kind of a turning point for music in general, where we're letting go of one type of music and we're starting to move into the New Wave-influenced era."

"Well, it was a struggle during the '70s, and that's one of the reasons we put our band together, is to just make fun of everybody else around us," Robin said. "We'd do our shows and Rick [Nielsen] had this thing called the 'carnival game' where girls would sit on his face and he would guess their weight. We'd do a parody of Queen where, you know, we would sing a whole different lyric to the thing. And not that we didn't like the band Queen, but we just thought—we were just tired of the same stuff happening."

Sean and I just sat back and enjoyed the storytelling.

"The big thing was disco," he continued, "and we had this song called 'Disco Paradise' that we used to play and make fun of the scene at the time. And I remember when the Ramones and the Sex Pistols and Cheap Trick came out, it was a backlash against basically dance music because no one was listening to rock music anymore. And if they were, it was all classical style, big, huge things.

And we were just a rock band. So it was sort of like Chicago. They were burning records, disco records and all this baloney."

"So you were taking the piss out of things?" Sean asked.

"Yeah, we were kind of doing that," Robin said. "It was a struggle—when we made our first record in '77, it came out in January—to get anybody to buy it. And to get radio to even play it. I think we sold 30,000 copies of our first record. And back then everybody was selling records. So that was nothing. But we had signed a three-record contract. And so they were forced to do two more records with us. But by the time the third record came out, we had won some fans, and especially overseas we'd done well. In Europe and Japan, we had a couple of hits."

We'd now reached the band's Budokan milestone. *Cheap Trick at Budokan* was the band's first live album, and remains their best-selling one. It was recorded over two nights in Tokyo in April 1978 and was intended for Japanese release only. If you've heard "I Want You to Want Me" on the radio, it was no doubt the live version of the tune recorded at the historic Japanese arena.

"We had a few hits here and there in the world, not in the United States," Robin said. "We had one song called 'Surrender' that was doing okay on the radio charts. I think it was in the '60s or something like that. But it was on medium rotation, a lot of major stations. So we went to Japan and we thought, 'Well, we're popular over there.' At least we had a couple hit songs. But we didn't realize how popular we were. I remember sitting on the airplane and we're sitting there and I'm wondering, 'Who are all those people out there? And it must be the president's here or something.' And it was for us. And we couldn't believe it. It was unbelievable."

Dream Police was in the can and ready to be released, he said, but now it had to be delayed. "We had recorded a live album in Japan that took over the world. It went like wildfire. And we had to delay the release of *Dream Police* by a year."

We were mesmerized.

"What did you learn from redoing *Dream Police*?" Sean asked.

"Those songs on that album are pretty difficult songs to sing. I don't know if anybody realizes that or not, but, I mean, of all the records we've done, that's one of the toughest ones for some reason, for me. I just remember when we did the record, I wasn't really pleased with the way the producer was handling it because he was rarely there."

The producer was Tom Werman, I confirmed with Robin, the legend who has produced a few dozen gold and platinum albums by the likes of Blue Öyster Cult, Molly Hatchet, Ted Nugent, Mötley Crüe, Twisted Sister, Jeff Beck, and Poison.

"He wasn't pleased with the fact we wanted to use some orchestration on the record," Robin explained. "And he didn't like some of the performances by us. You know, we are the band, not him. When we weren't there, he would bring in extra players to do stuff. Oh, yeah. So we'd have to go back in there and erase stuff, and it got to be, like, a pain in the you-know-what. But there you go, things happen. And we never used Tom after that. But no offense, Tom, but there you go."

These days, Robin and his family have found their own dream living nearby in Tampa Bay.

"Hell, it's beautiful here," he beamed. "Every day you wake up and the sun's shining and I wouldn't move and live anywhere else."

I told him the story about how I once followed him after a concert. REO Speedwagon was playing a free show in St. Petersburg after a Tampa Bay Rays game, and we were among those with a coveted field pass.

"Creepy story coming," Sean warned.

"You left literally 30 seconds before I did. I'm walking down the hallway and you're probably 20 feet in front of me. And I figured it out and blurted, 'Oh, my God, it's Robin Zander!' My friend begged me to run up to you and say hi, but I was like, 'Nah, nah. Let's be cool. Let him have his privacy.'"

"I'm just like anybody else," Robin insisted. "I don't mind talking to people and stuff like that, but people sometimes come over to your house uninvited, stuff like that."

We changed the subject, probably not to the happiest topic. The Rock & Roll Hall of Fame nominations were due soon. Though the band had been eligible for induction since 2002, their official acceptance was still a few years away at the time of the interview. We asked Robin about the snub.

"That's fine," he said. "You know, they have their thing in the way they do stuff. I don't even know if I would go if we were nominated, to be honest. I mean, to me, I was disappointed with them a long, long time ago. You know, look at a band like Kiss, for God's sake."

(Kiss was inducted three years later, in 2014.)

"I think it's more than just sales and figures. They do that, but then they also go back and see what influence you had on the music scene. And they have judges within their little thing. So there's a number of things that they look at. But who the hell cares? I don't need somebody like them to tell me how great I am."

We were fired up!

"You need us!" I blurted out.

"Yeah, every day!" Sean added.

"I mean, I think we're pretty damn good. I think our band's pretty damn good. We've been there for thirty-what, six, seven years now, so you know, we wouldn't be around if we weren't pretty decent."

When the interview ended, Sean, Robin, and I headed up to the newspaper's photo studio where we posed for pics with a staff photographer. A photo of Robin Wayne Zander, the future Hall of Fame frontman with his arm draped over my shoulder as

I pose with a deliriously happy grin, hangs on my office wall to this day.

JACK BLADES comes across as a guy who's still having a blast making music, and that joy is impossible to miss. Whether on stage or on the phone, it feels like the Night Ranger frontman never sits still. That made him a joy to talk with in 2008, when the band was touring and making a stop in Tampa Bay.

The phone call began with a bunch of technical snafus—sadly, not an entirely new tangle for us even three years into the podcast. I was working the control board and finally figured out which knobs to turn to get things into gear.

"Yeah, yeah, there you go!" Jack exclaimed. "You guys are geniuses!"

"We're calling from a payphone, and we only have three quarters," Sean suggested.

"Remember the day when people actually used payphones?" Jack continued. "That was before our cell phones. Think of all the stuff that went on, and we didn't have cell phones!"

From there, our interview turned into a *Seinfeld* scene for a few more minutes as Jack riffed on the cost of bottled water in airports and other daily troubles. Three minutes into the interview, Sean lobbed what he deemed "the first real question."

"You've been in all these kind of iconic bands and these great bands, but all different bands," he began. "You're at Night Ranger, which is this cohesive unit. You go to a supergroup like Damn Yankees, and then you and Tommy [Shaw] have this great duo with Shaw Blades. How do you change your musical approach to each one? Or maybe you don't. Do you have a different role in each, or are you still the same Jack Blades?"

"You know what, I'm still me," he said. "Night Ranger, it's like it's who we started out with, it's who we are, it's our music and everything like that. And then when we started Damn Yankees, it became sort of like this really rockin', with Tommy and Ted [Nugent] and, man, I gotta tell you, I learned so much. I mean, we learned so much from Nuge. Ted's the kind of guy—I mean, here I am in Night Ranger, and Tommy's from Styx and Ted's— we're playing with the Motor City Madman. Ted's the kind of guy that taught me if you're going to, like, scream, scream the loudest, most blood-curdling scream you can ever scream. If you're going to jump, jump the highest you can jump. If you're going to shove your bass neck through the kick drum, it better go right through and right up the drummer's ass."

Nugent's career, which was red hot in the '70s when he scored three consecutive platinum albums and the monster hit "Cat Scratch Fever," had cooled a little in recent decades. His sometimes cartoonish behavior onstage—he once rode a buffalo across the stage—has evolved into an ultra-right-wing political activism that has divided his fans. We were curious what Jack's take was on Nugent's state of mind.

"Well, Ted Nugent's been..." Jack began, choosing his words carefully. "He's been Ted Nugent since the late '60s. I mean, Ted and I are great friends. In fact, I coproduced his latest album, *Love Grenade*. We did it up in my studio."

We dropped the subject and pivoted instead.

"You recorded the theme song for the movie *The Secret of My Success*," Sean said. The 1987 movie starring Michael J. Fox got a mixed response from critics, but the title song by Night Ranger would be nominated for a Golden Globe. (Alas, "[I've Had] The Time of My Life" from *Dirty Dancing* triumphed that year.)

"A producer buddy of mine, David Foster, called and said, 'I'm doing the music for this movie, *The Secret of My Success*.' And then

Michael J. Fox called us and was a fan of Night Ranger and said, 'Hey, we're doing this movie.' And we're, like, 'Yeah, we're in.' So I went down there and wrote the song with Foster and we recorded that and it was just really great, very enjoyable, really fun. We've had a lot of songs in a lot of movies, and of course, Tommy and I cowrote a couple of songs with the guys in Aerosmith that were in the *Armageddon* soundtrack, and Damn Yankees had songs and movies. So the movie thing is a pretty familiar feel, a place for us to be. It just happened that that one was a real strong one for us, and I love the song 'The Secret of My Success.'"

Another famous Night Ranger soundtrack moment: The inclusion of "Sister Christian" in *Boogie Nights*, the indie flick that followed an unlikely rise to fame for an amateur porn actor (played by Mark Wahlberg).

"I thought that was the crowning moment of Mark Wahlberg bottoming out," Jack said. "We all saw that movie, and sweat beads are pouring out of our foreheads because, believe me, in the early '80s, we've been in houses like that. We were in houses like that with the frickin' piles of, like…[Jack stops himself here.] And some guy over there is shooting off firecrackers, and everybody tweaked out. I mean, believe me, my wife and I were looking at each other going, 'Whoa, this is a little too real.' And then the gunshot and everybody shooting, it's like, 'What the fuck have I'—excuse me, 'What the hell have I done?'"

"No, that's all right," Sean said. "You can say it."

(Our editor at the *Times* told us we could keep any F-bombs in our interviews—just the audio version, of course—only if they were used as adjectives. Any use as a verb? Nope! Strictly forbidden. Jack's F-bomb made the cut for the final podcast.)

Speaking of unwritten topics, we were curious about Night Ranger's reputation for being, let's say, "fun-loving" while touring in the '80s.

"You guys always came off as like you had your shit together," Sean started. "But was there a time with *Midnight Madness* and then *Seven Wishes* when you just really, you guys were partying tons?"

"You know what, you can't help it when it's just, like, you go out there and here we are like in 1982, 1983, and we hit the road and we were, like, on 18 months, two-year tours, and we're out there constantly playing and touring," Jack answered. "It's the perfect lifestyle if you're, like, a 21-one-year-old, single male. But after a while, you really realize that you can't. I mean, for all the people that are coming to your shows, that's the night that they save up to party for the whole month or something, and you're in a different city every night. So if you go out with them and rock 'n' roll the way they want you to, by about the fourth day, you're going to be frickin' toast or dead, one of the two. So, I think you learn real quick: water seeks its own level. You find out what works for you and what doesn't."

A day after our interview with Jack, he and Night Ranger were in Clearwater to open for Dennis DeYoung, the former Styx frontman who was now touring solo. (Please, please go read the chapter about Dennis where he jokes about that night with Night Ranger.)

That evening, I was backstage to introduce Night Ranger on stage. I'd had this privilege now at Ruth Eckerd Hall a few times, so my nerves were considerably calmer. Still, old habits die hard, and when it was time to hand the mic over to Jack I bellowed out, "Please welcome my good friends, Night Ranger!"

And standing there, mic freshly handed off, I realized that moments like this were why we kept doing the podcast through technical disasters and nervous stomachs. Sometimes the secret of our success isn't measured in downloads—it's measured in small, surreal moments when the music you grew up with suddenly feels like an old friend.

DON BARNES of 38 Special has been one of the answers to a trivia question I often use to test the history acumen of music fans: Name three bands that claim Jacksonville, Florida, as their birthplace. Most people get Lynyrd Skynyrd. Some might eke out Molly Hatchet. A third is 38 Special. (Others include the Allman Brothers Band, Blackfoot, and Limp Bizkit.)

I spoke with Don in 2023 to help promote the band's upcoming appearance on The 80s Cruise. I was curious what made Jacksonville—probably the most un-Floridian metro area in the state—such a crucible for rock music. I had lived there for four years and hadn't really caught any particular creative vibe. Great barbecue and affordable beach towns, yes. Music center of the Sunshine State? Not in my wildest dreams.

"It was a Navy town, I guess you knew that," Don began. "It has four or five naval bases there, and all the sailors would come in on ships, and they'd have their leave. And so as young kids, I'm talking about Duane Allman, Gregg Allman, Ronnie Van Zant, and everybody played the enlisted men's clubs at Mayport, Cecil Field, and NAS [Naval Air Station] Jacksonville. So at 15 years old, you could go and play cover songs with your little neighborhood band. It was an early proving ground, a kind of foundation to learn the craft of writing songs. Skynyrd and the Allman Brothers, Molly Hatchet, Blackfoot, everybody came from that area. I guess we all owe our careers to the Navy, playing for sailors. We were up there watching them drink and fight on leave."

I've seen 38 Special perform a handful of times, including a memorable show at—you guessed it—Ruth Eckerd Hall in Clearwater, where they opened for REO Speedwagon. I was late arriving to the venue and walked into the auditorium during one of their many rousing anthems. Donnie Van Zant—wearing his obligatory

Texas Rides Hi-Roller hat to honor his late brother Ronnie—was whipping the crowd into a screaming mass.

"All those guys—Kansas, Styx, REO—they say, 'We hate following you guys!' They're all good friends of ours," Don explained. "You can count on pretty much one hand all the survivors of '80s groups. I'm talking about big guitar bands with radio hit songs and all. We're lucky to be among some rare company there. Over the years, we never slack up, we stack up, man! That's kind of our unwritten, unspoken rule. Put the muscle in melody, we call it. Put the snarl of the guitars in the face with a great story and good melody. We feel like if it ain't broke, don't fix it. Right, Steve?"

I confessed I knew the words to just about every song on their setlist.

"Yeah, we're not one of those groups that play one song and then say, 'Thank you very much' and then 'Our next song is this….' We line them up; we push them back to back and just keep taking them for a ride," he said. "It's a great job to bring that kind of joy to people. You see them high-fiving each other, singing along, sometimes you see some tears in their eyes, or a song might remind them of something. But it is an emotional experience for us because we do see all that directly. It kind of gets me a little choked up every now and then."

I'm always curious about the origins of the monster hits that bands play every night. For 38 Special, that's "Hold On Loosely," which soared to No. 3 on the Billboard charts in 1981. It was also the 13th music video played by MTV on its first day of programming.

"All those songs represented milestones in our life," Don began. "'Hold On Loosely' I wrote with Jim Peterik and Jeff Carlisi from the band. Jim Peterik was from the band Survivor. He later had written 'Eye of the Tiger' so he's no slouch. The first time we met him, we sat at his breakfast table and we were just kind of meeting each other for the first time. He said, 'So how you guys been doing?' I was going through kind of a relationship that had gotten a little sour, and I had a little notebook of titles and I said, 'What is it about people, they just can't seem to tolerate their differences, they try to change each other. What do you think about this title: 'Hold On Loosely.' And he said, 'Oh, yeah, but don't let go.' And that was a perfect couplet, first thing out of his mouth. So we were off to the races there."

Did he ever tire of playing it?

"I see the people's faces, that's what I see, and that makes my heart sing," he answered. "We were young boys with a dream. And that's something that's a full, fleshed-out dream. It's a big risk to take, something like this. We didn't have anything to fall back on, and we didn't have schooling or training or anything. We had done three albums that went right over the cliff, Steve. But if it was easy, everybody would be doing it."

Those young days and dreams were created in Jacksonville, where I had toiled for four years working for the city's daily newspaper. I told Don about my pit stop in his hometown.

"The *Times-Union*, yeah!" he exclaimed. "Well, this is a full circle because if you remember, the top of the street was Jackson Street, and there was an old warehouse there and that was our rehearsal building, right across the street from the *Times-Union* building."

Sure, I drove past it every day.

"Yeah, Lynyrd Skynyrd had bought us the sandwich shop next door and gutted it and made a little eight-track studio," he continued. "So we were all working right on that corner. That's crazy!"

Back in those days—the early '90s—I was still trying to appreciate the music of the day (with little to no success). And my '80s obsession and writing days were still a good decade away. I'm not sure Jacksonville was the same conduit to dreaming for me that it was for Don and his bandmates. Turns out, it was Ronnie Van Zant who'd given them a nudge in the right direction.

"He was watching us come in on the tail end of the Southern rock bands, and it was kind of waning by the time the '80s came around," Don explained. "And he just kind of put his foot down and he said, 'Stop trying to be a clone of whatever else came before you. Do what makes your heart sing.' And we took that to task. We were more melody-oriented. Foreigner, Boston, and Styx, and everybody is coming up with the great arena rock. And we liked that kind of big guitars, big presentation. So we stripped it all away and came down to just eight notes. We crafted a style and a sound that actually worked."

It's worked for more than half a century now; 38 Special marked their 50th anniversary in 2024. That sandwich shop is now long gone, as is the *Times-Union* building. But the memories are still there, if you hold on loosely but don't let go.

TERRI NUNN has that rare combination of pop-star pedigree and genuine kindness that immediately puts you at ease. Of course, I knew her songs forwards and backwards before I interviewed her. "The Metro," "No More Words," "Masquerade"—the list of Berlin hits goes on and on. I'd seen her live a few times before interviewing her in 2017. Every show was a gem.

She came into my orbit thanks to The 80s Cruise. She and her bandmates played a standing-room-only late-night show on the cruise's 2017 voyage, and the crowd was wildly appreciative, especially when Berlin rolled into covers of AC/DC's "Highway to Hell" and Jefferson Airplane's "Somebody to Love." The owner of the cruise immediately called the band's manager after the show and booked them for the next several years of voyages.

"Wow, I didn't expect that reaction," Terri began. "We have never done a cruise before. Maybe you can help me understand. I'm used to people liking our show and loving our show depending on the show, but what about this was so different than the other ones?"

"That's a good question," I laughed. "I wasn't prepared to answer questions—only ask them! But it was a late-night show and everyone was jammed up front like the old days. And you guys came out and you played three of your biggest hits right off the bat, one, two, three. I mean, I think that whipped people into a frenzy."

"Okay, okay," Terri said, seemingly unconvinced.

"You can't doubt your own stage charisma," I said. "I mean, you're overflowing with it."

"It was just so great to have that experience. I wanted the cruise people to be happy. I wanted them to like it. I was hoping maybe they would think about asking us back," she said. "The next morning, I got a call from the cruise director, Michael, and he said, 'What's it gonna take to get you on the cruise next year?'"

Berlin is, thankfully, one of the bands that we get to see often these days. Their music sounds as sharp and relevant as it did in the early days of MTV. Terri doesn't seem to have aged a day. And in recent years, original bandmates John Crawford and David Diamond have rejoined the lineup, giving fans a rare look at a legacy band still largely intact.

Terri and I talked for an hour, covering everything from the first autograph she got (from Walt Disney) to her first influences.

"I was listening to David Bowie, Pink Floyd, Roxy Music, Fleetwood Mac, Heart, Cheap Trick," she began. "I know Iggy was well before the late '70s, but that's when I noticed him. And we also opened for him. He was one of the first shows we ever played with a punk guy. And I was terrified because at that time, it was all about spitting. People were all about spitting on each other and on the bands. And I mean, opening for Iggy Pop, oh my God, we're a New Wave band and who knows if they're even going to like us because we're not violent, we're not loud, we're not any of that. We did the show, and they didn't spit on us. They crossed their arms in front of their chest and just kind of looked at us. They didn't hate it. They clapped a little, but clearly they wanted Iggy. So that was my one brush with Iggy fame."

I told Terri that pretty much any U.K. musician I've interviewed has cited Roxy Music and David Bowie as igniting their musical sparks.

"Without David Bowie, we would not have had glam rock," she said. "Without him, we wouldn't have had Queen. We wouldn't have had Elton. We wouldn't have had New York Dolls. We wouldn't have had Roxy Music. We wouldn't have had any of that. He opened up the doors and started that whole 'it's okay to be gay' or 'it's okay to be bisexual, it's okay to not be sure.' He was all of that wrapped up in one guy, and after him it was, like, 'Oh, it's cool now.' And without Glam Rock, there wouldn't have been Berlin. There would never have been New Wave without Glam Rock. So all of it, to me, traces back to Bowie."

I asked how she felt when Bowie passed away unexpectedly in 2016.

"It fucked me up for a while, a couple of months," she said. "It was too shocking. It didn't compute. He never talked about the cancer diagnosis. And so it came out of nowhere for all of us. I owe not only my love for music in large part to him, but my career, because the kind of music I wanted to do was directly related to what he had started."

A less expected name also had an early impact on Terri.

"Danny Elfman was great to us because they [Oingo Boingo] were way bigger than we were," she said. "They sold out places, and we were just trying to get an audience, and they put us on their bills a number of times. And the first time I was ever in a studio, Danny showed me how to use a microphone. I was terrified. I had no idea what to do. I didn't know how to record, how to sing into a mic, my technique, any of that. And he was in the studio leaving when I came in and he could see I was nervous. He followed me back in and said, 'Here, I'll show you. Here's the mic.' And his engineer was still in there packing up. He said, 'Turn on the mic, just show her, let me show her a couple things.' And he showed me how to use it. And it was so valuable to me that I still remember how relaxed it made me feel. And I did a much better job because of him."

In 1983, Oingo Boingo and Berlin would share the same stage again for The US Festival. The weekend-long concert at Glen Helen Regional Park in San Bernardino, California, was primarily organized and funded by Steve Wozniak, the cofounder of Apple Computer. Wozniak's goal was to create a "We Generation" milestone rather than a "Me Generation" event. The massive event took place over four days and included more than 30 band performances.

"That was one of the greatest days of my whole life," Terri recalled. "I've got the T-shirt up on the wall."

What was it like playing in front of a half million people?

"It was surreal," she said. "I've never since seen that kind of vision. It was literally like the people went over the horizon. Like, there was no way to see the back. And then to get to not only play, but watch all of those people in one day play and be part of it. I can't even tell you, it was just like the biggest orgasm I've ever had. Because concerts to me are the biggest orgasms. They are the best drug that I ever have. Whether I'm watching one or I'm doing one, it's the same high. It is so great to be immersed in music that I love and watch someone or be someone that's doing it, and I can't even describe it to you. It's better than any drug I've ever had."

Terri had just given me one of the best quotes I'll ever get as a writer. How did I react? By *transitioning* out of the question! What an idiot. Here we go.

"Yeah, so you compare performing on stage to an orgasm. How does acting compare?" I asked, remembering that Terri had a string of acting roles in the late '70s and early '80s before turning her attention to music full time.

"Pretty good," she said. "It's not the same. I mean, music to me is the ultimate orgasm. It was really my mom who finally gave me the nod to try it because my life was becoming more and more about acting work. And I was doing well with it. And I liked it. I liked the creativity of telling a story that was good and doing it well. And I have a great, huge respect for anyone who can do it well, because it's a craft and it's hard."

Terri had a string of one-episode appearances in such shows as *Trapper John, M.D.*, *Lou Grant*, *Family*, and a big-screen appearance in *Thank God It's Friday*. Clever fans have uncovered on YouTube a screening tape of her auditioning for the first *Star Wars* movie alongside Harrison Ford. But the biggest acting opportunity she had, she ended up turning down.

"It was a crossroads in my life—we all have them—where I got insanely lucky," she said. "The casting director of a show called *Dallas* happened to know me and sold me somehow to the producers of the series, which had not started yet. They were just casting the main characters for it. And so I walked in and there wasn't even an audition. They just said, 'Do you wanna do this role?' And 'Do you want this contract?' And 'Do you want this money?' And it was seven years, and I was 17. So I thought, 'Oh my God, if I sign this, this whole music thought that I have is gone because then I'll be 24.' And in those days, that was ancient in music."

"It's, like, 'You're either doing this, Terri, or you're going to try the music thing,' which I had not even tried at that point. And it was my mom who said, 'Terri, I don't know if you're going to make it, but if you don't try, you will always regret it. So if you want to try this music thing, then try the music thing.'"

Any regrets?

"No, not at all," she said. "I mean, I lost my agent immediately. He was like, 'Are you out of your fucking mind?' My manager dropped me because she was pissed. And so I had nothing. And then at least I had nothing to lose anymore because I'd lost it all. I was completely, like, at square one now. I just thought, 'Okay, well, I'll give myself a year and see if I can get anything going, find a musical partner or a band or something.' And it was literally a year later to the month that I met John Crawford in Berlin."

John Crawford had formed Berlin—originally called The Toys—in 1976 in Orange County. Singers had come and gone until Terri answered an ad in 1979.

"He was doing something unique and something that I thought was worthwhile," Terri said of her bandmate. "He wasn't just talking, he was going for it. And he needed a singer, and I loved what he was doing. So it just worked out."

These days, Berlin has reunited. Terri, John, and David have together recorded two albums while still playing shows around the country. In 2026, they returned to The 80s Cruise for the trip's 10th anniversary.

In 2021, I interviewed the three of them at once. Terri was feeling reflective but had her eyes on the present.

"We've all grown and we don't have the fears and the same ego problems that we had before," she said of the group. "That's one great thing about aging is, you know, when you have kids and you have failures and you have evolved in your life, things actually get better."

So was she happy where she was now, I asked.

"I would never go back to my 20s," she replied. "That was fun, but this is way better. I'm not scared all the time. When we were in our 20s, every show was do or die. It took time to get there. And now we're there. And I really appreciate this time. I'm gonna make music with them now, because this is great."

It's a pretty great feeling, hearing someone who once hung on your wall talk like this—calm, unguarded, grateful. The '80s were supposed to be all hairspray and excess, but the things that stick with me now are the simplest: Robin Zander walking up the steps alone. Jack Blades turning an unexpected phone call into a stand-up routine. Don Barnes talking about sailors drinking and fighting like it was last week. Terri Nunn saying—plainly—she's not scared anymore.

Legends, without the limo. Turns out that's the best kind.

Our most uncomfortable interview has become one of our most enduring stories. Not because we stumbled, but because we learned...that even the sideways moments still move you forward.

THE POWER OF LOVE

Huey Lewis is one of the defining faces and voices of our decade, and I genuinely believe most interviews with him go swimmingly. In 2007, the *Stuck in the '80s* conversation with the legendary frontman went a little sideways.

Longtime listeners of the podcast enjoy a few laughs at us for this ancient show—granted, with very good reason. Huey was in Tampa Bay to play in a pro-am golf tournament and sprinkle some gigs in around the state.

My cohost Sean and I jumped at an offer for a morning chat with Huey. At the time, podcasts were still so new that those courageous artists who agreed to appear on them rarely understood what they were doing.

"Nice to be on a podcast, whatever that is," Huey said to us to start.

"Oh, man, we got at least 12 people listening a month!" Sean joked back. I remember holding my breath and hoping Huey had a generous sense of humor. Truth be told, we didn't have a good sense of our audience in those days. The numbers could have been more on point than we knew.

Back in 2007, Huey and his boys in The News were performing about 80 shows a year, he told us—considerably fewer than the 200 they'd done in earlier times. During the '80s and early '90s, the band had scored 19 Top 10 hits across the charts.

"It's enough to keep your chops, you know what I mean?" Huey said. "If you don't, as long as you don't work too hard at this ripe old age, it's like falling in love all over again. I mean, if we don't play for two weeks, it's the most fun thing in the world. So, it's a great job as long as you don't have to do it 200 shows a year."

In recent years, Huey had been making the headlines more often for his acting work than his music. After his surprise cameo as a disapproving teacher in *Back to the Future*, he'd recently played Billy Flynn in *Chicago* on Broadway.

Acting on a stage, it turns out, was more challenging than performing music on one, Huey told us.

"Broadway is way tougher. Not because it's the endurance part. I mean, you do eight shows a week, but the thing that's tougher about it is that you really have to be on your game. You're naked out there, and every bad note is way easier for people to hear. You can hide in the middle of a big rock band once in a while if you have to. But you can't hide on the Broadway stage."

Our conversation was going great up to here. Do you see any signs that the train is swaying on the track? Pay attention, here it comes.

After Huey admitted he had some reservations about taking the role, Sean started to have a little fun. "Well, you got more musical chops than Richard Gere, at least!" he said.

"He's a film actor. Anybody can do it on a film," Huey admitted.

"Throw down! Excellent!" Sean celebrated.

"No, I mean, Richard Gere is an excellent film actor, I'm not trying to belittle Richard Gere," Huey insisted. "There's no surprise that they'd want a film actor to do a film. It's the hard part—the sensitive scenes and in a film, that's all. I'm not trying to belittle him."

Oh, God, no. I tried stepping in and assuring Huey we were just kidding. "That's just me being a creep," Sean underscored.

"Yeah," Huey said bluntly. The shortest reply so far. I tried to change the direction. "Would you like to continue your acting career? What would you see in the future if you continue acting?" I asked. And then I held my breath. Huey seems like the kind of guy you don't push too far in the wrong direction.

Huey said he'd love to work for Martin Scorsese—"Who wouldn't?" he said—and then switched the subject to music and the desire to make a new album in the coming year.

The band's most current work was the album *Plan B* from 2001. Huey called it "our favorite work" and said eight of the band's most preferred songs to play come from that record. Alas, he said he was disappointed by its reception. *Plan B* would top out at No. 22 on the album charts in Canada and Norway. In the U.S., it peaked at No. 165.

"People truthfully want to hear the old stuff, and why wouldn't they?" he said. "I can't blame them. They don't hear us every night. However, as a storyteller, you do need a new story every now and then. So we will make a new record and blah, blah, blah. But I'm perfectly content to play my songbook a third of the year. And when I do it, I enjoy it. As long as you don't do it more than 80 times a year, you know what I mean?"

Sean cheered everyone up after that by namechecking Huey's work with Mutt Lange and Rick Rubin. Music fans were geeking out over the next few minutes as their producer heroes were feted by Huey. And then I decided to turn the car back down the wrong road.

"There's one question I've always wanted to ask an artist like you, and I never really expected an honest answer and it's okay if you don't wanna give me one either," I began. This was the world's longest question—that's never a good thing. Thankfully, Huey was patient and probably curious where I was going with it.

"I've always wanted to know: someone who's had an extensive catalog like yourself, is there one or two particular songs from the old days that you just wish you could just retire it and put it to bed and not have to play it again?"

"Yeah, I got you," Huey said. I'm relieved. Huey explained how he prefers to rearrange songs that feel wearisome or dated today, offering up the example of "Do You Believe in Love," the band's first Top 10 hit from 1982. "We cut it kind of—what's the word?—pompous. So we've changed the beat to it and made it into a kind of 'Stand By Me.'"

Rebranding and recasting a musical hit has become a common tool for bands from our generation. "Take On Me" from a-ha or "Don't Cry" by Asia benefit from their stripped-down acoustic versions. Hall & Oates took the approach to another level in recent decades by giving many of their hits the "Troubadour treatment" after a successful string of shows at the Hollywood venue.

"It's funny but today, I look out at the crowd oftentimes and we have all ages, of course, as any old-fart band does," Huey said. "When I'm singing those songs—'Doing It All for My Baby,' 'Stuck With You,' 'If This Is It'—they are more relevant to this crowd now than they were to us in our 20s. We wrote these songs in our 20s, but they're really more mature than that. So we were anachronistic then. So a roundabout way of answering your question, I don't hate any of my songs. Now that I've rearranged 'Do You Believe in Love,' I'm a very happy man."

We should have ended our conversation right there. When you get a musician to say "I'm a very happy man," take a bow, say goodbye, and hang up the phone. Nope. The next part of the interview is what listeners of our podcast remember and recall to us most often.

"All right. Easy question," Sean said. "What's your favorite song that you've done?"

"There's no such thing as a favorite song," Huey protested. He was polite but firm at this point.

"Come on," Sean persisted.

I don't want to be seen as recrafting or rewriting history here—such as it is—so here's the exact transcription from here on:

Huey: "There isn't. It's a lousy question, and you shouldn't ask me a question like that. No, no. First of all, the other thing you shouldn't do…"

Sean: "That's not…I know deep down, because even…"

Huey: "End of year to naming the Top 10 anything [laughter]. See, because you're a critic, and if you're a critic, you should point out the difference in things. What are the top five paintings of all time? Where's Mona Lisa?"

Sean: "Dogs Playing Poker is No. 1."

Huey: "What?"

Sean: "Dogs Playing Poker."

Huey: "All right. Hahaha."

Sean: "Oh, come on, Huey."

Huey: "It's a lousy question, 'What's your favorite song?'"

Sean: "That's not true. Because even if you ask, even, like, sometimes you get parents saying, like, in the deep dark recess of the brain, they have a favorite kid, right?"

Huey: "I don't think so. I mean, I don't know."

Steve: "I agree with you, Huey. It's a rotten question. I would never ask you."

Sean: "Look at you kissing Huey's ass [laughter]."

Steve: "No, I'll kiss Huey's ass all I want."

Huey: "But it's one of the lousy questions you hear over and over again, and it's just not—I mean, I'm trying to help you here."

Steve: "Yeah. Well, let me…"

Huey: "Really, a great critic would never ask a question like that."

Sean: "Oh, wow."

Huey: "It's right in there with, 'How did you get the name The News?' [laughter]. And…"

Sean: "I'm crossing that off the list right now."

Huey: "Yeah. I mean, who cares, for Christ's sake?"

Steve: "Well, let me ask you this, then. Every time I see a band, especially from the '80s, there's always one song that, when they hit the first couple chords of it, the crowd just explodes with anticipation. They know this is their song. Which song when you hit live that you get, do you really sense the greatest audience swell?"

Huey: "Probably 'Power of Love.' You know what? There you go. There's a way to ask that question if you want. What song are you proudest of? That's a better way to ask that."

Steve: "Sean, I am the new pop music critic for the *St. Pete Times*."

Ninety-nine times out of 100 in those days, Sean knocked my socks off as an interviewer. He could write three words on a piece of paper and then go conduct one of the best conversations with a musical hero that you'd ever hear.

That one day in February 2007, I had my two seconds of fame. I probably couldn't wipe the smile off my face for a week.

SEAN SAYS NOW: Huey's a man's man, right? There was a lot of testosterone flowing in our interview with Huey Lewis. It was a very lazy question that I wish I could have back. I remember looking at Steve and the look of fear in his eyes.

The conversation with Huey didn't end there. We covered his work with *Back to the Future*, his thoughts on the danger of downloading music instead of buying it in traditional outlets, and whatever else popped into Sean's mind. I think I had two more questions over the next 15 minutes. And I'm totally good with that. If you want to hear all the drama again, go to Episode 78 from February 3, 2007. It's still online.

Huey would go on to become the big headliner on the very first voyage of The 80s Cruise in 2016. Seeing an entire ship light up the instant "The Power of Love" kicked in, everything Huey told us finally made sense. Those songs weren't just hits—they served as anchors, carrying fans back to moments that still mattered. Huey understood that responsibility long before we did.

Two years later, he was diagnosed with Ménière's disease, an inner-ear disorder that causes hearing abnormalities. He has since ceased performing live.

A jukebox musical—*The Heart of Rock and Roll*—opened in Spring 2024 on Broadway. It's set in 1987 and features many of Huey's famed hits. While he doesn't sing or perform in the show, he has credited its creation as a "salvation" for him personally.

Listeners to the podcast sometimes ask if there's an interview I'd like to redo—whether I want a second chance to do a better job. They assume I'll answer "Huey Lewis." Nope.

That interview didn't need fixing. It needed time.

What felt awkward in 2007 now feels instructive. We learned something that day—about the kind of interviewers we were still becoming. Huey turned out to be exactly who you'd want him to be: thoughtful, protective of his work, and deeply serious about the craft.

Our most uncomfortable interview has become one of our most enduring stories. Not because we stumbled but because we learned. Maybe that's the real power of love—not the song, but the realization that even the sideways moments still move you forward.

OFF DAYS AND WRONG QUESTIONS

Over the years, *Stuck in the '80s* has been incredibly lucky. About 95% of our interviews have gone exactly the way you'd hope—fun, thoughtful, and occasionally magical. The other 5%? Those are the ones that still make my shoulders tense up when I think about them.

Not disasters. Just…misfires.

Every one of them has happened with an artist we admire, respect, and are genuinely grateful to talk to. Sometimes we've hit a nerve. Sometimes we've overthought things. And sometimes we've simply asked the wrong question at the worst possible moment.

SIMON LE BON fronts a band I never get tired of listening to or writing about. As I mentioned in the Andy Taylor chapter, Duran Duran's music is the soundtrack to some of my crazy teenage years. To this day, any of the tunes off of *Seven and the Ragged Tiger* trigger an avalanche of memories, all of which launch into my head when I hear the stuttering, remixed start to "The Reflex."

When Duran Duran was touring in 2011 to promote their new album *All You Need Is Now*, many of the press interviews were handled by drummer Roger Taylor. The band had a date booked at

Ruth Eckerd Hall in Clearwater, where I was still in good standing with the team, so I managed to score a 10-minute chat with Simon instead.

Simon always seemed to me to be the most elusive and aloof member of the Duran Duran team. Though he was not shy around the press, interviewers had to work a little harder to get insightful answers from him.

My previous cohost Sean had a story about Simon he loved to share. Sean had interviewed the whole band together at the top of the Sony building in New York in the '90s. As a new father, Sean had asked the band if they had any parenting advice, and Simon gave the best answer.

"Always make time to dance with your daughter," Simon said. I know Sean still prizes that tip.

Having only 10 minutes for an interview—usually I got closer to 20 or 30 minutes—was going to make it harder to get anything nearly so good.

Simon and I chatted about the band's setlist for the tour, the challenge of getting new material on the radio, and how the new album reminded fans of Duran Duran's work on 1982's *Rio*. As I reread the transcript today, I struggle to find any questions that generated noteworthy responses.

On the setlist: "We reckon you could do the ratio of new songs to old can be one third to two thirds."

On the importance of radio: "You want to get on the radio because it's still the way that most people get turned onto music, especially in this country."

When I pressed Simon on how the digital music world has impacted his life, he opened up a little. He described a connection younger fans make through digital pathways that is fundamentally different than the days of perusing record sleeves at the stores in the mall.

"My daughter listens to things like George Harrison and Joni Mitchell because of downloading music on the Internet," Simon said. "I've got another daughter who got into Nick Drake like that because they don't attach any age to it. They don't attach any kind of time. When she listens to Nick Drake, it's not music from the '60s. It's not a guy with big '60s hair who looks a bit old-fashioned, like pictures of your dad when he was young."

Digital, Simon insisted, has "democratized music."

Feeling like the door had been opened a little and I was getting answers that felt well conceived, I turned to a touchier subject. With a catalog of established hits over the decades, Duran Duran could easily tour every year and give fans a setlist of their greatest hits. But I told Simon I was under the impression that the band frowned on that.

"You said it. It is as simple as that, really," he confirmed. "We don't want to be a band who just goes out and plays the old hits. We want to play new music because we get excited by it. And not only do we get excited by playing it live, because it makes the show more interesting for us, but it's also exciting to go into studio to write it and to record it and to be part of the recording scene as well as the live music scene."

My time was running out. With an interview like this—and a band handling a slew of press inquiries on the eve of a tour—the 10-minute time limit would likely be strictly enforced. I had two questions. I should have only asked one.

I told Simon that the upcoming show in Clearwater would be my first-ever Duran Duran show—an odd admission considering how big a fan I was.

"Oh, wow. That's nice," he said.

I asked what he recommended for first-time fans of their shows. I honestly don't know what kind of answer I was hoping for.

"Just go and enjoy it," he said. "Have no expectations. Just go and just enjoy it all."

On the podcast version of the interview, the conversation ends there. In reality, I had asked another random question. I cringe thinking about it now.

"I have one last question that's been bugging me for years," I told him. "Yeah?" he replied with curiosity.

Oh, God help me, but I said this: "Aside from being 'a lonely child who's waiting by the park' or 'finding treasure in the dark,' what is 'The Reflex' really about?"

I can hear his answer today like he gave it yesterday.

"Oh, I've never heard that before," he said. "Sorry but time's up, I gotta go. Thank you!"

I still cringe when I think about that question. If I'd done even a modest amount of research, I would have known that Simon has never been interested in explaining his lyrics. "The Reflex," he's said over the years, is "a childish song." Bassist John Taylor has called the words "profoundly weird." And that's probably the point.

I can't escape "The Reflex," nor would I want to. It was Duran Duran's first No. 1 in the U.S., the gateway drug for a lot of us, and the song that still triggers an avalanche of memories. Whatever it means—or doesn't—has never mattered as much as how it feels.

Maybe Simon did answer the question: The best way to experience his music is to go in without expectations and just enjoy it all. I only wish I'd taken his advice five minutes earlier.

JOHN LINNELL of They Might Be Giants came to my attention thanks to the Columbia House record club. In 1990, while living in a $370-a-month apartment I could barely afford in Tampa and working my first full-time job in journalism, I'd joined the infamous club that provided a dozen or so albums for a mere penny. The member needed only to buy three or four albums at regular price in the coming year or so. We were *all* members; don't shake your head no.

One month, I'd forgotten to send in my "no-thanks" postcard on time, and a copy of *Flood* from They Might Be Giants arrived. I honestly hadn't heard of them, which is a little surprising. The Brooklyn-born duo of John Flansburgh and John Linnell had been cranking out quirky but catchy hits since 1982. Ninety-nine times out of 100, I'd send a CD back and carry on. But for whatever reason, I opened this one and put it in my stereo. "Birdhouse in Your Soul" played and I was hooked. I quickly collected all of their earlier works. TMBG became my favorite band.

In March 2008, They Might Be Giants was touring to support their 12th album, *The Else*. Back in 1999, Linnell had released a solo album called *State Song* that I adored. I figured I'd have a chance to talk about that during our conversation. I'm not sure he was keen to go along. Because I was still a little uncomfortable doing solo interviews, I had a *St. Pete Times* entertainment writer and occasional guest cohost, Stephanie Hayes, join me for the call.

We had prepped a bunch of questions we deemed thoughtful enough, but John wasn't feeling it. We were having a bad day. I began by asking about the motivation of reworking their classic songs during shows.

"I love how sometimes you rework an old classic, like the slowed-down version of 'She's an Angel' or hurrying up the pace of a song like 'Why Does the Sun Shine?' Is that something you guys do as sort of a way of keeping the song fresh?" Seemed like a good question, but no.

"I think we just forget how they go, mainly. No, I don't know," John replied. "We try and make it interesting each time. We're not really making a statement about rejecting an old arrangement.

I think often it's like we're trying to make it sound better. That's really the idea."

Okay, then. Maybe I put too much thought into it. *But don't give up just yet*, I told myself.

"Have you ever tried one of the old songs in a new way and then found out that it just sucks?" I countered.

"We have had that experience. Yes," John said. "I don't want to go into details, but we've certainly done the 'it sucks' kind of thing."

I was struggling at this point. Thankfully, Stephanie stepped in.

"What's your reaction when you hear people say that you kind of opened the door for other geek or nerd rock acts like Weezer or The Decemberists or The Aquabats?" she asked.

"I think that it's really up to any artist or band to just decide to go and do their thing, and they really don't need permission, or they don't need a precedent," John answered. Oh, boy, this wasn't getting any better.

"So are you guys actually geeks, or do you secretly have hot women hanging off you after every show?" Stephanie asked next. I admit I still wince thinking about this moment.

"Yeah, I don't know what that means, either," John said. "I mean, we've never really identified with that characterization. We don't feel that way. I don't even know what that is, exactly. And I feel like that culture has changed a lot since we started. It seems very mainstream, actually—to know something about technology, that doesn't seem so weird."

The interview did get better as we went along. I think John eventually understood we were genuine fans, not two interviewers looking to turn his band into a punchline. Still, when I listen back all these years later, it's an uncomfortable give-and-take—hesitant, awkward, and occasionally out of sync. Very human, in other words.

Not every conversation with a musical hero needs to be warm or affirming to be worthwhile. To this day, every time "Birdhouse in Your Soul" comes on, I'm still that broke twenty-something in Tampa, opening an unexpected package and discovering a band that would stay with me for life.

CYNDI LAUPER is one of the defining voices of the 1980s, but she's also one of its most uncompromising personalities. By 2010, she was deep into a late-career renaissance, releasing *Memphis Blues*, a blues album so authentic it earned a Grammy nomination and became the third-best-selling record of her career. Supporting it meant a relentless tour schedule—more than 100 shows—including a stop at Clearwater's Ruth Eckerd Hall.

Sean and I were slotted for a morning interview. And right from the first sentence, we knew this one was going to be…different. "I love hearing your voice," Sean began. "You have the greatest voice of all time."

"Okay," came Cyndi's reply.

To Sean's credit, he turned it around fast, telling Cyndi he had reviewed *Memphis Blues*, giving it a "big fat A," he said. That did the trick.

"Oh, thank you!" she said. "It seemed like the right time to do this, everybody's kind of having a hard time, you read the news. I went to Memphis because I wanted it to be legit. It's good to shine a light on Memphis. It's a wonderful music city."

Leave it to me to kill the energy and momentum.

"Hey, Cyndi," I said, "when you do a live show these days, how do you switch gears from the hard-core blues song to your '80s pop goodness?"

"I don't. These shows are mainly blues shows, and I do my old songs at the end and I don't switch," she answered quickly.

Ugh, I'd stepped in it. At this point, I was sliding down into my chair in the studio and giving Sean that weird "please take it from here" look.

Sean decided to explore her LGBT True Colors United work and her appearances on *Celebrity Apprentice*. Ah, causes close to her heart. Great idea, Sean!

"It seems like you're the kind of person that doesn't take a lot of BS," he said. "I love seeing you, I'm a fan, but at the same time I'm, like, 'Cyndi Lauper on the *Celebrity Apprentice*?' But then when I heard your reasoning, it made sense. It's a huge platform for you to get your ideas across."

A light switch flipped.

"Not my ideas, it's not my ideas! It's what's going on. It's not my ideas, sweetie. It's a reality," Cyndi said. "Do you know gay people in your life? Do you have a gay cousin, a gay brother, or a gay sister or an aunt, an uncle? They're part of our family. These are people we know and work with, and we are allowing them to be discriminated against in a big way. And that isn't good in our country. No matter what dogma you are throwing at people, it's not about my opinion, it's about what's going on. It's not my opinion or my thoughts, it's a reality. Talk to somebody, sweetie."

Sean and I looked at each other, and we could read each other's minds: *We are dying here*. We've stepped on a landmine. I feel like I want to throw up. Cyndi is, of course, right. Best-case scenario: we worded our question awkwardly, and now we'll pay for it. Worst-case scenario: last podcast ever.

We tried to change the subject back to the album, with little success. Finally, I looked at the clock and realized that our time was almost up. Thankfully sometimes, the bigger the name, the fewer the minutes you get with these interviews.

"Hey, Cyndi, we can't wait to see you here in Clearwater on August 4 at Ruth Eckerd," I said. "It's going to be a hell of a night."

"Well, it's a wonderful band," she replied, probably also relieved the chat was over. "And yes, at the end I do the old songs. But if I did the same thing every year, it would be a drag."

Would it really, though? A few years later, in 2013, Cyndi toured to celebrate the 30th anniversary of *She's So Unusual*, performing the album in its entirety. I caught that show in Orlando, and yes—she spent a lot of time between songs talking about the causes that matter to her. The set ran long, the pacing got messy, and she seemed frustrated by the end. So were parts of the crowd.

But that's the deal with Cyndi Lauper: You don't just get the hits—you get the person.

In late 2025, when Sean returned to the podcast for an episode to celebrate our 20th anniversary, I asked him what he remembered about the Cyndi Lauper interview. "She was a hero back then, but now she's been elevated to the saint status like Stevie Nicks and such," Sean said. "We want to talk about 'She Bop' and she's talking about Dizzy Gillespie or whatever. It was tough."

Our interview didn't go smoothly. It wasn't especially fun. And it certainly wasn't comfortable. But it was honest—and in its own way, completely on brand.

ANDREW DICE CLAY has enjoyed an unpredictable and always-evolving career. He got his stand-up start in the 1970s and worked up his "Diceman" portrayal in late-night sets in the early '80s at The Comedy Store in L.A. His acting credentials are pretty impressive too. He has credits for appearances on *M*A*S*H* and *Diff'rent*

Strokes, but he is obviously better remembered for his scene-stealing turns in *Pretty in Pink* and *Casual Sex*.

In 2007, Andrew was doing a club tour that included a stop in Tampa, so naturally I sought out an interview. It would become one of the most frustrating courtships in *Stuck in the '80s* history. His agent would agree to an interview then cancel it, reschedule, then cancel again. Days before Andrew's appearance in town the show was already a sellout, so no more promotion was really required or needed. I had pretty much dismissed the idea completely when the phone rang.

"Andrew's available to talk if you have the time," the agent said. It had been only hours since I'd finished interviewing Brian Johnson from AC/DC earlier in the day, so my mind was distracted with that victory. "Sure," I agreed anyway. "Just one question: Does Andrew do interviews in character or as himself?"

It was a clumsy question but the agent answered: "There is no character. Andrew is Andrew." Okay, then. I was told to wait by the phone and he'd call in about 10 minutes. I had zero questions written in advance.

"I really appreciate you doing this podcast with me today," I told him when he rang.

"No problem," he said. It was the Diceman all right. The accent, the attitude. This could be fun.

I asked if he still included his profanity-tinged nursery rhymes bit in his act. You've heard them, I'm sure. They were a staple on late-'80s cable comedy shows.

"Yeah, I do that. That's all part of my show," he said. "Little Miss Muffet sat on her tuffet, eating her curds and whey. Along came a spider, who sat down beside her, he said, 'Hey, what's in the bowl, bitch?' Awww!"

Now seems like a good time to restate the rules for profanity on *Stuck in the '80s*. Generally speaking, we bleep the F-bombs. At the time of this interview, though, I was still working for the *St. Pete Times*. My boss had given me one guideline on the F-bombs: if a guest says the word as an adjective, leave it in. If it's used as a verb, bleep it out. Andrew would make me work for it throughout our 12-minute chat.

"When people ask me about who my favorite comedians are, I'll be quiet," he said. (Side note: I didn't ask him about his favorite comedians. I have no idea how this started.) "I don't give a fuck about comedians. I never studied them. I don't know the history of them. I don't even like to go to comedy movies, you know what I mean?"

Umm, not really. But he was giving me an opening to talk about his acting career, which I was truly curious about. "How did you make that break into acting back then?" I asked.

"Just auditioning," he said. "There's no big story about it."

Sigh. Okay. I asked if he had wanted to try both standup comedy and acting to see which one worked out better.

"No, I just wanted to do both," he said.

"At what point did you kind of say, 'I'd rather do this than that'?" I pressed.

"I haven't said that," Andrew said. "You just follow life, and you go the way it goes."

"Any fond memories of those days?" I asked. Remember, I hadn't written down any questions ahead of time. I was just trying to fill the minutes at this point. Andrew brought up the 1984 movie *Making the Grade*.

"I really liked Judd Nelson, but when we worked together, he has got, like, a crazy temper. I do too. But, like, he likes to slam doors and things like that," he said. "We were sharing our trailer together, and he came in and nearly bashed my hand with the door. He was going so nuts. So I nearly had to just throw him a vicious beating, but of course we really dug each other. And anytime we see each other, it's always great."

"Did you get to improvise in the movie?" I asked.

"It's really not a good story. I could tell you a million great stories, that's not one of them," he answered. "He slammed the door. Who gives a fuck? Who is even thinking about him right now? Nobody. I don't think his own family is thinking about him. Who gives a fuck for him? I like him. He's a friend of mine."

At this point I couldn't even understand the flow of our conversation. I've relistened to it since and read the transcript over and over. The interview ended with a random comment from Andrew that might be the hidden gem in the conversation:

"Comics are angry fucking people. If they're any good, they take real life and they just throw it right in audiences' faces and let them know what asshole people they really are."

To this day, I've never seen Andrew Dice Clay perform live. I don't think I even managed to pull enough clean copy from that conversation to properly promote his sold-out show in the paper.

Ironically, the part of his career he seemed least interested in discussing—the acting—has aged the best. Over the years, he's earned real respect for his dramatic turns, popping up on *Entourage*, delivering a quietly excellent performance in *Blue Jasmine*, and continuing to surprise people who assumed they already had him figured out.

Despite what his agent told me, Andrew Dice Clay isn't just a character. He's someone who's spent a career playing himself.

COLIN HAY was a tough nut to crack. Or maybe it was just us that day back in 2009. The Men at Work frontman kept rescheduling our interview that afternoon. He was in his car, running errands, if memory serves. I'm not sure we had his full attention when we finally got him on the phone.

His answers were short and maybe funny? It's hard to tell sometimes, especially on a phoner.

Colin had been in Clearwater the year before as part of Ringo Starr & His All-Starr Band. He dazzled Sean and me that night but only played two of his hits. We felt—probably unnecessarily—short-changed, and we began by ribbing him about it.

"Last year we saw you with Ringo Starr at Ruth Eckerd Hall in Clearwater," Sean began. "We were there for you and you only did two songs!"

"Yeah, but why are you picking the bone with me?" Colin shot back. "Because that's not my call, that's Ringo's call. So you've got a bone to pick with Ringo, not me."

Ouch. Not a great start. Sean wasn't going to give up.

"I'm furious! I'm furious with the fourth Beatle!" he said. "So is that how it works now? Were there nights where you would get, like, three or four songs, or does everybody get two?"

"No," Colin said. "Everyone gets two."

Move on, guys. We got the message.

The man had been on top of the world in the early '80s as Men at Work became the first Australian band to have a No. 1 album (*Business as Usual*) and No. 1 song ("Down Under") simultaneously on the U.S. charts.

In 1983, Men at Work won the Grammy for Best New Artist, beating out Asia, The Human League, and Stray Cats, among others. However, the honor has become a jinx for some acts who found they never could continue past that milestone. I asked Colin if he felt the Grammy win was a curse.

"I didn't then, but I have a few times since," he said.

History would give him reason to reconsider. The band began to fracture in 1984, and by 1986 Colin had launched a solo career and relocated to the U.S., eventually settling in Los Angeles. Colin and his bandmate Greg Ham would reunite the band and tour from 1996 to 2002.

"We went all over the world," he said. "It wasn't all the original members, but it was Men at Work, under the banner of Men at Work."

Though Colin now often tours with a whole new lineup as Men at Work, he told us—at least back in 2009—not to expect a return of the original members.

"It's not like I have anything particularly against it," he explained. "Men at Work was a very important band for me at that very important time, and I loved being a part of it. But the thing is, when people ask me about it, I think to myself, 'The reason why I say no is because I know the people. So I know that it wouldn't happen, not because of me but because of other people.' So it's not like I am necessarily stopping something like that from happening."

"Hey, Colin, here's kind of an artsy question for you," Sean began at the end of our interview. "How do you know when something is done? Like, how do you know when an album is complete and ready to be mastered?"

"How do you know when the record's done?" Colin asked.

"Yeah, how do you know when a song is finished?" Sean pressed.

"Well, you have to listen to the song because if you listen to a song, it'll speak to you and it'll say to you, in between the grooves, if you listen very carefully, you'll hear this little voice saying, 'I'm done, I'm done.'"

It wasn't our smoothest conversation, and it certainly wasn't our funniest. But as we wrapped up, it felt complete. The song was done.

WHEN THE MUSIC WAS THE MOVIE

Will the 1980s go down as the "Decade of Soundtracks" (a label I much prefer to that dreaded "Decade of Decadence" moniker)? I hope so. Many of the most memorable films of those 10 years were inseparable from the music that gave them their pulse—*Purple Rain, Pretty in Pink, Footloose, Flashdance*. Whenever I get an artist on the phone whose work shaped a movie soundtrack, it's almost impossible not to pick their brain about the process.

STEWART COPELAND of The Police is one of maybe a dozen Rock & Roll Hall of Fame inductees to appear on *Stuck in the '80s*. When we interviewed him in 2009, he had just published a memoir—*Strange Things Happen: A Life with The Police, Polo, and Pygmies*—and we were lucky enough to snag some time with him for the podcast.

Stewart was chatty and polite and possessed a wicked sense of humor. The book was a blast to read. But when it came time to interview him, I could barely work up the nerve to speak. Thankfully—for my sanity—my co-host Sean Daly did most of the heavy lifting.

"Stewart, you write just like you play drums: it's all about rhythm and instigation, I think you like pissing people off," Sean said. *Oh, boy, here we go,* I thought at the time.

"I do like pissing people off [chuckle] but with love in my heart," Stewart said. "I like rattling people's cage, and sometimes, occasionally, I slip over the line just a crack, maybe."

"In the span of, like, 100 words, you call Sting at one point the Flying Dutchman, the Lion of Judah, and Captain Queeg. I know you love pushing his buttons," Sean continued.

"Oh, yes, it's my lot in life; it's my job," he replied gleefully. "And he also rattles my cage, and if it weren't for each other, The Police wouldn't be what it is."

What The Police was, at the time, was a newly retired band. Bassist Sting, drummer Stewart, and guitarist Andy Summers had completed a 30th anniversary tour in 2008 that would also serve as a final trip around the world. After legs in North America, South America, Europe, and Asia, the trio had called it quits.

Both Summers and Copeland moved on to solo projects, including working on soundtracks. In the '80s, Summers contributed to *Down and Out in Beverly Hills* and *Weekend at Bernie's,* while Copeland's list of credits includes *Wall Street, Talk Radio,* and *9 1/2 Weeks,* just to name a few.

"You're kind of like the master of the soundtrack: *Rumble Fish, The Equalizer, She's Having a Baby,*" Sean began. "How do you take somebody else's vision and kind of adapt to that?"

"That's the fun of film composing—it's a collaborative experience," Stewart said. "It's just like playing in a band, only unlike the band, the other collaborators have nothing to do with music, and so I get to do all the music myself."

"It's brilliant work. I love it because of the variety," he continued. "One film is a sci-fi film, and it's all electronics and sound effects. The next film is a romantic comedy, and it's a light orchestral. The next minute it's a sleazy urban thing with hip-hop. And so film music takes you into every realm of music, and you get to play with all the toys."

Rumble Fish was the movie that caught our attention the most. The 1983 movie—directed by the great Francis Ford Coppola—was based on a 1975 novel by S.E. Hinton (who also authored *The Outsiders*.) It had an incredible cast, including Matt Dillon, Mickey Rourke, Vincent Spano, Diane Lane, Dennis Hopper, and another actor whose career was about to take off—Nicolas Cage.

"The main memory is Francis Coppola and the latitude he gave me—he gave me enough rope to hang myself, certainly," Stewart recalled. "The way he works is that he finds the right people and then turns them loose, but loose with a very clear mission."

"He explained exactly what he needed emotionally for the different scenes and for the overall arc of the picture. I was able to come up with stuff and fortunately he loved it. There are other directors, like Oliver Stone, for instance, who is right in there analyzing every bar of everything, but Francis is the other kind."

We wondered aloud how Stewart—the drummer—could coexist with Stewart—the composer.

"The drummer guy is very different from the film composer guy," Stewart agreed. "The mission of doing a film is very specific. The emotional requirements for the music in a film are very, very specific. It's happy, sad, with a little silvery ray of humor in there but an underlying sense of doom."

"Now, when I get on the drums—and normally I don't get on the drums in a studio, I hire other guys to do that—but in front of an audience, that's a completely different mission," he explained. "The idea there is that I gotta light up the room. I gotta wake up the crowd. I gotta bring down the thundering, clanging gongs of doom and burn down the house. That's a visceral, animal, instinctive experience, and there's quite a bit of chaos in there, and you gotta deal with that if you're in a band with me."

There's a line in Copeland's book about how only eight years of his then 57 years alive had been with The Police.

"That's right," he said. "Eight pretty critical years that affected the entire other part of my life."

Did it bother him, Sean wanted to know, if his life felt defined by The Police.

"No, because I'm not really defined that way in any meaningful way. As a film composer, I'm defined by *Wall Street, Rumble Fish*, and the film scores that I've done," he said. "The Police has nothing to do with it....In the life that I live every day, I wake up and I walk out into the world, I'm with my friends who know me as me and my family who know me as Dad, and once again, the world that I live in is completely unaffected by The Police."

Would he go insane if it were otherwise?

"I live here in my house in Brentwood [Los Angeles] and live the life that I live, and it may be that that's what people are thinking but I'm not in other people's minds. I'm only in my mind, I guess."

Did this book mean The Police were done for good? It was the question we'd been tiptoeing around for the whole conversation. We were looking for a verdict. Would there be another tour? Was there a desire for another album?

"Probably not for a new album," Stewart said. "Sting writes those songs. The last person he wants in there fucking it up is me. And I hate going into a studio to record drums, and I think the most painful version of something that I already hate is going into the studio with The Police."

"It's incredible to go out there on the stage with those two bastards who are monsters of music. That's really a charge, but to go into the studio without 80,000 people cheering us on, it's a hell pit.

I got other creative endeavors that are a lot cozier and a lot easier. The Police is fucking hard."

We reluctantly said our goodbyes, and despite the dark turn near the end of the conversation, Stewart remained chipper. If he has demons, he keeps them on a leash. His final words to us—"I hope you got a story"—felt like an understatement from a man who has already lived several of them.

KENNY LOGGINS was the first home-run interview for *Stuck in the '80s*. We hadn't yet had an artist on the show who laughed and shared as much as Kenny did. He even sang for us!

In 2007, Kenny was touring to support a new album, *How About Now*, a record inspired by a recent reunion tour with Jimmy Messina. The pop duo had enjoyed incredible success in the mid-1970s with tunes such as "Danny's Song," "House at Pooh Corner," and "Your Mama Don't Dance." When the pair called it quits in 1976, Jimmy would find limited success as a solo artist while Kenny's career seemed to have no limits.

"It was a little bit weird," Kenny said of returning to the road with his old partner. "We hadn't worked together in many years. It was strange in the way you might be thinking of going back and doing material that I wrote when I was 18, 19, and 20. And seeing the difference in my writing, how far I'd come since then."

The difference began, Kenny said, with the movies.

"During a period of time where disco was coming in and was just totally taking over radio, I got lucky and took a big step left and went into *Caddyshack* and *Footloose* and *Top Gun*," he said. One anthem after another put bread on the table, he said, for most of the '80s.

"With *Caddyshack*, Jon Peters produced that," Kenny said. "I think that was his first production that he did on his own after he split up with Barbra Streisand. I met him when he was with Barbra, and we worked on *A Star Is Born* together and became friends through that."

One call led to another, and Kenny got a chance to see a rough cut of the movie—before an ending was even filmed.

"They just said, 'Rodney, say something, we need an ending.'"

"Hey everybody, we're all gonna get laid!"—as improvised by Rodney Dangerfield—would become the signature punchline of the early decade.

"I loved that rough cut," he said. "All the Bill Murray stuff was intact. All the Chevy Chase stuff was intact."

But it was the character of Danny—played by Michael O'Keefe—that caught the songwriter's attention and inspired the thumping tune "I'm Alright."

"The character was trying to figure out where he fit in. But at the same time, he wanted people to leave him alone and just let him find his own way," he explained. "So I wanted to kind of grab that character and summarize him, and that's what 'I'm Alright' was doing."

Kenny explained that the song originally had a bit of a Bob Dylan feel to it—quite possibly "It's Alright, Ma (I'm Only Bleeding)"—but with "a bit of a snarl" to work off the character's theme. Oh, and it has a single, uncredited line by Eddie Money: "You make me feel good!"

"That was before he had his hits," Kenny remembered. "He was in the studio working on one of his early records when I recorded 'I'm Alright.' Bruce Botnick was working with me at the time, and Bruce said, 'That guy's really good. You ought to bring him in.' And I met him, and he was like, 'Hey, man, how are you doing?' I said, 'Hey, would you do me a favor and sing a line on my song?'

He said, 'Sure.' And he came in and did that line. Isn't that ironic, how things go?"

"I'm Alright" would go on to be a Top 10 hit for Loggins and remained a fixture in his touring setlists for the rest of his career. He wrote three other songs for the soundtrack—"Lead the Way," "Make the Move," and "Mr. Night"—but they remain trivia questions in the big picture.

With his next big project—1984's *Footloose*—Loggins would score bigger.

"The energy of 'Footloose' was delivered to me in the screenplay," Kenny said, remembering the movie. "[Movie writer and songwriter] Dean Pitchford and I just wrote a lyric that tried to capture that emotion. So it's much less autobiographical than, say, a real thing from 'Leap of Faith' or [the song] 'Conviction of the Heart.'"

"I love to perform 'Footloose' because to me it's such a lighthearted tune. It's like doing a Chuck Berry song every night," he said. "I never get sick of it. I still love 'I'm Alright.' Again, the lyrics kind of pull me up. I'm less inclined to want to do 'Danger Zone' [from *Top Gun*]. I didn't write it. It was a Giorgio Moroder tune. It's a good rock 'n' roll song, but I don't think it holds up that well."

Pitchford and Loggins would co-write "Footloose," which spent three weeks at the top of the charts. Another Kenny tune—"Playing with the Boys," the playful volleyball-scene romp from *Top Gun*—would later peak at No. 22.

Truth be told, Kenny said, there weren't any movie projects he turned down in those days—even when the movie itself was a stinker. Yes, I'm talking about the unwatchable *Caddyshack II*.

"I got a funny story," I told Kenny at this point. "I was up late last night. I got home from work around 1:30 and I was ready to go to bed, and I'm flipping around the channels and I see *Caddyshack II* is coming on in 30 minutes. And I said, 'You know what,

I'm gonna stay up till 2:05 just so I can hear Kenny sing 'Nobody's Fool' one more time."'

"What a piece of shit that movie was," Kenny laughed. "Oh, my God."

"It is a piece of shit," I said, "but Kenny, that's a great song."

"I really thought it was a strong tune," he said. "I expected it to go further than it did, but I think it was saddled to just a really bad movie."

So, we asked breathlessly, any chance he was still performing "Nobody's Fool" in concert?

"No, I haven't, but you're making me think I should," Kenny said. "I'd have to drop it at least a whole step now, though. That was the highest note I could sing back then. Probably a B. No, that would be probably a C-sharp."

And then suddenly...

"I'm going all the way!" Kenny belted out in his signature song voice.

I just about passed out.

"Best podcast ever," I declared. To this day, I get the chills listening to it again.

JOHN PARR was an interview I didn't see coming. In 2020, The 80s Cruise arranged a Facebook Live conversation with John, who was booked on the next sailing. I'd never interviewed someone live in front of an audience—people could watch in real time and even submit questions. I was a little freaked out. I might have even tried to weasel out of it. I'm glad I wasn't let off the hook.

John was an absolute delight. His career was so much more than "Naughty Naughty" and "St. Elmo's Fire (Man in Motion)," two MTV favorites. He has worked with the great David Foster (his co-writer on "St. Elmo's Fire [Man in Motion]"; toured with Tina Turner, the Beach Boys, Journey, and others; and written tunes for Roger Daltrey of The Who, Marilyn Martin, and Meat Loaf.

But it's his movie soundtrack work that boggles the mind. Aside from the anthem to 1985's *St. Elmo's Fire*, John has provided music for *Quicksilver, American Anthem, The Running Man, Three Men and a Baby* and others.

John joined our Facebook chat from his house in Yorkshire, England, where he was hunkered down during the COVID-19 pandemic. Behind him on the video, I noticed a few guitars that he'd brought with him. He was going to perform during our interview. Another first.

After the usual pleasantries, I told John that The 80s Cruise guests exploded with excitement when the upcoming lineup of musicians included him with a snippet of "Naughty Naughty."

"Wow! Well, it's funny in England, that song's not so well known, but I know in America it kinda broke me," John said.

That song would also help connect John to super-producer David Foster. It turns out Foster loved "Naughty Naughty" and was using it as a template for a song he was working on with Paul McCartney.

"'Naughty Naughty' opened the door to David," John said. "He said, 'Look, I'm doing this movie, I'm doing the score for it, and I'm doing 10 original songs—will you come over and write a song for it with me?'"

The song, of course, was "St. Elmo's Fire (Man in Motion)," and it was written in about an hour, John said. Many casual '80s fans know the real story behind the song is the Canadian wheelchair athlete Rick Hansen, who circled the world in a wheelchair to raise money and awareness for people with spinal injuries.

"We'd written the music and all the arrangement really quickly, but I just couldn't get a handle on what the subject was," John told me. "I'm from Worksop, a mining town. I left school at 15. So trying to identify with rich kids in collegiate schools, and worried about where their next 100 grand is coming from—it just didn't really register with me."

Foster then showed John a video about Hansen.

"The hairs on the back of my neck stood up, and I just thought, 'I've got to write this song,'" he said. "So 'St. Elmo's Fire' was a prediction, really, of what did happen, because two years, two months, and two days after Rick Hansen set out from Vancouver, he wheeled back into Vancouver with a million people in the streets, and everybody's singing 'St. Elmo's.' The power of music and the inspiration of a man who wouldn't sit down and take no."

John and Rick Hansen remain friends to this day.

"The greatest thing Rick ever said to me was, he sent me a telegram when he was on the road," John said. "He'd had enough one day. And he said to me, he said, 'Whenever I feel I can't turn another wheel, I play the song and I can go out and do another 20 miles.' That was the greatest accolade of my life."

It opened the door to Hollywood, too.

"I'd had the dream of working in movies, and suddenly I did 10 Hollywood movies in two years," he said. "Unfortunately, my record company didn't like me doing it, so I would have a song in one of the biggest movies in the world, but it would never be released as a single because Atlantic wanted me to be a rock 'n' roller, and I just saw myself a bit wider than that. And that's really why my, kind of, recording career stalled a little bit. But my movie career went great."

The process of writing a movie song is fairly straightforward, he said. Usually it involves seeing a rough cut of the film before he begins work on the music.

"With *St. Elmo's Fire* I saw nothing, and that was the blessing," he said. "I just knew the basic outline with *St. Elmo's*. So when I wrote the lyrics—'All I need's this pair of wheels,' 'just once in his life, a man has his time'—they think I'm talking about Demi Moore's Jeep or Emilio Estevez getting the girl, when really I'm talking about turning the wheels of the wheelchair and when Rick breaks through the tape."

"But generally—like with *The Running Man*, the Arnold Schwarzenegger movie, they took me to the preview theater. I watched the movie and heard the song play in my head straight away."

That song, "Restless Heart," was co-written and produced by Harold Faltermeyer. It appears in the 1987 film during the movie's closing credits. Sadly, it didn't chart. But that didn't deter John, who picked up the acoustic guitar and played the song for me.

"That was the first time I ever played that acoustic," he said afterward.

"Yeah, I got chills," I admitted before remembering how hundreds of people were watching me fall apart live on Facebook. I rallied, turned to my web camera, and said: "If you're just tuning in, you just missed the greatest three minutes of my life."

John went on to stun me a few more times during that conversation. He brought his legendary Les Paul guitar, aptly called "Stars and Stripes." I think I audibly giggled with glee when he held it up to the camera so I could see it.

He finished our call by playing an acoustic version of "St. Elmo's Fire." And yes, I cried during it. On camera. My brain stopped working. A few days afterward, I received an email from John's publicist with a message that John wanted to send me. It reads:

> "Dear Steve. I just wanted to say a personal thank-you for having me on your show and making it a very memorable hour for me. It truly was a highlight, and many

people have told me it was made by your humanity and genuine love of music. My very best, John."

My wife printed it and added a few screen captures of the Facebook Live chat. She framed it and gave it to me as a present. Every time I pick it up, I cry again.

THE RIVALRY THAT WASN'T

TIFFANY trivia time. Pardon the pun, but time for a "pop" quiz: What is teen pop star Tiffany's last name? It's Darwish. Yeah, I have to Google it every time. I guess that's good branding. Tiffany's star rose in the second half of the '80s, thanks to hits like "I Think We're Alone Now" and "Could've Been." She's crossed my path a few times over the past 10 years because she's a frequent host and performer on The 80s Cruise.

Tiffany's story has often been framed as a rivalry or a brief snapshot of the era. What surprised me was how little she seemed interested in either. In 2016, I finally had her as a guest on the podcast. She had sailed on the inaugural 80s Cruise that year and was due to return in 2017. I asked her what the attraction of the cruise was for her.

"I have to say it's pretty magical to have the MTV VJs" on the ship, she said. "To me they were always, growing up, the coolest kids in school, right?"

Did she remember her first MTV moment?

"When Nina (Blackwood) came to my school, and she did a real long interview with me, and I thought that was just—I thought it was a great day to be Tiffany," she said. "I had some people who never noticed me before, they're like, 'I want to be your friend!'"

Another revelation I learned that day: Tiffany never went to her prom.

"I went to my graduation and not my prom," she said. "That was my last two years of high school, and things were moving way too fast, and I was on the road most of the time. So I missed all the cool dances and prom, and I barely made it back for my graduation."

During our short chat, we covered everything from her then home in Nashville to her favorite childhood bands and even the R2-D2 pajamas she brought for Pajama Party Night but chickened out of wearing. She was just enjoying the parts of adolescence she'd missed.

"I know it's all a media-manufactured thing but Debbie Gibson will also be on The '80s cruise [in 2017]," I began. It was a phone call so I couldn't see her eyes rolling, but I wouldn't blame her. "I know you've answered the question a billion times about the rivalry but I'm just wondering, since you're both on the ship: I mean, have you had any thoughts about trying to do something with her, performing on stage with her on this trip?"

"Probably not," Tiffany answered. "To be honest with you, Deb and I actually did some stuff together about three, four years ago. And it was really great and lots of fun. And I'm sure she's got, like, her whole show planned. I think more than anything, you're just going to see us hanging out together. I mean, we really are friends. So I think that in itself will be shocking for a lot of people."

Huh, I thought. I'd be shocked as well. But should I have been?

"All that rivalry stuff before was ridiculous," she continued. "I think that was something that was part media and part maybe our labels because it was good media."

"It's good business in a way," I added.

"Deb and I never got a chance to even really talk. We were so busy. We would kind of be in the same hotel here and there or wherever, walk the same carpet, but really sit down and talk, no," she said. "And that's just really happened more in the last 10 years."

What happened was the 2011 movie *Mega Python vs. Gatoroid*, a campy TV monster-disaster romp that featured the two pop princesses.

"It's been great doing the movie together," Tiffany said. "Days that we were shooting, we just had time to just kind of hang out. We found so much in common besides music. We've had so many mutual friends and fans. So it really was a cool thing. And we randomly text each other and just give each other encouragement."

I was admittedly surprised. Skeptical maybe? But Tiffany insisted there was no rivalry.

"You couldn't get two more opposite people, but yet, that's the cool thing about it, that we kind of respect that about each other. And that somehow that works for us."

What struck me most wasn't that Tiffany and Debbie Gibson were friends—it was how long it took for anyone to believe it. They were teenagers dropped into a rivalry that made sense on paper but not in real life. Once the headlines faded, they finally got to know each other. Turns out some of the most persistent '80s myths were also the least real.

DEBBIE GIBSON visited Tampa Bay in 2008 and wanted to stop by the newspaper office to join the podcast. At that point, we'd never had a guest come into our studio. (It wouldn't happen again until Robin Zander paid us a visit in 2011.) I even tried to talk her out of it. But it happened, and we have the transcript and awkward photos to prove it.

To be honest, much like Tiffany, Debbie made music at a time when my co-host Sean Daly and I were probably not in her key demographics. By the late '80s, we were both in college listening to angsty tunes by college radio favorites, not crooning along to "Electric Youth." But we were still intrigued by Debbie—and fell instantly in love with her moxie.

"Either Steve or I, or both, will stroke out at some point," Sean assured Debbie.

"I'll just carry on without you when you guys pass out," Debbie quipped.

First thing we had to do was figure out whether to call her Deborah—as she was going by at the time—or Debbie, her nickname during the chart-topping years.

"Let me just explain this and get this out of the way," she began. "Everybody in my real life, my family and friends for the first 16 years of my life, called me Deb or Deborah."

Really? Sean and I looked unconvinced. Apparently it was her record company's idea after Deb rejected their suggestion of Debbie G. By the time they came back around to Debbie Gibson, she had grown weary of the battle and agreed.

"No one calls you that now?" I asked.

"Except dumbass journalists," Sean added.

"It was a good thing growing up when the success started happening, and people started getting our home number," she explained. "If somebody called the house asking for Debbie, my sisters and my parents knew we didn't know them."

"Imagine what it's been like having the last name Spears for the last 10 years, and the phone calls I get at home," I said.

"Oh, God," she said, realizing the Britney Spears curse was on me. "'Oh, baby, baby. How was I supposed to know that something wasn't right?' That's my favorite impersonation I do, by the way."

It was dead on.

Speaking of her teen years, we were curious how stardom changed her.

"I've never touched a drug," she said. "I've actually never been drunk in my life."

"Come on," Sean protested.

"I've never had a whole drink," she insisted. "I don't like alcohol. I don't like any of that."

"Your halo looks awesome," Sean teased.

"Thank you. Is it glowing?" she asked. "But more importantly, how does my skin look?"

"Did you have a spa treatment?" Sean asked.

"No, just clean living, you know what I mean? Like, seriously," she added.

"I look like shit, don't I?" I finally said. "There's a reason that we look like we're on our deathbed and she doesn't."

It turns out Debbie was mature for her age. She was singing different languages in a children's chorus at the Metropolitan Opera before she even reached her teenage years. She auditioned for *Les Misérables* on Broadway at age 15. And in 1988, her tune "Foolish Beat" topped the charts. She became the youngest person to ever write, produce, and perform a No. 1 song.

It was another feat, though, that made me stutter out a question I never thought I'd be in a position to ask.

"I gotta ask this question..." I began slowly and painfully, "because you were a Miss Squeaky Clean whether you wanted to be or not..."

Debbie was giving me the raised-eyebrow treatment and a taunting smile as she watched me suffer.

"In 2005 you did something that kind of threw people for a loop: You appeared in *Playboy*," I finally spit out.

"I was torturing you, making you get the words out," she said with a devilish look. "You like that?"

"Yeah, I do," I shamefully confessed. "That was really uncomfortable."

"That's part of why I did it, because it's so fun to me," Debbie said. "It's funny for me to watch other people squirm when I was so comfortable with it."

Debbie appeared in the March 2005 edition of the magazine, which also named Paris Hilton as "Sex Star of the Year." For what it's worth, Debbie's gal-pal Tiffany had done the *Playboy* gig in 2002.

"I got that call at age 18, 22, 25, 28, 30," Deb began. "They called in like '98 or '99. At that time I was actually playing Gypsy in *Gypsy*. Gypsy Rose Lee was, like, a burlesque queen. And the timing of that was very interesting because I was suddenly on stage having to really come to terms with being at home with my sexuality. It was, like, a very in-your-face kind of role."

Debbie told the magazine she'd do it—if they would do "a theatrical, stylized-type thing" that matched the tone of her *Gypsy* stage role. *Playboy* passed at the time, insisting its readers weren't into that, but came back in 2005, offering Debbie freedom over everything.

"'You can show as much or as little as you want, do whatever you want,'" she said they told her. "And I just went, 'You know what? Why not?' I came up with 8,000 creative ways of creating G-strings. I was like, 'Oh, this necklace would make a great G-string.' So yeah, I kind of, you know, as I put it, it's like boobs and booty day on South Beach, you know?"

"Did you talk to Hef at all?" Sean asked.

"No," she said. "Actually, now I go to the Playboy Mansion all the time. I go for their dinner, like 20-people dinner and movie nights. I can just pull up to the house anytime and talk to the rock that has the speaker in it and go, 'Hey, it's Deborah Gibson.' And they go, 'Come on in.'"

By the end of our conversation, the jokes about halos and *Playboy* had faded into the background, replaced by Debbie's sense of purpose. She talked about songwriting, mentoring young performers, and building a future that felt earned rather than nostalgic.

Naturally Sean asked the obvious follow-up: "Have you thought about making new music?"

"The whole end of last year I was in the studio working on new stuff," she said. "I'm at the point where I want to do like—I was a teenager when Tina Turner's 'What's Love Got to Do With It' came out. It was, like, that resurgence, that moment. Like when Cher came out with 'If I Could Turn Back Time.' I feel like I'm right on the verge of that moment. And it's about feeling like I have the absolute perfect song that makes the statement I would want to make."

"I like showing people where I've been, where I am, where I'm going. Not just where I've been because that would be boring."

"I never wanted to make a solo album. I only recorded *Desert Moon* to have something to do."

THE MAN BEHIND THE MASK

Ever felt like every big life moment has one band handling the soundtrack for you? That was Styx for me. And talking to Dennis DeYoung for about 90 minutes in 2011 was surreal—like briefly consulting with my life's orchestra conductor. Thankfully I have the whole thing on tape to remember all the details.

As a preteen, I was a freak for Kiss. As my teen years approached, a neighbor friend named Scott took pity on me and lent me some Styx albums. *Pieces of Eight* is the one I remember most. The album cover, with its robotic, aging faces and hollow, shadowed eyes, still haunts me in some weird way. I loved every song on it, even the kooky "Aku-Aku."

When I fell in love for the first time, it was "First Time" on *Cornerstone* that talked me through it. When my heart was dragged through the coals by the same girl, "Don't Let It End" off *Kilroy Was Here* was my lamenting plea. When I want to chase all the women from a room, nothing works better than "Castle Walls" from *The Grand Illusion*.

The idea of talking to Dennis DeYoung had never seemed practical. I had heard he was a little surly during meet-and-greets. Frankly, I didn't want to ruin the image I'd had of him in my head for decades.

So in 2008, when I learned that Dennis and Night Ranger were coming to Clearwater's Ruth Eckerd Hall, I chose to interview

Jack Blades for the podcast. Jack was a real "get" for us, and he regaled us with plenty of memorable stories from the band's run in the '80s. As I mentioned in chapter 15, I was even invited to introduce Night Ranger onstage that night. I remember patting guitarist Brad Gillis on the back as he stepped onstage. (He must have been thinking, "Who is this schlub?")

After the show was over, I was backstage chatting with the Ruth Eckerd Hall staff when Bobby Rossi, the venue's executive vice president for entertainment, asked if I wanted to meet Dennis.

"Nooooooo," I pleaded with perceived visions of the legend giving me the cold shoulder.

Bobby insisted and took me over to the guy who wrote just about every Styx song I had memorized for the past 25 years.

"Dennis, this is Steve Spears," Bobby said. "He's a writer for the *St. Pete Times.*"

"Ahhh, a journalist," Dennis replied. "So you probably have a few questions for me."

I didn't. I hadn't expected this meeting to happen. I did my best two-step anyway.

"Well, it was a great set list tonight," I stuttered out, "but why didn't you play 'Desert Moon'?" The song was a standout hit when Dennis recorded his first album apart from the group in 1984.

Dennis's smile turned into a frown the moment I spit out the last syllable. He pointed at Bobby.

"Because this *asshole* booked Night Ranger to open for me," he declared.

My face turned white.

"I'm kidding!" he said.

That was my introduction to Dennis and his unique sense of humor. I have zero memory of our conversation after that. I seem to recall complimenting him on playing "Castle Walls," but that's about when my brain ceased to function.

Four years later, in 2012, Dennis would return to Ruth Eckerd Hall, this time backed up by The Florida Orchestra. Having fully recovered from his Night Ranger joke, I was ready to tackle a head-on interview with him.

Our conversation lasted more than an hour. About 45 minutes of it was on the record. It began with me retelling the story of his Night Ranger-Bobby Rossi joke.

"Did I really say that?" Dennis asked incredulously.

"Yeah, and you did it with a totally straight face," I replied.

"I didn't mean it seriously," he insisted. "Oh, God, I'm glad I don't remember half the things I say."

I assured Dennis that it was a fun memory and a story I told frequently when listeners of the podcast asked about what goes on backstage.

"I learned a long time ago that when you meet people—fans or anybody—it doesn't really take much to be affable and nice to them," he said. "And it's a lesson I learned as a very young man. And the thing is, if you don't have time for fans or the media or whoever, how else do you get to have the career you have? You just don't have it without those people...but that doesn't include that bastard Bobby Rossi."

When I reread the transcript of our chat today, it's full of Dennis and me trying to crack each other up. Only when we turned to the subject of his former bandmates in Styx does the interview take a more somber tone. Most of those moments came after we agreed to continue our chat off the record.

I took the conversation back to Roseland, the Chicago neighborhood where Dennis grew up and met his future band co-founders—twin brothers John and Chuck Panozzo. A VH1 *Behind the Music* episode featured the brothers with Dennis, who was holding an accordion. Did he still have it, I asked.

"It was in a flood," he told me. "The accordion in that picture, I still have, but it's pretty moldy. It's packed away in storage someplace. I can't really play it anymore. You have to understand, I was 14 years old, okay, and the Panozzo brothers were 12. ...It was before the Beatles by almost two years. We didn't know they were going to be this phenomenon of rock bands that would play and sing their own music....We were not a rock band. We were a wedding band. People forget the most popular instrument in the '50s after the piano was the accordion. It was not the guitar."

"Here's the humiliation that it teaches you," he continued. "You spend your life learning an instrument that becomes obsolete and almost something to be derided and made fun of. That'll set you on a course of trying to be an overachiever."

I'd never make fun of the accordion again, I assured him. I also confessed to being subjected to having organ lessons at a young age. That's another level of humiliation.

"Lowrey organ in the living room!" Dennis exclaimed. Yes, I sighed.

"That's the story of my life here, what you just said," Dennis continued. "When I was 13 years old, I was recruited to go and play on this football team, and I told my mother that I was giving up playing music because I wanted to play football. And I went and played that year and we won the city championship. And it was the next year when I was walking down the street, and I hadn't played the accordion for a year, and I heard the Panozzo brothers, so I went and dug my accordion out and went back to music. Otherwise, who knows?"

It was the Beatles and their Ed Sullivan appearance in 1964 that further turned on the light for Dennis, though he admits his first assessment of "I Wanna Hold Your Hand" was that the popular tune was "baloney."

"I listened and I didn't get it," he says. Still, the phenomenon was intoxicating.

"I remember we were sitting and watching the TV in my house. I looked at it and I thought, 'Well, there you go. That's what I'm going to do. Just like that.' And that's when we started to try to play rock songs."

We fast-forwarded the interview to 1979 and the album *Cornerstone*, maybe the first Styx album I bought. I had been pulled in by the ballads. Only in recent years had I learned that the album's turn away from prog rock had begun causing divisions in the band.

"After we did *Pieces of Eight* and we went to England for the first time, we were greeted with such derision by the press. They were in the throes of the punk revolution when we got there and we were labeled dinosaurs," Dennis recalled. "Hell, we'd just become successful in 1977 in a big way.... When we came back at the beginning of 1979, I just saw the handwriting on the wall, and I believed that if we continued in that direction our career would be finished. And so I kind of led the band to make *Cornerstone*, which was an album, from my point of view, which was not trying to be necessarily softer but more natural. If you listen, there's real stuff like 'Boat on the River,' stuff like 'First Time,' stuff like 'Babe'—even 'Lights.' I was going for something more organic, more naturalistic, because I knew we weren't going to evolve into a punk band."

I'd pushed a button. I buckled up.

"What people fail to realize is, any album that we did—any album—really 90% of it reflected the songs people brought in," he said. "What people don't understand is, we never over-recorded. In other words, we wrote almost to the song. If there were eight songs or nine songs on a Styx album, those were primarily the eight or nine songs that were brought in by the writers. There weren't 15 or 20."

Dennis was on a roll. I wasn't going to stop him.

"The funny thing about *Cornerstone*...you like that record, and the funny thing about it is 'Babe' was never supposed to be on that record. It was a song I wrote for my wife as a present, never intending it to be a Styx song. And 'Boat on the River,' when Tommy played it for me on a bunch of song ideas he had on a cassette, I just said—He said, 'I have this song, but it's not a Styx song.' And I said, 'Why not?' I said, 'Not a Styx song? Well, maybe it isn't, but it's a great song and we'll make it ours.'"

I'd struck at the heart of the fissure point of Styx. This is where Dennis took over the leadership of the band, creating platinum records and underlying resentments from his bandmates.

It's here where Dennis asked the next question before I could ask it: For a guy who was so motivated by the Beatles, Styx sounded nothing like them. And yet it appeared the old McCartney-Lennon rivalry was unfolding regardless.

"Our music did not sound like the Beatles in any way, shape, or form," he said. "I could never find it in myself to use those Beatle tricks in Styx records because they were sacred to me. But what they did always influenced my thinking. So, I mean, you could have 'Revolution' right next to 'Ob-La-Di' and I could enjoy it."

"If I just brought you from another planet and sat you down and you knew nothing about Styx, and I play three songs for you—I play 'Babe,' 'Renegade,' and 'Mr. Roboto'—what would you say those songs have in common?"

Nothing, I replied.

"Nothing. You are a fan of my vision, which was I wanted Styx to be the band that lots of different people could come to the same party in. You know what I mean?"

How could anyone disagree? Dennis was at the pulpit. I didn't really need to ask him anything more to keep the sermon coming. I sat back and just listened.

"I'd like people to understand that Styx, in my mind, was never intended to just be one thing. What is your favorite Styx song? Quick."

I couldn't pick one. Dennis challenged me to pick three. I confess I panic when the tables get turned on me as an interviewer. I blurted out "Castle Walls," "Don't Let It End," and "First Time."

"Okay," Dennis said, preparing to make quick work of me. "If you listen to 'Castle Walls' and 'First Time,' you wouldn't think they were from the same band."

No, of course not, I confirmed. We were inching closer to the million-dollar question: How was it that Dennis wasn't a part of this amazing band anymore? The popular theory is that his bandmates grew weary of his softer-rock tendencies—'Babe' was a huge hit but not with the band members. Documentaries usually point to *Kilroy Was Here* and the plan by Dennis to dramatize the start of every live show to match the record's concept. It was the bridge too far for Tommy Shaw and James "JY" Young.

I kept looking for an opening for the *Kilroy* discussion. Dennis was still teaching a history lesson for me on the band's sound. He described the early years as "The Who meets Emerson, Lake & Palmer meets Yes meets Three Dog Night."

"When the public at large discovered us, Queen, Kansas, Foreigner, Boston had all come, had huge successes before us. It was a musical style that we were doing unsuccessfully, but it wasn't derivative of anybody," he said.

I saw my opening.

Kansas, Journey, REO Speedwagon—all bands that transitioned from a harder edge to a softer, FM-friendly sound. Styx did the same thing beginning with *Cornerstone* in 1979, continuing with *Paradise Theater* in 1981, and finishing with *Kilroy Was Here* in 1983. It's worth noting that *Kilroy* was the band's fifth platinum record in a row, a streak dating back to 1977's *Grand Illusion*. The band has yet to release another platinum album since *Kilroy*.

"I want to talk about *Kilroy* for a second," I told Dennis. This interview was long before Zoom was an option for recording interviews, so I listened for any sigh or verbal inflection that would signal his objection. Nothing. I went on.

The *Kilroy* tour was the first time I'd been allowed to drive myself to a concert. It was in downtown St. Petersburg, about a 45-minute drive. I took a date—Janette, the former girlfriend who triggered so many Styx musical cues for me. It was raining like hell that evening. It was a miracle I found the concert hall at all in that weather. I remember every detail of the show—I even kept the concert T-shirt far longer than it was wearable. Dennis listened patiently.

"'If you could go back to that record and that tour, would you do anything differently?" I asked. "Knowing the series of events that would follow *Kilroy*, would you go back and do anything differently?"

With no pause whatsoever, Dennis said: "I'd have had the Roboto mask made larger because it didn't fit well on my face."

We both busted up laughing.

"Yeah, I think," Dennis paused. "Look, I can go back. Rarely will an artist look at what he's done, no matter how much it's appreciated and respected, and not believe in their heart that they couldn't have made it better."

"Here is the fundamental problem with *Kilroy*," he continued. "More than any song about a robot, more than my encouragement and almost insistence that we try to act on stage a little bit and tell a story in a real dramatic setting, more than any of that, the greatest failing of it is…"

I was holding my breath.

"I've said this before: I needed 'Renegade' on that album. The worst thing about that record is my premise being that rock 'n' roll music was being subverted, and it was being censored to the point of putting rock stars in jail. This is my premise. Correct?"

"Right," I agreed.

"There weren't any songs on that record that really encapsulated the spirit of true rock music. There isn't a 'Blue Collar Man,' 'Rockin' the Paradise,' or 'Renegade.' The truth of the matter is, nobody brought those songs in. What we really needed musically was a song like 'Renegade' because the characters in *Kilroy* were based on the personalities. I mean, Tommy Shaw is the 'Renegade' rebel. I was the least likely guy in the band to write that kind of song. I'm better at ballads in the big Art Rock statement. That's the thing that I would like to change. I would like to have had a couple more really great rock songs on there."

Would a couple more rock songs have made a difference? Try exploring the history of Styx and decide for yourself. Some reports say Tommy wasn't happy beginning with the songs "Babe" and "First Time" back in 1979. Another report says Dennis was briefly fired and quickly rehired in 1980. I wasn't going to spend my precious time with Dennis asking for a scorecard, but he surprised me again.

"I want to be clear: Tommy quit the band onstage during the *Kilroy* tour," Dennis said. "He quit the band, and we were faced with what was going to happen next. And John and Chuck wanted to replace Tommy and just move forward, go right back in the studio, do a summer sort of greatest hits tour with a live album with a replacement, and then move forward. And I couldn't understand that because to me, fundamentally, I believe that the fan base really liked Tommy and liked us together, and asking them to suddenly like somebody else, it just felt wrong to me."

Tommy went on to record and release three solo albums in the '80s after leaving Styx. In 1989, he formed the supergroup Damn Yankees along with Jack Blades of Night Ranger, Ted Nugent, and Michael Cartellone. The band's biggest hit—"High Enough"—was a Shaw composition.

Dennis would record his own solo album—*Desert Moon*—in 1989, scoring a Top 10 hit with the title track. He stunned me with his next reveal.

"I never wanted to make a solo album," he said. "I only recorded *Desert Moon* to have something to do."

Those songs of his from the solo record, they could have been Styx songs, I thought. Dennis read my mind.

"'Desert Moon' would've been a huge hit for Styx," he said. "We'd have gotten together and that song would've been fundamentally the same, but it would've been different because we'd have gotten in the room, and everybody's personality would have been brought to bear to the sound and the interpretation. I think it might've been a Top 3 record for Styx. Tommy and I would've been singing together on the choruses. We'd have been in harmony."

I told Dennis I'm a huge fan of the music videos he did for *Desert Moon*. He showed off his acting chops—a hobby he'd embrace further in decades to follow.

"The thing about acting is, I did some stage acting, but I didn't commit to it. I'd have to go to L.A., get an agent, and I probably should have but I didn't. I always wanted to be in the Beatles more than anything, and I got that from being in Styx. I would've rather been in the Beatles than be Brad Pitt."

Dennis insisted his only real contribution to the *Desert Moon* videos was insisting on using a 1965 Mustang instead of an MG for the story.

"That car is incredibly important symbolically to that video," he said.

"A return to the past?" I asked.

Not exactly, he said. "It's the idea of letting go of things that are in the past that you really are...no longer part of them. Those are moments in time and they cannot be relived."

I gulped.

"That's painful to hear in a way," I confessed. "I pretty much make my living these days writing about the past and trying to come to grips with it and maybe come to peace with it in my own way."

"The fact is this: when you're young, of course you're gonna write about the future because that's what's coming up," he said. "And then the older you get, the more reflective you get if you're not some sort of a retarded adolescent."

"What I was saying in 'Desert Moon' is, you really can't hold on to those things. In your heart you can, but you can't continue to replay the same movie in your own life."

I wanted to replay the movie, though. I wanted Styx to reunite. I wanted to see Dennis standing onstage with Chuck, Tommy, and JY.

"I can't impress upon the fans enough that I did not and I'm not standing in the way of that happening," Dennis said.

Deep down, I don't think it'll happen.

Weeks after my interview with Dennis, he invited me to watch rehearsal from backstage as he ran through some songs with The Florida Orchestra for a show later that night in Clearwater. It was the same venue where I had first met him and experienced his razor-sharp sense of humor years earlier. Exhausted from the show, Dennis still took time to pose for photos with members of the orchestra, graciously shaking every hand.

Dennis turned out to be the opposite of what I'd originally heard about him. He was thankful, humble, and gracious—even taking another 10 minutes of his time to chat me up about the article and my thoughts on the show.

A career and legacy like his deserve one more act. One more chance to wear that Roboto mask—as tight as it might be—and dazzle the fans. One more bow. If it happens, I want to be there too. It's a performance that needs an encore.

CONVERSATIONS BETWEEN THE HITS

BRET MICHAELS has a reputation for being unfailingly warm, generous with his time, and game for just about anything—and in 2010, he lived up to it. That year, the Poison frontman and solo rocker was set to perform a free concert after a Tampa Bay Rays game in St. Petersburg, and he joined my co-host Sean and me on the podcast to promote it. He didn't just answer questions. He invited us to throw a baseball around with him after the game before he took the stage. (Why we didn't follow through on that invite is still mind-boggling to me.)

Bret was struggling with his health at the time—he had recently been diagnosed with patent foramen ovale (a hole in his heart) and would go through surgery to repair it a few months later. The year before—at the Tony Awards in 2009—he'd suffered a near-fatal brain hemorrhage when he'd collided with a descending set piece after a performance. Months before our interview it had been an appendectomy that had sidelined him. But the guy is just indestructible.

We asked if he'd had to pull back on his performances a little to accommodate his health issues.

"Here's the thing: I haven't altered it a bit," Bret answered. "I give everything that I've got."

We asked if he had a bucket list of things still to conquer.

"I have a whole slew of things, and I upped that ante right after the brain hemorrhage," he said. "I figured I better get adding into this thing pretty quick at the rate I'm losing organs. I've never sky-dived, so that's gotta be on there. And I'll tell you, for me—and I say this without a doubt—one time I wanna sing the national anthem at the Super Bowl. I got to do it at Three Rivers Stadium right on the weekend they were taking it down, so that was huge. But to be able to sing the national anthem at the Super Bowl, that'd be huge."

On our bucket list was getting him to tell us the "Every Rose Has Its Thorn" story. It didn't take much prodding.

"There's a lot of pain behind that song," I began asking, "and I'm just kinda curious: How much of that do you channel each time you perform it? Does it still make you ache a little bit?"

"That song, for me, is bittersweet," Bret began. "I wrote that literally in a laundromat in Dallas, Texas. And I had convinced Poison—this is one of my brilliant moves—to play a country bar in Dallas, Texas. Besides the band members there were nine other people at the bar. It was early on in our career."

"I went back, called my girlfriend, we broke up, and I wrote that song, and so it's bittersweet," he said. "When I play it, there's still that feeling, that emotion that you get anytime you hear something that reminds you of something, especially if you wrote it. But at the same time, I'm really thankful because it really struck a chord somewhere in America and around the world because it became the No. 1 song in, like, 52 countries or something. It was ridiculous."

In 2023, I finally saw Bret Michaels perform live. He was on The 80s Cruise that year. My wife and I made it about three songs through before our ears gave out on us. Two days later, my wife got her photo taken with Bret and Lou Gramm as they both disembarked the ship at the same time. Speaking of Lou...

LOU GRAMM always struck me as one of the good ones—but the memory I associate with his voice has nothing to do with kindness or nostalgia. It goes back to March 1982, when Foreigner was scheduled to headline Rock Super Bowl XIV in Orlando. Two days before the show, Randy Rhoads was killed in a plane crash, and my dad woke me up early to tell me the news. Foreigner still performed but Ozzy canceled. I was crushed, and I've never quite separated that feeling from Foreigner's music since.

In 2010, long after his time with Foreigner had ended, Lou was touring with his own band and had a gig coming up in Tampa Bay. My cohost Sean and I were both eager to talk to him—for very different reasons.

I wanted to ask him about that Rock Super Bowl and how Randy's tragic accident had affected everyone backstage. I ended up not finding the right opening. It's also possible I completely chickened out. Lou was having a great time chatting with us, and it's likely I didn't want to bring him down.

Sean, on the other hand, had been waiting for this moment since he was a teenage boy—for very different reasons.

"I've told this story on our show before, and I have to tell it to the man himself," Sean began. "When I was a young lad, on my very special night with a young lady, when I became a man..."

"Oh, boy," Lou replied.

"The song that was playing as I lost my precious virginity was 'Midnight Blue'!" Sean announced.

"And I was told only 'Waiting for a Girl' and 'I Want to Know What Love Is' work," Lou said. "But you see that, 'Midnight Blue' is all right too, isn't it?"

"Listen, no offense," Sean continued. "It's not like I queued it up. It was just kind of serendipity that the radio was on and I was on, and all of a sudden Lou Gramm was in the room with us and something just happened."

Sean was a genius that day, and to be honest I've never met anyone as comfortable in his own skin during interviews with our heroes. I'd have never had the guts to open with that story with Lou. (Hell, I interviewed Tom Bailey of Thompson Twins a few years later and never confessed to him that "Hold Me Now" bears that same distinction.)

I'd have to wait until 2023 to hear Lou perform "Midnight Blue" live. It was the ninth song in his setlist for The 80s Cruise, sandwiched between "Just Between You and Me" (another absolute classic from his solo career) and, yes, "I Want to Know What Love Is."

KEVIN CRONIN has written songs that don't just play on the radio—they show up at turning points. REO Speedwagon's music has scored first kisses, last goodbyes, and a thousand moments in between—including plenty of my own. When REO came through Clearwater's Ruth Eckerd Hall in 2007, Kevin joined the podcast and was generous with his time, which only encouraged my co-host Sean to see just how far he could push the conversation.

"I gotta believe, Kevin, somebody like you, you must have people come up to you all the time saying that they got married to this song, or they lost their virginity to this song," Sean began. "I mean, you make these songs that really get to people's hearts. Do you have stories like that?"

"What I was hoping for was that people would come up to me and want to have sex with me when they listen to the song," Kevin shot back. "That unfortunately hasn't happened a whole lot lately."

Wow, hadn't seen that coming.

"We do get—we get some wacky stories," Kevin continued. "This was up in Syracuse, New York. As I was singing 'Can't Fight This Feeling,' I kind of out of the corner of my eye noticed that a lot of the people in the audience weren't really focused on the stage anymore. Everyone looks to their left. And so I kind of looked over there, and there was a guy on one knee in the aisle proposing to his girlfriend as we sang the song."

Sean was in the middle of saying "I thought you were gonna say..." Yeah, you can fill in the blanks there. But Kevin continued.

"You can laugh about it and stuff like that. With the internet it's a lot easier to stay on top of the fan mail that comes in, and so I get all kinds of messages, and I recently got a message from a guy who was going through chemotherapy. And he would play our song 'Keep Pushin' over and over again as he went through it just to help him to make it through the process. I'm, like, 'Man, that's pretty awesome.' I got an email recently from a guy in Iraq who plays our music inside of the armored vehicles and inside of the tanks as they're, like, going into battle. They're playing 'Ridin' the Storm Out.'"

We were awestruck at this moment.

"Oh, check this out," he continued. "The surgeon who just recently did surgery on my dad said that when they're in surgery doing, like, open heart, like heart transplants and stuff, they're playing our *Hits* record while they're doing surgery. He said, 'It just kind of calms everybody down.'"

"So it's nice to see that people just go out and dance and have a great time and sing along at our concerts too. But it's nice to know that there are other things that the music is used for that take it a step beyond just 'drink some beer and go out and dance.'"

I felt almost bad to bring it back to myself, but there was something I had always wanted to relate to Kevin if I got the chance. In the early '80s, when our social lives revolved around Saturday afternoons at Super Skate and never-ending spins of the *Hi-Infidelity* album, I had a girlfriend for a brief few weeks. Janette would be the first girl I'd kiss, probably the first I'd even confessed to being in love with. But then I heard it from a friend who...heard it from a friend who...heard it from another Janette had been messing around. With a guy named Harold! (Seriously?)

I told Kevin the story and said I always relive a bit of the pain when they play "Take It on the Run."

"I hear that, dude," Kevin said with whatever empathy he could have for a stranger interviewing him over the phone. "That's pretty raw, but it happens. 'Time for Me to Fly' is another one that I'm hearing people using as the kiss-off song. So, but hey, you're better off for it. Who needs her anyway?"

"But Steve," Sean interjected. "How many girls have you seduced while 'Keep On Loving You' is playing?"

"Countless," I replied, giving Sean and Kevin the punchline they were hoping for.

Janette and I have stayed in touch over the years. She didn't end up with Harold, to my relief, but she once asked to borrow $100 to fix her air conditioner, money she never repaid. I'm not getting that money back now, am I, Janette?

TIM BUTLER of The Psychedelic Furs turned out to be as thoughtful and open as the band's music is restless. I'd seen the Furs circa 2009 at a venerable theater in Ybor City, Tampa's historic Latin district, and the band had blown me away with their onstage energy and seemingly endless bucket of memorable anthems.

Two years later, in June 2011, the Furs were returning to town, and I had a chance to chat up the bassist and co-founder. Tim Butler and his brother Richard founded the English band back in 1977 but had a reputation for not being the closest of siblings. It felt like a fair place to start.

"Several bands that are composed of brothers are famous for not getting along: Oasis and The Kinks," I began. "So how do you and Richard get along, traditionally, on and off the road?"

Thankfully Tim didn't chafe at the question.

"Very well," he said. "Years ago, when we first started touring in the mid-'80s when we were drinking and stuff, we'd get into fights and give each other black eyes and stuff, but they're all over in 10 minutes. But since we got back together and we don't drink and party like we used to, the old egos and the sibling rivalry have disappeared because we've both discovered that we're equally as important to the first sound."

So it was all in the past. But I was curious about how their dynamic worked today.

"I'll come up with the chord structures for songs, and then I'll play them to Richard, and Richard will say, 'Why don't you extend this piece?' or 'Can we go somewhere else with this chord-wise?' It's, like, teamwork."

That year, the Furs were touring to mark the 30th anniversary of *Talk Talk Talk,* so the band was playing the entire album each night on stage. The 1981 album was the band's second and had the nominal hits "Dumb Waiters" and "Pretty in Pink," which would become a huge hit for them when it was reworked in 1986 for the movie of the same name.

How did the band land that prime spot in the *Pretty in Pink* soundtrack, I asked.

"Originally we weren't going to be (involved), but Molly Ringwald was a big fan of the original recording of 'Pretty in Pink,' and she played it to John Hughes and said, 'You know, can you write me a movie vehicle around this song?' which he did."

The song had a different sound in 1986, though, as any fan of the original tune could tell you. What happened?

"They couldn't use the original version because they were saying one of the guitars was slightly out of tune, which I think it gives you character," Tim said. "But they were gonna find some other band to re-record the song. And we said, 'Hey, no, we'll re-record it. There's nobody else who's re-recorded our songs in the movie.' So we went in and re-recorded it. It wasn't as good as the original, but at least it was us doing it."

STEVE KILBEY always felt slightly out of reach—and that was part of the appeal. I'd been a big fan of his band The Church since I was been a teenager. They were cool and ethereal in a way other Aussie bands weren't. But it felt like Steve rarely did interviews, and the chances of one falling into my lap seemed remote.

But in the fall of 2023, The Church announced a tour of the U.S. that included an unlikely run of six shows in Florida. I got an email asking if I'd like to talk with Steve. I couldn't say yes fast enough.

The conversation got off to an unexpected start, thanks to an awkward admission on my part.

"I keep going back and forth on whether or not I want to confess that in the mid-'80s, I used to drive my car around listening to 'Unguarded Moment' all the time while trying to match your vocals," I said, then singing, "Tell those men with horses for hearts…."

"Nobody wants to be doing that," Steve replied. "I don't wanna be doing that."

Singers not loving some of their biggest songs isn't a new discovery. Jim Kerr of Simple Minds has a complicated relationship with "Don't You (Forget About Me)." Billy Joel has an on-again/

off-again relationship with "We Didn't Start the Fire" and "Uptown Girl." And there are scores of stories about bands nearly imploding when a song written by an outsider—Berlin's "Take My Breath Away" by Giorgio Moroder and Tom Whitlock comes to mind comes to mind—pretty much split the group in half.

"I hate 'Unguarded Moment,'" Steve said flatly. "I don't mind 'Under the Milky Way.' The other ones, I don't mind them. 'Unguarded Moment'—I don't know why I am not terribly enamored of that song."

The tune, the second single released off the band's 1981 debut album *Of Skins and Heart*, was in fact written by Steve and the group's bassist, Mikela Uniacke, to whom Steve was married at the time. I wish I'd known that when I asked about the song.

"Unguarded Moment" would peak at No. 22 on the Australian charts while not making it at all here in the U.S. (The Church finally penetrated the U.S. market with 1988's *Starfish* album.)

"Well, we keep it," Steve said of the tune. "I enjoy the pleasure other people get out of hearing it."

Steve went on to admit that "Under the Milky Way"—by far the band's biggest hit here—likewise held no charm for him, but that they continued to perform it.

"When a song has deep meaning to the audience, it's churlish to not get some enjoyment out of that," he said. "I think most people would say that. I mean, does Paul McCartney really love playing 'Hey Jude' every night? I don't know. I think it's just something you do for other people's pleasure."

At this point, I wondered if I'd dug a hole I couldn't climb out of. Letting an interview go negative wouldn't be a good look for me, so I tried to rally.

"That's a great answer," I blurted out. "That's as good of an answer as I think there is."

"I think you've got to hope that the song that you're known for isn't such a bad one, because you've got to do it," he said. "If I live for another 20 years and I keep playing America, every time I come there, no matter what else I'm doing, I've got to do 'Under the Milky Way.' I'm very grateful that that song is a song that I can play as an old man as much as I could play as a young man. I'm glad it's not a novelty, stupid song that I have to regret writing. I'm glad it's kind of a nice, okay, pleasant song to do. One can only imagine if your big song was some horrible number. There was a guy in Australia who had one big hit. Have you ever heard that one, 'Shaddap You Face'?"

Of course, I said. "Shaddap You Face" by Joe Dolce was No. 1 for eight weeks in Australia in 1980. A year later it would top the British charts, keeping Ultravox's anthem "Vienna" out of the No. 1 spot.

"Imagine if you had to do that every night. 'What's-a matter you? Ah, shaddap-a you face!' If that was me, I think I'd rather work for the post office than have to go around playing that every night," Steve said. "I don't know. I imagine those guys in Men at Work. Do you really want to play 'Land Down Under' every night? I don't know. I wouldn't."

CAROL DECKER is exactly the kind of artist you hope will join you on The 80s Cruise.

Warm, generous, and happy to trade stories, the T'Pau front-woman came on the podcast in late 2024 ahead of her appearance on the 2025 sailing. I wanted to see if she'd be a good fit to host trivia one afternoon at sea. She was—and then some.

During our short chat together, she professed her love for late '70s disco and festival concert bookings. She also described her inability to appreciate the '90s grunge movement that perhaps put a premature pause on her band's momentum. But it was her stories about England's *Top of the Pops* TV show that really dazzled me.

"America had *American Bandstand,* but Britain's *Top of the Pops* always seemed so much cooler to me," I began.

"It was the one show that grandchildren and grandparents, all the generations, could sit and watch," Carol said. "It was a pivotal point for the charts, so to be on it—I think I grinned so hard my cheeks hurt. And we finally got to perform 'Heart and Soul,' our first big international hit. I couldn't stop smiling all the time."

Top of the Pops, for those who haven't seen the clips on YouTube, was a music chart TV show. Broadcast weekly on the BBC from 1964 to 2006, it was the world's longest-running music show. Each episode featured performances of the week's best-selling tunes. Just about every British act of our beloved decade has made an appearance on *Top of the Pops.* T'Pau's first performance came in 1987.

"They would rehearse you all day—absolutely all day," Carol said of the show's staff. "You'd be in at 9 a.m., and they had you there all day. Everything was union. So I had to smuggle in my own makeup artist as a personal assistant and hide all her makeup and brushes and stuff."

Performing alongside T'Pau that night were Wet Wet Wet and Then Jerico. Also another band you might have heard of: The Bee Gees.

"They had a huge entourage, and they had the most gigantic security men as well, who just politely but firmly moved everyone out of the way," Carol recalled.

Another pair of celebrities were also on hand that night.

"Paul and Linda McCartney, his lovely late dear wife, stood watching us for ages because Paul was promoting one of his solo albums," Carol said. "And they were staring. Anyway, when I finished sound checking, they came over and said, 'Oh, we hope we weren't intimidating you. Sorry, I didn't mean to stare. It's just that you remind us so much of our little girl, Stella.' Their daughter Stella, the amazing fashion designer, was a toddler at the time and had bright red hair, as did I. They'd been away from home touring for ages. And so they were just going, 'Oh, Stella's gonna look like Carol when she grows up.'"

"We became pals," Carol said of the McCartneys. "For the longest time I was quite friendly with the McCartneys, and Linda used to send me a Christmas calendar of all her fantastic photographs."

"When you're in the charts, you tend to get invited to all the red carpet events when you're hot, so you bump into each other and rekindle," she said. "It was like a very nice acquaintanceship. Not gonna say I was ever around for tea. But for several years, I got Christmas cards and calendars."

JOE ELLIOTT of Def Leppard was 10 years away from being inducted into the Rock & Roll Hall of Fame when he joined *Stuck in the '80s* for a visit in 2009. Def Leppard was visiting Tampa Bay for a show alongside Poison and Cheap Trick. It was a powerhouse lineup that *Entertainment Weekly* called the show to see that summer.

"All bands have been through that period where you take out an opening act, and nobody's ever heard of them and everybody's sitting, twitching in their seats if they're not sat in the beer tent," Joe began. "We've done our best to, for these last five years or so, to try and make this, like, an eventful tour."

Def Leppard has continued to headline tours fairly consistently since the mid-'80s, when *Pyromania* and *Hysteria* were the darlings of the album charts. Both records got their unique sound from Robert John "Mutt" Lange. We had about a billion questions for Joe about the South African producer, whose fingerprints are all over hits by Heart, Foreigner, the Cars, Bryan Adams, and countless others.

"We were fans of his work before we worked with him," Joe said. "Let's not forget, it's a little-known fact that we actually tried to get Mutt for our first album, but knowing full well he wouldn't get on board. He hadn't ever heard the demos, and Mutt is pretty picky about who he works with."

It turns out that opening for AC/DC, for whom Mutt had produced *Back in Black*, was the key.

"He came to an AC/DC concert and we were the opening act," Joe said. "The manager kind of dragged him onto the side of the stage to watch us for 20 or 30 minutes. And Mutt was actually quite impressed with what he saw. And he was saying, 'Yeah, they do have something. It's just they need a bit of work, but they've got something.'"

Mutt's first job was producing the band's 1981 album *High 'n' Dry*. While not an instant hit or chart climber, critics at the time lauded the added confidence that Mutt gave the band.

"We were, like, just young kids," Joe said. "We were like rock 'n' roll students who were much more willing to listen to him than most seasoned musicians would be. It was kind of like going back to musical rock high school, if you like. As much as we were making records and, little did we know, making history, we were more than prepared to actually work with him in the sense of suggestions and stuff. It wasn't like we were just puppets to him or anything like that. But we would use him as the ultimate referee on a decision rather than beat the shit out of each other."

In 1983, when it came time to record *Pyromania*, Mutt had a proposal for the band.

"He said to us, 'Look, we can go out and make another *High 'n' Dry*, or we can go and try to make a record that nobody else has ever made before,' to which the five of us would be looking at each other with big, wide eyes going, 'Yeah, that sounds like way more than an option!'"

Mutt warned Joe and the band that the process would involve a lot of dead-end roads, but that they'd turn it into a hell of a trip.

"We did all sorts of experimental stuff with sounds and samples, but back when we made that record nobody in rock was doing it," Joe said. "So we knew that we had gone at least one foot further than most people because we were the ones that were prepared to go there and not just set the gear up and play live in the studio and then overdub some vocals and stuff."

Mutt Lange would end up getting writing credits for all but one song on *Pyromania*, which had three songs that landed in the Top 40—"Photograph," "Rock of Ages," and "Foolin'." The record sold more than 10 million copies in the U.S., landing as high as No. 2 on the album charts.

What kept it out of the top spot? In 1983, only one album had that power: Michael Jackson's *Thriller*.

TAYLOR DAYNE has a deep respect for '80s fans—the kind that show up, sing every word, and trust the moment. I saw that firsthand on the 2020 voyage of The 80s Cruise, one of the last ships to sail before the pandemic hit. Taylor had joined the lineup at the last minute, stepping in for a band sidelined by early travel restrictions. The artists boarded first, hours before the passengers, and she stood just behind me in line for the gangplank. I didn't have the courage to introduce myself then—and I didn't confess that later when we finally talked on the podcast.

"It was a lot of trust amongst the people there," Taylor said of the times we were then in. "I don't think we knew anything. We knew nothing." Nothing of the panic that was gripping people around the world. Nothing of the growing travel bans. Nothing of the impending toilet paper shortages.

Taylor's performance that week was particularly memorable to me. I planned to propose to my girlfriend that first night. The entire time Melissa and I sat at the show listening to hit after hit—"Prove Your Love," "Don't Rush Me," "Love Will Lead You Back," and of course her biggest anthem, "Tell It to My Heart"—I had an engagement ring sitting in the world's most oversized jewelry box in my pants pocket. I got a little misty-eyed during one of Taylor's numbers—caught up in the event that was to happen later that night—and Melissa noticed.

"I thought, 'Wow, I had no idea Steve was so into Taylor Dayne!'" she would later tell me.

"Wow, that's beautiful," Taylor said when I recounted the story. "When did you ask her?"

"At midnight that night," I said.

"I figured you were doing it during the show," she said. "Wow, that's incredible."

"Oh, no, I think she would kill me if I interrupted your show for that," I said, not really joking.

Taylor is one of the truly dazzling success stories of the second half of the decade. Her first two albums went double platinum. Her first seven singles all landed in the Top 10 of the U.S. charts. Still, she bristles at suggestions her fame came too easily. She began performing professionally as young as 16 in such little-known bands as Felony and Next.

"It was an overnight success on some levels, but for me it was that little girl who was fighting her way to be seen all these years," she said. "I learned my chops in the clubs and went to everything from Bitter End, Bottom Line, CBGB. I saw everything. I lived it. You know, I was a New York girl."

I asked if the rumors were true that her voice track for "Tell It to My Heart" had been recorded at five in the morning.

"Oh, yeah," she said. "This was during the times at a studio where we could afford to be in there. I worked in a Russian nightclub in Brighton Beach. My typical Friday, Saturday, Sunday didn't end till 3 or 4 a.m. And so doing the vocals at five was no big deal. That was our life."

The success of that first hit—particularly in Europe—scored Taylor an opening slot on Michael Jackson's Bad tour in 1988. Instead of playing Brighton Beach, she found herself playing before crowds of up to 100,000.

"It was past surreal. I was like, 'Bye-bye Russian club!'" she said. "I think I threw up and shit myself the first time I was walking out because it sounds like the Colosseum. You're, like, 'the roar of the lions.' That's what the sound of all these people sounds like."

How do you focus in situations like that? I asked.

"The little person inside you says, 'What am I doing here? Do I deserve this? What is this?' I have to deal deeply with issues about feeling deserving of something like this and not just taking it for granted. It was frightening. But behind me was my family, my band."

Overcoming a difficult childhood and coming to terms with her success became common themes during our conversation. She details much of it in her 2019 memoir *Tell It to My Heart: How I Lost My S#*T, Conquered My Fear, and Found My Voice*. I had skimmed the book before our interview but I wished I'd read it cover to cover. Still, I complimented her for wearing her heart on her sleeve.

"It's taken me years to build the sustainability," she told me as we were finishing up our talk. "Years and years and years of really working on mental, emotional, spiritual health and feeling deserving. Not everything adds up, but you have to add up. You have to find the worth. You have to develop that strength."

"We all had 18 minutes to do our allocated four songs. And I think we were just so petrified that something was not gonna work..."

VOICES FROM LIVE AID

Where were you on July 13, 1985? I was sitting on a creaky old couch in my college dorm lounge in Gainesville, Florida, watching Live Aid and wishing I was there. If there's a high-water mark of the 1980s, I've always considered it to be Live Aid, the massive two-venue charity concert that attracted 1.9 billion TV viewers and raised more than $100 million for Ethiopian famine relief. Back then, my generation thought we could change the world. Today I'm not even sure we can save it.

Over the years of podcasting, I've tried to take extra time with artists who performed at Live Aid. I want to know what they remember and what still stands out to them today. I've been lucky to talk to a handful of participants.

TOM BAILEY of Thompson Twins fame was touring in 2014 with two other veterans of Live Aid—Midge Ure and Howard Jones—on the Retro Futura tour. His interview remains one of my favorites—he was an original "bucket list" hope of mine. During our talk, he admitted to me that he had to go out and buy a Thompson

Twins greatest hits CD to help relearn the songs for his tour. It was his first time on the road in about 30 years.

"I was doing other things, and I obviously wanted to move away from, kind of, mainstream music for a while," Tom said by way of explanation. "Also I was raising kids, and I thought I'd earned a little bit of a rest."

We both laughed, and a wave of relief swept through me at this point. Tom, like so many other U.K. artists, would be a joy to speak with.

"I really was distracted by other creative projects," he said. "So I got involved in other things, which kept me very busy but didn't involve such a high profile in terms of the mainstream media. I wasn't chasing chart positions with the same vigor."

One thing my generation doesn't usually absorb very quickly is the high level of energy required for our favorite musicians to remain at the top of the business. Tom confirmed as much.

"People want the same thing out of you again and again and again, and it became a little bit restricting," he said. "And I knew I wanted to do other things that I wasn't allowed to do within that context. The other thing is, of course, psychologically you start to deny your past. You start to say, 'Oh, well, I don't do that stuff anymore.' So it almost becomes a kind of survival necessity to say, 'I'm never doing that again. I put it behind me and blah, blah, blah.' And I'd more or less completed that denial project, and given it no thought for a long, long time. I never thought we would ever be doing this. So only about six months ago did it occur to me that I was going to change my mind."

I asked what his personal expectations were for this tour—and his comeback. I wanted to know what he wanted to accomplish by playing these songs again.

"Well, in a way I've already discovered that reengaging with the songs was a more powerful and satisfactory thing than I ever expected it to be," he said. "So the validity of them is absolute for me. I've only chosen the ones that I felt I could inhabit or reinhabit successfully, 100%. I don't want to do this half-heartedly. Luckily the songs are powerful enough, and partly because I discover new meanings in them with the benefit of hindsight and 30 years more experience."

One of the songs Tom found new meaning in was "If You Were Here." It wasn't released as a single but instead found popularity and fans because of its placement at the end of John Hughes's *Sixteen Candles*.

"I thought it was really about the question of honesty in personal relationships," Tom said of the song. "But going back to it, it really struck me very, very powerfully that it was also about reassessing the honesty of our optimism about the future. And I thought 30 years ago, we had this optimism that the world was going to be a better place, and yet I felt that we hadn't fully delivered. I'm not just talking about the Thompson Twins. I'm talking about the human race."

I was struck by his revelation and its correlation with how I felt about Live Aid and its mission and message.

"We haven't fully delivered on that optimism, there's still an awful lot to be done," Tom continued. "And so I've actually written two more verses to more fully emphasize that feeling that I got from the song, that was about questioning our unfinished business as responsible people."

At the time of Live Aid, Tom and his generation of artists and musicians also knew there was an awful lot to be done. During the benefit, he performed onstage for 18 minutes in Philadelphia.

I asked what memories popped into his mind first about that day.

"Well, our 18 minutes should have been longer," Tom said. "We had a song cut off because the previous band went on too long or something [laughter]. We were running late, just like I've been having the same problem with these interviews, just as yours [laughter]. Here's a funny thing: we were introduced in front of the curtain by, I think, Bette Midler."

Oh, God, he was right. One of the details I overlook when I wax poetic about Live Aid was the use of actors as emcees between the acts. Crazy.

"Then the curtain goes up, and on the other side of the curtain is my microphone stand. I'm standing back by my guitar amplifier, with the guitar, and I'm walking towards the microphone stand during 'Hold Me Now,' thinking by the time we've been 32 bars into this introduction, I have to sing the first line. And I realize that the mic stand was so far away that the guitar cable wasn't long enough to get there."

I was laughing but loving every second of this unexpected tale.

"So this is where you're in front of 90,000 people in the stadium and many millions watching on TV—that's not the time you want to have such a basic problem. So I had to decide to unplug the guitar and walk to the microphone stand."

Watch the DVD of the performance or the YouTube video, and you'll see Tom don a headset microphone to solve the dilemma. He would eventually be joined onstage by Madonna, Steve Stevens, and Nile Rodgers.

"We were working with Nile on the album. He'd just made an album with Madonna. So they were friends. I think we'd bumped into her a few times in the past and so we were kind of friendly. And Steve had made an appearance on that album," he said, explaining the seemingly unusual collaboration.

Even odder, I'd heard the musicians decided to go back to their hotel and play Scrabble when the set was over. I asked if that urban legend was true.

"That's absolutely correct," Tom said, laughing. "Nile, who was going through a difficult time with drugs and drink, was on a promise to return and not to party too hard. So we went back to his room, and we played Scrabble."

JIM KERR and Simple Minds were just beginning to really take off in America thanks to the movie *The Breakfast Club* and its anthem "Don't You Forget About Me." The Scottish band had formed in 1977 but hadn't found commercial success until the early '80s. They performed at Live Aid in Philadelphia. When I had a chance to interview Jim in 2011, I wasn't going to wait long to ask about that day.

"You know what, it was obviously overwhelming because it's the biggest gig we'd ever done, biggest gig I think most people had ever done," Jim said. "I'm not gonna say it passed me by, but it almost passed me by. I mean, of course we're only on stage for whatever it was, 15 minutes or 20 minutes as well. So there is that. But, I mean, when you think about it, we were either brave or mad. We went on stage and we started with a brand-new song that wasn't even recorded. No soundcheck."

The song was "Ghost Dancing," a tune off the album *Once Upon a Time* that wouldn't be released until the fall. It would go on to be a Top 20 song in the U.K., but it didn't make a mark in the U.S., despite being an instant classic when performed live on tours.

"Anyone else should have said, like, 'Are we sure about this, fellas? You've only got 15 minutes.' But I'm thinking of it now, I think we were a bit neurotic about the success of 'Don't You Forget About Me,' and we still are, but we thought, 'Oh, everyone's going to think that we're just a pop MTV band, and so let's go on and just show that there's something a bit more than that going on.'"

I decided to share my theory with Jim—my argument that Live Aid was my generation's Woodstock. That it was a musical event that we all experienced in our own way, but it still had political and global themes. I also pushed another theory.

"I also believe it can't be duplicated in any meaningful way today," I told him. "Is it fair to say that the current generation of music-makers don't really have the same concern, for lack of a better word, for the global issues that artists did back in the '80s?"

"First of all, I agree with you on that first part," he said. "It can never be repeated because even within its thing, it was the first televised global music event. It had never been done before and the first is the first, and it seemed like the whole planet was tuning in to it. And so, yeah, that was the first. It'll never be repeated with the same effect."

I could tell by his tone that the second part was something he was having trouble agreeing with.

"I'm reluctant to seemingly castigate the younger generation but I think it's true, what you're saying. However, I think the very nature of politics has changed so much since back then. I mean, back then everything seemed a lot more..."

"Black and white?" I asked.

"Yeah, a lot more black and white, a lot more polarized. There was a cold war that was left. There was apartheid, there was anti-apartheid, there was Greenpeace. Politics can be the coffee you buy in the supermarket. Politics can be if you go to The Gap or you don't go to The Gap."

So where did that leave us with Live Aid and the future of politics in music?

"I don't know if it's a reaction to the likes of the Bonos and the Peter Gabriels, and to an extent the Jim Kerrs and others. We were just one generation from the hippie thing. We still had a bit of that hippie ethic, even though it wouldn't have seemed so at the time.

We were so brought up to sort of fight the man, even though we made it look ridiculous as we were in the most capitalistic industry out here, and we're all making a fortune [laughter]. But we were brought up with the remnants of that hippie ethic. That doesn't seem to have trickled down to the current generation."

HOWARD JONES was the first musician I interviewed who had played the London venue of Live Aid at the famed Wembley Stadium. For years at every place I'd lived, I'd had a giant poster of the final moments of Live Aid with Freddie Mercury, Bono, and Bob Geldof standing there at the lip of that stage. Right next to them is a beaming Howard Jones. In 2010, I asked Howard about that night.

"I was very, very happy to be part of that," he said. "I know I only played one song…'Hide and Seek.' I was really, really proud to have a small part of that day and to contribute….I wasn't one of the ones who was pushing to get hold of a microphone. I was just happy to be there and share the stage with all those amazing artists."

Years later, in 2023, Howard was on the lineup for the annual voyage of The 80s Cruise. We were lucky enough to land him as our VIP guest for the trivia sessions we hosted on the ship. Again, I asked Howard to recall his memories of the night.

No transcript exists of that early afternoon on a Royal Caribbean ship in the middle of the ocean, but Howard dazzled the crowd with the story behind his performance. It seems the piano on stage that he'd have to use was the very one that Queen and Freddie Mercury used when touring. Phil Collins warned Howard, he said, that the keys were sticky and that he'd have to bang particularly hard on them to hear any sound.

Even now, when I watch Howard playing the piano by himself that day, I can see him concentrate on banging those keys and making his mark.

MIDGE URE really needs no introduction. The Scottish artist made his mark with Ultravox, Thin Lizzy, The Rich Kids, and Visage in the 1970s and '80s. He's also co-writer and producer of the charity single "Do They Know It's Christmas?" and the co-organizer of Live Aid. If you want chills to run up and down your body, queue up the live performance of "Vienna" from Wembley Stadium that July day in 1985. Without the benefit of a soundcheck or much time to warm up, Midge delivers each chorus with such power and vigor that I start tearing up every time I watch it.

I've had a few chances to interview Midge over the years, and it never gets old. He is one of the most generous souls I've ever chatted with, and the honor of spending an hour with him always makes me proud.

In 2014, Midge was touring with the Retro Futura tour—yes, the same tour that allowed me to catch up with Tom Bailey. In fact, I interviewed the pair on consecutive nights. I was probably losing my mind at the time over my good luck. With Howard Jones also on that tour, fans were about to see three of the Live Aid performers in action again.

"I still get very surprised today when I'm doing an interview with someone or I meet someone and they say, 'Hey, I was there.' You think, 'Oh my, wow,' because in the U.K. there was only 80,000 tickets, 80,000 people," Midge said of that summer day. "That's not a lot of people. And you think, 'Oh, wow, somebody was actually there and saw it and experienced it and breathed the same air I did that day.' That's fantastic."

While Midge made a huge contribution with Live Aid, his career is one so worthy of greater respect. Ultravox inspired generations of bands that followed. Even the late drummer of Rush—Neil Peart—name-checked Ultravox as an influence in conversations with reporters. Still, I've always felt they didn't get the credit they deserved. Did Midge feel the same way? He had written in his 2004 memoir—*If I Was...: The Autobiography*—that journalists had been rough on the band over the years.

"I think they saw us as bombastic and pompous and a bit above our station," Midge told me. "And possibly at some points, they were quite right. But they couldn't see that—take away the poor-faced guys in the videos and take away some of the imagery—that if you just listen to the music, the music was actually intelligent and smart and creative and pushed an awful lot of boundaries."

We went on to talk about the difference between Duran Duran and Ultravox—"They were younger and prettier," he said—and the role of social media for artists today. "I think you've got to embrace almost all of it," Midge said.

I didn't want to use up my time talking about social media, so I gently turned us in the direction of Band Aid. I asked what his first memory is when he hears "Do They Know It's Christmas?"

"That opening clang," he said instantly. "The bell—the multi-track vocal, the drum that I stole from Tears for Fears, all of that. It makes the hair on the back of your neck stand up because it's so evocative, and it just stimulates exactly as it was meant to do back then."

"It's the only piece of music that I've ever written that was designed to do one particular thing. And it's a very strange thing to sit down and be as cold and calculated as that. We had to write something that opened with a clanging chain of doom but finished with a 'Happy Xmas (War Is Over)' sing-along. It was a tall order, and of course it's a song with no chorus, which is the most bizarre thing ever."

The conversation moved to Live Aid, and I asked about meeting Freddie Mercury of Queen for the first time backstage at Wembley.

"He thought I was the guitarist from The Boomtown Rats, so it kind of burst my bubble somewhat," he told me. Even writing about it today, I'm also crushed.

"I think it's perfectly acceptable," Midge said of the mix-up. "Had it been someone else I might have been annoyed, but it was Freddie. He just lived in his own little Freddie world, so why would he know anything?"

Still, the magic of Freddie's performance that day is an epic memory.

"We saw him that day walking on at Live Aid in Wembley, and he was magnificent," Midge said. "I defy anybody to say he wasn't the highlight of the day because he was. Queen was fantastic. They're always great, but Freddie was just in his environment. He was in his zone in front of all those people, and he had them in the palm of his hands doing all this singing and scat stuff and the audience singing back, and it was just in seventh heaven."

But what did Midge make of his own performance that day?

"I think it all flew by so quickly. We all had 18 minutes to do our allocated four songs. And I think we were just so petrified that something was not gonna work because 'Vienna' is a very sparse song. If the bass synth didn't work, then half the song's missing. If the drum machine didn't play the 'kah kah!' noises, it wouldn't be 'Vienna' because there was no sound check or anything. We were just really happy that everything seemed to work during our set. To me, the key thing about the 'Vienna' performance was seeing the audience putting their hands in the air and doing the double-clap thing for the syndrome part, the 'kah kah!' It was fantastic to watch that sea of people singing along."

I was leading up to the question I really needed to ask: if Live Aid will always be my Woodstock, what is the event's legacy to Midge? What did he take from it?

"It's a question that I've been asked many times over the last 30 years: did it make a change?" Midge said. "Did it make a difference? And you could look at third-world countries—you look at Africa and you think, 'Well, there are still famines and there are still crops failing and the rains fail and all of that stuff. And nothing seems to have changed.' The difference is, I've met the change. I've spoken to the change. I've spoken to the people who were in aid camps as babies who survived because somebody put their hand in a pocket and bought that record. And that is worth it."

He wasn't done. And I was just taking it all in.

"There's a great story someone told me," he continued. "Two friends walking down a beach, and these starfish have all been washed up on the shore. And one of them says to the other, 'Well, we better try and save them.' And the other one said, 'Well, we can't save them. We can't do that. There's thousands of them.' The first one picked one up, put it back in the water, and said, 'Well, that's the first one.' And that's kinda how you've got to look at it. You can't fix these things overnight. It has to start somewhere and then it has to kind of move on. It has to roll on."

I still don't know if Live Aid saved the world. But to me—and the millions of others watching from couches, dorm lounges, and living rooms that day—it remains a revelation. It made us believe, if only for a moment, that music could be more than entertainment.

I remember wiping
the tears from my face
afterward as I edited
the show together—
unable to catch my breath
at times.

THOSE WE'VE LOST

Memorial episodes of the podcast gut me—every one of them, without exception. If we're honoring a person I've interviewed, the pain is twice as acute. One thing I've grown to accept is that these tributes are going to be a fact of life as long as we do a show about a decade that is currently more than 40 years old.

It's tough explaining the ins and outs of our memorial episodes—why some artists get one while others don't. When Michael Jackson died unexpectedly in 2009, we didn't record a tribute show. We had highlighted his *Thriller* album back in 2006 and felt there wasn't anything more to say. Were we sad? Devastated. Maybe too much so to record.

We skipped doing a show for David Bowie, too, upon his passing in 2016. None of us hosts at the time had anything more to add to all the exhaustive profiles written by journalists who knew Bowie's work so much better than we did. We felt it'd be disrespectful to try to add more perspective to his work. He was our hero, and we didn't want to diminish his memory with amateurish words.

But in 2009, when John Hughes suffered a heart attack one summer morning in New York and died on a sidewalk, the grief was overwhelming. The moment felt like we had lost a family member. A podcast seemed to be the best therapy. We had no special guests. Just me, Sean Daly, and Cathy Wos sitting at a table, sharing what his movies meant to us. I remember wiping the tears from my face afterward as I edited the show together—unable to catch my breath at times. And when it was finished, I took the unpublished show back to my condo, poured a stiff drink, turned off the lights, and laid down on the couch. I listened to the show over and over until I felt better again. It took a while.

OLIVIA NEWTON-JOHN was the first podcast guest we lost. Of all the people I've ever followed, the British-Australian hitmaker and actress seemed the most immortal. Her squeaky-clean image, warming smile, and optimistic attitude felt impenetrable. But in 2022, her long battle with breast cancer ended. I felt like my chest was going to explode when I heard the news.

In 2009, she'd called into the podcast to promote her upcoming tour. ONJ, as we liked to call her, was always a challenging interview. She was as sweet and giving as could be, but she wasn't going to give us any scoops or scandalous stories. As much as you wanted her to be "Bad Sandy" from *Grease* during an interview, she was always going to be more like "Sandra Dee." We loved her just the same.

Speaking of "Bad Sandy," we probably stupidly began our chat about that. Looking back—even later that afternoon—it didn't seem really clever or sensitive. But Sean wanted to know if—in reality—she was more "bad" than "good."

"Oh, I'm not telling you that one," she quickly replied. I remember my face scrunched up. It was as if she could feel it, so she added some more. "It's interesting because when I first read the script and I realized I had to do both those characters, I was really nervous about the second character, Sandy 2, as I call her, because I never really played any roles like that. But it was interesting. Once I got the clothes on it just came naturally. I had a ball with it."

We knew she and her *Grease* (and *Two of a Kind*) co-star John Travolta had remained friends through the years. But we couldn't get any stories out of her about him, either.

"We have a wonderful friendship going back a long way, and we'll always have that. And he's a wonderful man."

I told Olivia I thought the real secret of the success of *Grease* was the chemistry the audience felt between her and Travolta. Did she sense it too while filming?

"Yeah, we did have a great chemistry," she agreed. "I had just made a film that was a bit of a disaster called *Tomorrow*, and I just had my first hit record or second hit record in America, and I was really scared of doing a movie in case it was a bad one. So I actually asked for a screen test. I said, 'I want to do a screen test with whoever you are thinking of for Danny, and I want to see it, and then I'll decide.' And we had great chemistry from, you know, even from when we met. And so I was happy to do it. I was all of 29, can you believe? And I was worried about being too old."

Olivia wasn't even the oldest actor on the set. Stockard Channing, who played Rizzo, was 33 when she was cast. Olivia and John would team up again for 1983's *Two of a Kind*. The chemistry was still strong but the movie was a dud, remembered today best for its "Twist of Fate" song by Olivia and "Ask the Lonely," a hit composed by Journey for the movie soundtrack.

On a music stream now, we were curious about her setlist for her upcoming tour. Here she opened up a little about her reluctance to put new spins on her classic hits.

"I don't change things much because I remember when I was a young girl and I went to see one of my favorite singers. I wanted to hear the songs the way that I remembered them, and she changed them or she didn't do them at all," Olivia said. "I thought, 'Gosh, if I'm ever lucky enough to be that successful, I'll remember to do my songs, to do them and to do them the way they want to hear them.'"

Who was the singer that disappointed ONJ as a kid? "I'm not telling," she said.

At this point I couldn't resist myself: I needed to gush about *Xanadu*, the movie and music she made in 1980 along with Gene Kelly and Michael Beck. The movie was considered a bomb at the box office, but it resonated with fans for its music—much of it from Electric Light Orchestra's Jeff Lynne—and it would later achieve cult-movie status.

I blurted out that I owned the soundtrack on vinyl, cassette, and twice on CD. To this day, I still have the movie on DVD and digitally.

"I love it. I know it word for word," I told Olivia. "You'll see me there in Row S singing along."

"I can remember the words by watching your lips," Olivia teasingly replied. I turned a bright shade of red.

"Steve here, one of his favorite songs about you is 'Suddenly,' your duet with Mr. Cliff Richard," Sean told her, adding to my embarrassment. "Steve sings it, like, once a day at work. It's really annoying. Even though I adore you, Steve, it's really annoying hearing that all the time."

"I sang it on my last tour," Olivia said, "but the wonderful singer who usually sings with me couldn't come on this tour, so I'm not doing 'Suddenly.' I'm so sad."

We're not coming anymore, we told her. Well, maybe if she played "Twist of Fate."

"Oh, God," she said. "You like all the rock 'n' roll, don't you?"

As our interview wrapped, we promised to sneak backstage when she was in town to say hello and get a hug. "Do come back," she said. "That would be lovely."

Neither Sean nor I made it to the concert. It's been so long, I can't remember why. Was it raining that night? Maybe we were sad she wasn't playing our favorite songs. Either way, we figured we'd get another chance on a future tour. It never happened.

When Olivia passed in 2022, I knew we needed to do a memorial show but I couldn't find the right angle. I was lucky that my wife knew Cindy Gaber, who co-wrote Olivia's 2018 memoir *Don't Stop Believin'*. Cindy added some much-needed perspective on Olivia, explaining that the singer was most herself and happy at home surrounded by loved ones and her animals.

The Olivia tribute has become a must-listen fan favorite because it fills in the missing pieces—and it gave us some closure. We ended the podcast with Olivia's own words—spoken by her audio recording of the book—from the memoir's final pages. In those final thoughts, she reflects on her dream to see an end to cancer. She speaks of horses, tennis, grandchildren, her beloved dog Raven, and her husband John. She wishes for "health and happiness" for all.

Our tribute episode wraps up with the final bars of "Magic" from the *Xanadu* soundtrack. Her final lines of the song. And then silence.

CARL WEATHERS was one of only a handful of actors who have ever joined us on the podcast. Had he not passed away in 2024, our memories of Carl would be in the earlier chapter with his fellow actors. He was kind and giving during our short chat in 2009 and had no reservations about sharing his memories of the movies we loved as kids, even though the business at hand was promoting his then-current TV series *Brothers*.

Carl had been a college football player at San Diego State in the late '60s and then a pro player with the Oakland Raiders in the '70s before pursuing a career in acting. I asked him if football players made better actors than other athletes do.

"Well, that's a good question," he said, seemingly a little surprised by the query. "I don't know the answer to it, really, but I think there is something about the world of football and the form of entertainment that it is. If a guy is smart, and the guy is articulate, and the guy is a quick study, the camera seems to love him. Football, I guess, provides the kind of world that best suits what guys in front of the camera who are actors do, and maybe much more so than a lot of other sports do."

Okay, then conversely, we wondered, why do the co-stars of the 1987 sci-fi action-horror movie *Predator*, which Carl co-starred in, make good governors? Jesse Ventura and Arnold Schwarzenegger would later in their careers lead the states of Minnesota and California, respectively. Sonny Landham would briefly run for governor of Kentucky before withdrawing.

"I think those egos in *Predator* were so substantial that the guys in that movie all seemed to think we could do anything," Carl said. "You had guys there involved, myself included, who always had tremendous aspirations. As they perspired, they aspired [chuckle]. So maybe that's the answer."

While the politics were set aside on set, the egos definitely were not, Carl said.

"Nobody would let anybody get the best of them," he said. It was a "constant, constant, constant" pissing contest, he assured us. "Just a lot of sweat. You didn't have to worry about your wardrobe, didn't have to worry about makeup. It didn't matter. You just got there and mowed down the jungle."

Aside from the all-star cast of *Predator*, Carl was also iconic in a few other classics from the era: as Apollo Creed in the *Rocky* franchise, as Chubbs Peterson in *Happy Gilmore*, and even as an exaggerated version of himself in *Arrested Development*. We wanted to know which role fans recognized him as on the streets.

"It depends on where I am and the different age groups," he said. "It's funny, if you're anywhere from a 16- to a 20-something, it's either Chubbs or *Arrested Development*. If it's a family group, it's mostly *Rocky*. And if it's just those sort of geeks who love action movies, then of course it's going to be *Predator*. There's just no question about it."

There was one more role I wanted to know about.

"The other guy that you appear with in *Happy Gilmore* is Richard Kiel, right?" I asked.

"Richard Kiel, my God! Yeah," Carl exclaimed. "Richard Kiel and I go back to a movie that I did back in the..."

I didn't let him finish: "*Force 10 from Navarone!*"

"That's right," Carl said.

"It's Steve's favorite Carl Weathers movie," Sean added. I confessed I still owned it on DVD.

"No kidding," Carl said. "We shot that movie in Yugoslavia. We were all over Yugoslavia. We were on the isle of Jersey. We were in London at Shepperton Studios. That was about five months it took to shoot that movie."

"You play Sgt. Weaver," I said. "If I saw you walking down the street, I would say, 'Hey, Sgt. Weaver.'"

"I love it," Carl said. "It's just amazing. Boy, when you've been around as long as I've been around, and done so many different roles and people like the movies, it's really gratifying."

If he's not Sgt. Weaver to you—frankly, he's only Sgt. Weaver to me—he's likely Apollo Creed, so we focused on that, asking him his favorite memory while shooting the first four *Rocky* movies.

"Being on the same stage with James Brown," Carl said without hesitation. Carl's character danced along while Brown performed "Living in America" in *Rocky IV*.

"Growing up as a kid and [adoring] an icon like James Brown, and then to actually wind up on the stage with him—how many people can say that you shared the stage with and had a great time being on stage with him? So that was a special moment."

Even if he was wearing stars-and-stripes boxing britches?

"I do have my patriotic shorts," he said. "How could I lose them, man? No way [laughter]. No way could I lose the patriotic shorts."

Did he ever get a chance to really pop Sylvester Stallone during the filming?

"It happened that he popped me a few times too, so it wasn't like I was the only one doing the hitting. Boy, I'll tell you, this guy, for all his power and everything else, he made quite a few mistakes there with pulling those punches. Sometimes they didn't get pulled."

We were impressed but still convinced that in a Weathers vs. Stallone battle, you bet on Carl every time.

"Well, from your mouth to God's ear [laughter], I would pick Weathers every time."

Carl passed away at his home in Los Angeles on February 2, 2024. He was 76. That night, I rewatched *Force 10 from Navarone*. His co-star Richard Kiel—better known as "Jaws" in the James Bond franchise—passed away in 2014. He, too, would have been a wonderful person to have on the show.

GREG KIHN was an interview I—sadly—had to revisit. He was one of those yeses you don't take for granted. The '80s singer turned San Francisco Bay Area DJ was promoting *Kihnplete*, a three-disc digital anthology of the Greg Kihn Band. Usually we only snag an interview with a touring artist who is making a swing through Florida, so we were happily surprised that he took the time to talk with us.

We began with an obvious question: For an artist who had used his own last name for so many puns—his album titles include *Kihnspiracy*, *Next of Kihn*, *Citizen Kihn*, and *Kihn of Hearts*—were there any Kihn puns he had rejected?

"Well, you know, our standards are extremely low, so rejection is almost impossible," Greg answered. The laughs were only beginning. Speaking of humor and satire, we were curious to know what he thought of Weird Al Yankovic's parody "I Lost on Jeopardy," playing off Kihn's big hit "Jeopardy."

"I was flattered, you know, because when Weird Al parodies you, you've arrived," Greg said. "You've got to get permission from the artist before you do the song, and I remember Weird Al called me and I said, 'Geez, of course, I'd love you to do it.' And I wound up making a cameo appearance in the video for that, which was a great day because I got to meet Don Pardo."

Greg wasn't done spinning the tale.

"He's done a million parodies of all kinds of different artists, and the only person that ever, ever turned him down was Prince. He wanted to do a 'Purple Rain' parody but I guess Prince doesn't have much of a sense of humor and he took it pretty seriously. Michael Jackson loved Weird Al and would call Al in the middle of the night with ideas for other song parodies. So I was flattered. I thought it was a great feather in the cap to have Weird Al do the parody. And frankly, I love the man. He still sends me checks. I get mailbox money from Weird Al to this day. And you know what? That song was on an album that went multi-platinum. It was like the song was a hit all over again. It was wonderful."

While we were talking hit songs, I wanted to know more about "The Breakup Song" (aka "They Don't Write 'Em"). It was Greg's first hit, reaching No. 15 on the Billboard chart in 1981. Did he know it was a hit when he finished recording it? I asked.

"No, I didn't, and I'll tell you the truth: I always meant to finish those lyrics, and I only had, like, half a song's worth of lyrics," he said. "The day we cut the tracks, I went in there and it was, like, you know, 'Hey, just go out in the studio and do a guide vocal, you know, just so we know where we're at.' And it was supposed to be a rough vocal that was supposed to be redone the next day. And I was supposed to have lyrics. Well, I just go out there and I was making stuff up. I mean, I had pretty much every other line written. So I just threw the 'uh-uhs' in there to, you know, fill a little space. And then I get back in the studio, and the band are all hugging me and they go, 'Man, those are the deepest lyrics you ever wrote.'"

The tune—off the album *RocKihnRoll*—was later joined by moderate hits "Sheila" and "The Girl Most Likely." The record, his sixth album, would peak at No. 32 on the album charts.

"Think about this, guys," he said. "We didn't have a Top 10 hit until seven albums into the game. That's absolutely unheard of now. You couldn't do that. And then 'Jeopardy,' which came along, I believe, in '83, that was our first actual No. 1. [It topped the dance chart, but it would peak at No. 2 on the Billboard Top 100]. The atmosphere is pretty rarefied up there in a Top 10. You need special breathing apparatus."

For an artist whose sense of humor was always on the front line, did Greg ever get any crap back from the fat cats in the music biz?

"Yeah, but you know, screw it," he told me. "You got to be true to your school. You got to be who you are. And that's who I am. I mean, I've never been anything except really what I am. I've always been Greg Kihn. I've never tried to be anything else. I'm a lousy rock star, guys. I am not good. You put me in a limo, I'm uncomfortable. You know, I do too much coke, I get a little weird, you know, and I'm like, you know, I play Madison Square, I get a little, you know, antsy. I'm not what, you know…I'm much more comfortable just being myself. Whether we were No. 1 or No. 701, it didn't matter. We played every gig like it was the only thing we were ever going to do, and we gave everything the same shot. And I think that's where you really got to be like that."

God, we loved Greg. Reading his stories today makes me tear up a little.

"We considered ourselves artists," he continued. "We were making art. And if some A&R guy came in there and said, 'Hey, I don't hear a single,' it's like, well, tough titty, mister. You couldn't even have that attitude nowadays. Everything is marketed, you know, pretty much 100% and probably even test-marketed before it comes out. If I had to start all over again, I could never make it, never."

Greg Kihn passed away on August 13, 2024, after a battle with Alzheimer's disease. Damn. They don't write 'em like him anymore.

I just interviewed Steve Perry. I thought back to all of the career decisions that had led me to this moment. ... Worth it. Worth it all.

PATIENTLY

There aren't too many dates burned into my brain, but as I mentioned at the start of this book, October 22, 1981, is one of them. That was the day I saw my first concert: Journey on their Escape tour at the Lakeland Civic Center, with Loverboy opening up.

To this day, I probably have hearing damage from that night, but it was worth it. I'd wormed my way to the front of the general admission crowd and was maybe 15 or 20 feet away when Mike Reno and the boys from Loverboy hit the stage. I have zero clue what they opened with. The amps blew my brain matter to the far corner of my skull, where it stayed until about four days later. Journey opened with "Escape"—it was the band's tradition to begin each show with the first track of the newest album.

From that day on, I had an odd connection to Steve Perry, the band's charismatic frontman. He had a limitless energy, as if he was operating at an entirely different voltage. I wanted to know what made him tick. Trouble was, he hadn't spoken to the press much since leaving Journey in the mid-'90s. He was more myth than man.

In November 2011, six years after the podcast launched, I sensed an opening. Journey had released its *Greatest Hits 2* album, and Perry remastered most of the tunes himself. He also had just revisited his first solo album, *Street Talk*. If he was ever going to be willing to talk, this was the time.

Just a small little wrinkle: Perry wasn't easy to find. He didn't seem to have an official website with any contact information. I didn't have any connections with his record label. But he did have a fan club run by Fan Asylum in San Francisco.

I scoured the website for names and email addresses—these weren't hard to find. But who was the right contact? *Screw it*, I thought, and I emailed them all.

"Hi. You might not be the right person, but I hope you'll pass it along to whoever is. I'm a podcaster working for the *St. Petersburg Times* and a lifelong Journey fan. I know Steve Perry just finished remastering the second volume of greatest hits and I'd love to talk to him about it. Here's a link to my review. Any help appreciated."

It was a total shot in the dark. I was gobsmacked to get a reply within a week.

"Yes, Steve is doing press. Tell me more about the podcast. Would the whole conversation have to be on the podcast? Will the newspaper run the interview? I think we can make this happen."

Holy hell, are you kidding me? It took me another week to set it up—seven nights of basically restless sleep and total nausea. The night before the interview, I rewatched the director's cut of VH1's *Behind the Music* documentary of Journey. I went to sleep that night with Journey's song "Patiently" playing in my head nonstop. I still hear the emotional vulnerability in the lyrics today as I type.

The next day, I settled alone into the control booth of our podcast studio to wait for the call.

The phone in the control booth was crazy loud, and the ringing nearly gave me a heart attack. I picked up and got some static. Then I heard him. He was talking to his publicist, Laura. When podcast listeners ask me what my favorite interview was, this conversation with Steve is always my first answer.

"Hi, Steve...Steve and Steve!" Laura exclaimed.

"Steve and Steve live!" Steve Perry shouted out.

"Wow. Thirty minutes alone with Steve Perry," I began. "This is a dream I've waited about 30 years for."

"This is like a date or something," he agreed.

"I appreciate your time," I continued. "Your relationship with the media...you've almost kind of become the Howard Hughes of rock 'n' roll." Steve burst out laughing. "I've been called a lot of things, but that's a first!" he exclaimed.

It turns out my online review of *Greatest Hits 2* caught the attention of his rep. "She said you wrote some amazing stuff about this [greatest hits album]. You used words like 'GH2 Dazzles.' I thought that was a beautiful headline she read to me."

Laura had told me I'd be the last interview Steve did this particular day. It could have gone a few different ways. He could have been exhausted and burned out from the questions, or he'd be willing to stay longer on the phone. We talked for an hour.

I recounted the story of seeing him perform live in Lakeland in 1981. Steve told me a story in return of his memories playing in an old rodeo venue in Hollywood, Florida. The wheels of our nostalgia fest were just beginning to spin.

"It was a tin building that was used for rodeos out in the middle of nowhere," he said. "And you had to ride in there with a dirt road, and it was just a mess. The people were stomping around, there was plywood on the ground, and they would be stomping up and down on plywood, so it would make dust, and the room was just—you'd literally leave and there would be boogers in your nose [laughter]. It was just horrible. But boy, didn't it rock like a son of a bitch? I mean, Florida used to rock hard."

It still does, I assured him. I told him how Lakeland was the halfway point between Orlando and Tampa, and yet it was the home to so many epic concerts during the first half the '80s.

"And you know what? You came from a little podunk town in Florida, and now you're the main guy at the *Times*, Steve," he said. "I came from a little podunk town in California called Hanford. And then what did my mom do when I was about 12, 13? She was afraid the town was getting too dangerous and too big. Oh shit. It was only 12,000 people. So we moved to the one that was 7,000 people, a town called Lemoore. So I would be a lot safer at Lemoore High School. Talk about little farm towns. Well, I think, Steve, we did okay."

The conversation turned to "Don't Stop Believin'," Journey's enduring anthem of optimism. In 2011, the song was getting a second and third life on the charts thanks to appearances in Fox's *Glee* and HBO's *The Sopranos*. CBC Radio One in Canada had produced a segment on the song featuring interview snippets with Steve and me talking about the song. CBC interviewed me separately from Steve, so we weren't live together. Still, it was possibly the most surreal moment in my life up to the day of our chat.

"When [Radio One] asked me about the longevity of the song, I said something about how it's this perfect combination of piano and vocals and guitar. How the chorus is at the *end*. And that there's this reaffirming theme," I began. This wouldn't be the last time Steve would be asked about the tune. It was about to become the cornerstone of *Rock of Ages*, the Broadway musical that was headed to the big screen in 2012. Why this song, I asked.

"I don't really know why except that I'm so grateful that the song has just caught on and people love it," he said. "I've had seven-year-old, nine-year-old kids come up to me and say how much they love that song. And at a baseball game, they want me to sign their glove or a ball. To see that happen in my lifetime...I'm just profoundly grateful for that."

It's really hard to even think of another song from any generation that has had the ability to continually resurface and become just as popular as it has.

"All the songs when we were recording them were given the same love and treatment and consideration and heartfelt performances," he said. "We as a band worked hard on every single track, whether it was 'Chain Reaction,' 'Separate Ways,' or 'Send Her My Love' or 'Open Arms.' All of them—different as they may be to each other—were all given the same kind of emotional performance. We loved them all the same. But the world chooses what it chooses and time does what it does."

The world chooses what it chooses and time does what it does. Holy hell. I scribbled that down on an envelope next to my microphone. If I ended up losing this audio recording, I damn well wasn't going to forget that line. This guy wrote some of the songs that defined my decade, my generation—and he had no ego about any of it. Maybe Steve Perry didn't have the answers to all my questions. Maybe he didn't have answers to his own questions—but there was a reassuring peace in that.

As my mind momentarily wandered off with these thoughts, the talk moved to memories of Steve's early touring days after joining Journey. He painted a gritty picture of a band determined to pay its dues.

"We toured really hard. The grueling tour schedule cannot be attained by anybody anymore," he said. "We never stopped. Four or five shows in a row and a day off wasn't a day off, Steve, it was a travel day. The only reason there wasn't a show is because it was impossible for the trucks to get there in time. Otherwise it would've been six, seven days a week."

I must have sounded unconvinced. It certainly was eye-opening.

"That's the truth!" Steve insisted.

No, I believe it, I assured him.

"It was like running for public office," he continued. "You really had to travel every single day and perform every night. And there were times that we just lived on the bus and we'd get what's called day rooms. People don't realize that we'd just get a day room and the day room was so that everybody could take a shower because there was no shower on the bus. I'm not making this up, Steve. And there wasn't enough towels to go around, and so we'd have to use damp towels: 'Whose towel is this? Who showered before me?'"

What tour was it that Journey was finally able to afford real rooms, I asked.

"Boy, that's a good question. It wasn't the Infinity tour. By Evolution, I think we might have got hotel rooms. I know by the time we got to Escape we had our own rooms, and we were in nice hotels, which was just, wow. That was touring."

We started talking about the engineering of producing the greatest hits record. Some of it went over my head, but Steve could make even a story about visiting a Radio Shack mind-blowingly entertaining.

I hung on every word. I didn't want to miss a beat, but I needed to change the subject. I wasn't sure how he'd react.

In the spring of 1984, Steve Perry released his first solo album, *Street Talk*. It's an album full of memories I wasn't sure he would want to revisit—and maybe rightfully so.

"You also remastered *Street Talk*," I began.

There was a pause.

"Yes."

Steve became quieter now. He was taking more time to answer. He knew what was coming.

"Obviously, 'Oh Sherrie' is the huge hit off that album," I continued. "And the video is almost as memorable as the song because it featured your then-girlfriend, Sherrie Swafford. What kind of feelings go through your head to have a huge hit like that so prominently linked to a public relationship that ultimately didn't work out?"

"Yeah." A long pause followed. When I listen to the audio of this part of our conversation today, I still can picture what his face must have looked like. How his head probably dropped. Maybe he took an extra few breaths. Then, unexpectedly, I heard a few chuckles.

"That's a tough question, man! Sherrie and I were crazy in love, I can tell you that. And it was very tough times because the band was peaking. And if any woman out there thinks that it would be real exciting to be the girlfriend of somebody in a band like that—the truth is, it was a hard thing to navigate a relationship while you're in the midst of such a ride. It was emotionally hard on her, emotionally hard on our relationship. I'm prancing around every night, ripping my shirt off, shaking my ass on stage and enjoying every goddamn minute of it. Chicks out there wanting to do things to me with a fork [laughter], that was exciting. I didn't partake in it, but it was there. It's challenging. It's challenging to the security of someone's heart. I think it was difficult on the relationship and eventually, it just unfortunately got damaged.... But you know, relationships get damaged. Isn't that what they do sometimes? It's just sad but it can happen."

We'd made it through that, but tougher questions remained ahead. I was committed to going where the conversation took us. I was also aware that we had already talked for more than half an hour. Steve's publicist could interrupt at any moment to wrap things up. This chat couldn't end on such a somber note.

I turned the conversation to the rumors that he'd been making new music. He hasn't released anything new since *Trial by Fire* in 1996, 15 years prior at the time.

"How important is music in your life nowadays? Do you need to make music to be happy these days?" I asked.

"I think it was May 8th of 1998 that it was kind of officially over," he recalled. "I didn't do anything for the longest period of time, until about two and a half years ago, maybe three years ago. I loaded up a computer with Pro Tools....I just stayed out of the way and let the Journey guys do their thing, and I'm just going to fall back into life and let it all go. And I had my hip replacement shortly after they moved on, and I started writing music thanks to some people that I was listening to at that time."

I'd heard Steve had been listening to music by Eels and their singer-songwriter Mark Oliver Everett, better known as E.

"People like the Eels. I love E. I think his writing is bold and edgy," Steve said. "And he gave me courage to try to do the same, just to write whatever comes to mind, in any musical direction, even if it's out of the fingerprint that people have known me for. I had to give myself the right to suck and write some music that maybe isn't so great. I don't think it's so great. I play it for friends, they love it. But then there's other songs that I know are better."

I stopped Steve here. I needed to tell him something: "You don't understand how much your fans adore you and want you to be happy," I blurted out. Suddenly I was a therapist—to Steve Perry. "If you knew that, I think you'd take the pressure off your fear of sucking."

I braced for backlash. If he had hung up, maybe I would have deserved it.

"You know, Steve, God I wish that was true," Perry said instead. "I wish I could embrace that as true. I'm slowly starting to see that that's possible. But if I could tell my fans anything right now, it would be that I want them to know I am happy. I was happy being in front of them every night. They lifted me to places I could not go without them. My voice was actually their voice, because I had to go get it because they wanted to hear it. I can't get that without them. I've tried to sing like that in my living room with my Pro Tools rig."

His words flowed, but more slowly, more deliberate than before.

"They don't even know how much of a part of my life they were. They think I was a part of theirs, but they'll never know how 50-50 it really was. They need to know that. Without them, I was not who I am. That needs to be said. They literally made me happen."

I sensed he felt the sun was shining again. Therapy time was over. But Steve wasn't.

"I just want them to know that for the years that I have not been around, it was a difficult comedown in the beginning. It was like coming off the Earth's orbit and coming back through the atmosphere and burning some heat tiles off your face on the way in....And now I'm okay. I love my life. And I'm so pleased that everyone still loves the music."

I needed to ask him about Journey, the possibility of a reunion, and the Rock & Roll Hall of Fame. These are questions he's no doubt answered dozens of time, so I rephrased my words.

"I am not going to ask you about reunion stuff because you've answered that a thousand times, but let me frame it somewhat differently," I said. "When Journey gets inducted into the Rock & Roll Hall of Fame—and I say when and not if because I believe it will happen—will you be there to rejoin your bandmates at the ceremony? And will you play a couple of tunes with the boys?"

"I don't think I can answer that question. I have to see where my life is at that point," he said. "I've never been that excited about any of those accolades, be it Grammys or anything else. It was never, ever about any of that to me. In fact, if anything, I was really against that stuff and still kind of am. You don't need to worry about awards if you do the music right. Let the music do your talking for you, then there's nothing else to say. I've moved on already. I'm in the bunk sleeping in the bus into the next city."

"Steve, as long as you're happy," I said. "That's all I give a damn about."

"Yeah," he laughed. "I'm happy, Steve."

We said goodbye and hung up. I probably sat in my chair for another 30 minutes. I just couldn't move. I checked the recorder—YES!—the audio was recorded. It sounded perfectly crisp and clear.

I just interviewed Steve Perry. I thought back to all of the career decisions that had led me to this moment. The weekend and holiday shifts copyediting the work of full-time writers. The obnoxious bosses. The minuscule paychecks. Worth it. Worth it all.

Finally, I found the energy to head back to my cubicle and face my co-workers, who were well aware of where I had been for about two hours. They took one look at the expression on my face and knew it had been something special.

Again, the lyrics from "Patiently" began crawling through my brain, and the song now made sense. It's about hope without entitlement. It's the realization that life unfolds on its own timetable.

A few years after my interview with Steve, in April 2017, Journey was inducted into the Rock & Roll Hall of Fame. Steve was there, with the boys, and addressed the fans directly:

"You're the ones who put us here! You are the Rock & Roll Hall of Fame! You put us here! We would not be here had it not been for you and your tireless love and consistent devotion. You never have stopped. And from my heart, I must tell you, I have been gone a long time, I understand that. But I want you to know, you've never not been in my heart. I want you to know that. And I love each and every one of you."

Steve did not perform with Journey that night. In October 2018, he released his new music—the album *Traces*—his first in 25 years.

It was full of messages of love and loss, grief and remembrance. The music and lyrics pushed emotional evolution over nostalgia, acceptance over bitterness, introspection over showmanship.

It was Steve Perry.

POSTSCRIPT

Forty-four years after that first Journey concert, in 2025, I found myself in Lakeland again, staying for one night at a hotel next to an aging cement mausoleum-looking lyceum called the RP Funding Center that was hosting scrapbooking conventions and reptile shows. It all seemed eerily familiar, though.

"Hey, the building next door…," I said to the front-desk clerk at the hotel. "Did it used to be the Lakeland Civic Center?"

"Yep," she answered. No further comment. No back story. No sharing of memories. No sad, wistful smile. It felt like a morose and unacceptably insufficient eulogy for a once-powerful palace of whimsy and wonder.

I wanted to stand there and tell her about Loverboy and their killer amps. About what Steve Perry sang first that night. I even imagined walking the 20 yards to the arena doors, grabbing the handle, and seeing if the past would reopen for me again.

I thought again about "Patiently." Love comes without guarantees. Memory sometimes has no controls. Sometimes meaning arrives years or decades later.

So instead of walking over to the civic center, I drove home the next day and finished writing this collection of memories.

Not every story gets closure.

Maybe that's why I'll always be hopelessly stuck in the '80s.

STUCK in the '80s
Moments in Time

Steve's original column photo for the Tampa Bay Times. (2005)

With co-host Sean Daly and Robin Zander of Cheap Trick.

Photo: St. Petersburg Times

Sebastian Bach sings "The Final Countdown" and the theme song to WKRP in Cincinnati during his mad-cap afternoon hosting trivia with Steve and Brad on The 80s Cruise.

Photo: Chuck Coverly

Steve and Brad Williams with Pete Byrne of Naked Eyes.

Photos: Chuck Coverly

With Brad along with Martha Davis and Marty Jourard of The Motels.

Former TV critic Chase Squires joins Steve and Gina Vivinetto for a podcast about TV theme songs in 2005. Dave "The Maestro" Morrison is handling production duties.

Photo: Dave Morrison

Cathy Wos, Sean Daly, and Steve backstage at Ruth Eckerd Hall in 2006 for a live podcast during the We Are The 80s concert.

Cathy Wos and Steve podcast live from the 80s Prom Party at the Tampa Theatre in 2006.

Photos: Dave Morrison

Rick Springfield joins the podcast hosts in 2006 before his show at the We Are The 80s concert in Clearwater.

Sean Daly, Steve, and Cathy Wos in a promotional shot for the podcast, circa 2006.

Photos: Dave Morrison

Steve and Gina Vivinetto during a promotional shoot for the podcast.

Photo: Chuck Coverly

With Brad and Midge Ure after Big 80s Trivia on The 80s Cruise.

Photo: Kristin Mackin

With Air Supply's Russell Hitchcock during soundcheck before a show.

Steve inside the podcast studio at the Tampa Bay Times, circa 2012.

With Richard Marx backstage at the Capitol Theatre in Clearwater, Florida, in 2010.

With Dennis DeYoung backstage at Ruth Eckerd Hall in Clearwater at the singer's performance with The Florida Orchestra in 2012.

Photos: Chuck Coverly

Brad and Steve interview Nina Blackwood, Mark Goodman, and Alan Hunter on The 80s Cruise in 2019 for the podcast's 500th episode.

Terri Nunn and Berlin join Brad and Steve for a live podcast interview on The 80s Cruise.

Howard Jones and Steve interact during a trivia session on The 80s Cruise.

Steve, Mark Goodman, Alan Hunter, and Brad

Steve at his 20-year high school reunion, locking the door to the hotel bar after the long weekend.

Steve with his press pass backstage at Ruth Eckerd Hall in 2008.

Podcast producer Dave "The Maestro" Morrison with Steve's cat Nick Rhodes for a podcast taped at Steve's condo in 2008.

Cathy Wos, Sean Daly, and Steve backstage at Ruth Eckerd Hall for the We Are the '80s Tour, where they interview Rick Springfield and Loverboy for the podcast.

Photos: Dave Morrison

Rick Springfield is among the first artists to be interviewed in person for the podcast in 2006.

With Asia drummer Carl Palmer backstage at Ruth Eckerd Hall in 2007.

Photo: Chuck Coverly

Larry "The Duck" Dunn of SiriusXM's First Wave joins Steve and Brad for trivia on The 80s Cruise.

Photo: Dave Morrison

Sean Daly, Debbie Gibson, and Steve in the *Tampa Bay Times* podcast studio after Debbie's appearance on the show in 2008.

Steve live blogging backstage during the Regeneration Tour stop in Clearwater in 2008.

ACKNOWLEDGMENTS

It was a visit to an author's book fair in Tampa in early 2023—starring my wife and her book about dating—that finally gave me the push I needed to begin this project. Seeing her on the other side of the table made the idea of this book feel less hypothetical and more inevitable.

The partners I've had over the years for *Stuck in the '80s* have been endlessly generous with their support and enthusiasm. I could write a book about every one of them. Gina Vivinetto, my first cohost, supplied the spark that got the podcast off the ground. Brendan Watson, our first producer, helped it take flight. Dave Morrison—"The Maestro"—produced the show during its early years, building a framework for excellence while patiently teaching me the basics of audio editing. His photos also appear in this book, further proof that this whole thing actually happened.

When Sean Daly and Cathy Wos joined me behind the microphone, the result was always an hour of bellyaching comedy, genuine camaraderie, and a pure love of the '80s. Sean, thank you for holding my hand through the early interviews and teaching me how to polish a story. Cathy, you are exactly how Gina sold you—cooler than her and me put together.

To Brad Williams, my current cohost and constant friend, thank you for stepping in when the podcast was truly rudderless. Together, we've grown the podcast into something bigger and stronger than I ever imagined. Your humor and constant encouragement keep me grounded when things feel uncertain.

To the past and present staff and executives of ECP—Entertainment Cruise Productions—thank you for a partnership with The 80s Cruise that gave the podcast a much-needed kick in the pants and opened the door to so many unforgettable conversations with our '80s heroes.

To the musicians, actors, writers, and celebrities who have shared their time and stories with us over the past 20 years: thank you for your generosity and for patiently answering our questions. A special nod of gratitude goes to those early guests who came on the show without yet knowing what a podcast actually was.

To the professionals at Clearwater's Ruth Eckerd Hall, who have helped facilitate so many of those conversations—Jennifer Gulick, Katie Pedretty, Bobby Rossi, Jill Holcombe Suel, and many others—your support has always felt unconditional, and the hall feels like a second home to me.

Thanks to the incredibly talented and dedicated journalists and editors of the *Tampa Bay Times* for your encouragement during the podcast's first years. *Stuck in the '80s* was born and spent seven amazing years there. Special thanks to Christine Montgomery, my manager, who greenlit the podcast and always stood behind it.

Special thanks to the patrons of *Stuck in the '80s*, whose financial and emotional support have kept the show alive.

A high-five to Chuck "The Mayor of The 80s Cruise" Coverly for contributing many of the photos in this book—and for stepping in as a cohost when I need a strong pinch hitter.

And thank you to Jen "With One N" Boggs, Gayle "In DC" Weiswasser, Drew Friedman, Stephanie Hayes, and many others for taking over the microphone and lending your expertise when we've needed seasoned pros.

Praise and thanks to Tamara Dever of TLC Book Design for the cover and book design—and for the friendship and timely pep talks that buoyed my spirits when I needed them most. And thanks to her team, Lisa Hochgraf and Peter Vogt, for editing and making every page better.

To my family, who has never stopped believing there was a book in me trying to get out—even when I wasn't sure myself. To my mother, Bonnie, who asked for writing updates on every phone call and never once doubted I'd finish. And to my late father, John, who showed me that dreams are built with patience and stubborn faith. Together, they taught me that anything is within reach if I want it badly enough—and quitting is never an option.

"At Last" my ship has come in, Mom and Dad.

And finally—most importantly—to my wife, Melissa. Without your love, patience, and encouragement, this book would still be sitting in the darkest corner of my brain. You believed in this project long before I did, and you never let me forget that the stories mattered—even on the days I was convinced they didn't.

You listened to drafts, lived with deadlines, tolerated the long days and emotional detours, and somehow always knew when to push and when to simply sit beside me. This book exists because you made room for it—and for me—every step of the way. Together, there are no gaps.

ABOUT THE AUTHOR

Steve Spears is the creator and host of *Stuck in the '80s*, a long-running pop-culture podcast that began in 2005 as an experimental work project at the *Tampa Bay Times* (then the *St. Petersburg Times*). What started as a way to explore nostalgia online turned into a 20-year journey through music, movies, television, and the memories that refuse to fade.

Over nearly 800 episodes, *Stuck in the '80s* has featured hundreds of interviews with artists and personalities who helped define the decade, including Steve Perry, Huey Lewis, Martha Quinn, Brian Johnson, Kenny Loggins, and many others. The podcast reaches a global audience, with listeners regularly checking in from around the world to share their stories of growing up in the MTV era.

Steve has spent his career as an editor and online producer, shaping stories rather than starring in them. *Stuck in the '80s* has been recognized with 11 major industry awards, including top honors from the Online News Association, *Editor & Publisher*, and the Florida Society of News Editors.

Steve lives in Orlando with his wife, Melissa, and their dog, Benji. He still listens to '80s music every day, hosts trivia events aboard the annual voyages of The 80s Cruise, and remains proudly, unapologetically nostalgic. He wrote this book to tell the stories behind the interviews—and to finally explain how *Stuck in the '80s* became more than just a podcast.

STUCK in the '80s

Find and follow us online to keep reliving the music, movies, and memories that have shaped us.

 @stuckinthe80s

 @SIT80sPodcast

 @stuckinthe80spodcast

 Check out the podcast at Sit80s.com

www.ingramcontent.com/pod-product-compliance
Lightning Source LLC
LaVergne TN
LVHW021235080526
838199LV00088B/4354